Journal on AI Policy and Complex Systems

Also from Westphalia Press
westphaliapress.org

The Idea of the Digital University

Dialogue in the Roman-Greco World

The History of Photography

International or Local Ownership?: Security Sector Development in Post-Independent Kosovo

Lankes, His Woodcut Bookplates

Opportunity and Horatio Alger

The Role of Theory in Policy Analysis

The Little Confectioner

Non-Profit Organizations and Disaster

The Idea of Neoliberalism: The Emperor Has Threadbare Contemporary Clothes

Social Satire and the Modern Novel

Ukraine vs. Russia: Revolution, Democracy and War: Selected Articles and Blogs, 2010-2016

James Martineau and Rebuilding Theology

A Strategy for Implementing the Reconciliation Process

Issues in Maritime Cyber Security

A Different Dimension: Reflections on the History of Transpersonal Thought

Iran: Who Is Really In Charge?

Contracting, Logistics, Reverse Logistics: The Project, Program and Portfolio Approach

Unworkable Conservatism: Small Government, Freemarkets, and Impracticality

Springfield: The Novel

Lariats and Lassos

Ongoing Issues in Georgian Policy and Public Administration

Growing Inequality: Bridging Complex Systems, Population Health and Health Disparities

Designing, Adapting, Strategizing in Online Education

Pacific Hurtgen: The American Army in Northern Luzon, 1945

Natural Gas as an Instrument of Russian State Power

New Frontiers in Criminology

Feeding the Global South

Beijing Express: How to Understand New China

The Rise of the Book Plate: An Exemplative of the Art

Journal on AI Policy and Complex Systems

Volume 9, Number 1 • Winter 2024

Percy Venegas, Liz Johnson & Joseph Cochran, editors

Westphalia Press
An imprint of Policy Studies Organization

Journal on AI Policy and Complex Systems
Volume 9, Number 1 • Winter 2024

Westphalia Press
An imprint of Policy Studies Organization
1367 Connecticut Ave NW
Washington, D.C. 20036
info@ipsonet.org

ISBN: 978-1-63723-657-4

Cover and interior design by Jeffrey Barnes
jbarnesbook.design

Daniel Gutierrez-Sandoval, Executive Director
PSO and Westphalia Press

Updated material and comments on this edition
can be found at the Westphalia Press website:
www.westphaliapress.org

Journal on AI Policy and Complex Systems
Volume 9, Number 1 • Winter 2024

TABLE OF CONTENTS

Editor's Letter

This issue of the *Journal on AI Policy and Complex Systems* is dedicated to applied research, experience, and frameworks.

In "Adaptable Artificial Intelligence" Azish Filabi, Nick Masi, Ellie Pavlick, Rico Picone introduce the concept of Adaptability in the context of modeling complex AI systems.

"In search of lost relations. Educational approaches against the background of quantum mechanical equivalents" by Zrinka Stimac, offers a path of inquiry to consider complexity in education as quantum-like.

In "Experiences in Designing Complex Software Systems" Andrew Boake offers a practitioner perspective on Complexity.

"Leveraging AI in Deciphering Geopolitical and Counter-terrorism Complexities in the Middle East" by David Alkaher, Uri Ben Yaakov, Elizabeth J. Taylor, proposes a novel application of large language models in scenario planning for security and strategic studies.

We include a new Literature Review section, and the paper "The Transformative Effects of AI on International Economics" by Rafael Andersson Lipcsey.

Finally, in the Letters section Tim Craske shares his experience as a practitioner learning about Complexity, in "Developing Interest in Complex Systems: It's where the wicked problems live".

As we get closer to our goal of opening the Journal to become a sharing space for academics and practitioner-scholars alike, we are grateful for the interest of our readers in these different perspectives on AI, Policy and Complexity.

Best regards,
Percy Venegas
Editor-in-Chief, *Journal on AI Policy and Complex Systems*

Este número de Journal on AI Policy and Complex Systems está dedicado a la investigación aplicada, la experiencia y los marcos de referencia.

En "Inteligencia artificial adaptable", Azish Filabi, Nick Masi, Ellie Pavlick y Rico Picone introducen el concepto de adaptabilidad en el contexto del modelado de sistemas de IA complejos.

"En busca de relaciones perdidas. Enfoques educativos en el contexto de los equivalentes mecánico-cuánticos" de Zrinka Stimac, ofrece un camino de inves-

 doi: 10.18278/jpcs.9.1.1

tigación para considerar la complejidad en la educación como algo similar a lo cuántico.

En "Experiencias en el diseño de sistemas de software complejos", Andrew Boake ofrece una perspectiva profesional sobre la complejidad.

"Aprovechamiento de la IA para descifrar las complejidades geopolíticas y antiterroristas en Oriente Medio", de David Alkaher, Uri Ben Yaakov y Elizabeth J. Taylor, propone una aplicación novedosa de modelos de lenguaje de gran tamaño en la planificación de escenarios para estudios estratégicos y de seguridad.

Incluimos una nueva sección de Revisión de Literatura y el artículo "Los efectos transformadores de la IA en la economía internacional" de Rafael Andersson Lipcsey.

Finalmente, en la sección Cartas, Tim Craske comparte su experiencia como practicante aprendiendo sobre Complejidad, en "Desarrollar el interés en los sistemas complejos: es donde viven los problemas perversos".

A medida que nos acercamos a nuestro objetivo de abrir la Revista para que se convierta en un espacio de intercambio para académicos y profesionales por igual, agradecemos el interés de nuestros lectores en estas diferentes perspectivas sobre IA, políticas y complejidad.

Saludos cordiales,

Percy Venegas

Editor en Jefe, *Journal on AI Policy and Complex Systems*

本期《人工智能政策与复杂系统杂志》致力于应用研究、经验和框架。

在《适应性人工智能》一文中，Azish Filabi、Nick Masi、Ellie Pavlick和Rico Picone在建模复杂人工智能系统的背景下介绍了“适应性”概念。

Zrinka Stimac撰写的《寻找丢失的关系——根据量子力学等效原理的教育方法》提供了一条探究途径，将教育中的复杂性视为量子复杂性。

Andrew Boake在《复杂软件系统的设计经验》一文中提供了从业者对复杂性的看法。

David Alkaher、Uri Ben Yaakov和Elizabeth J. Taylor撰写的《利用人工智能解读中东地缘政治和反恐的复杂性》提出了大型语言模型在情景规划中的新应用，以用于安全和战略研究。

本期包括一个新的“文献综述”版块，收录了Rafael Andersson Lipcsey

撰写的论文：《人工智能对国际经济的变革性影响》。

最后，在“信件”版块，Tim Craske分享了他作为一名从业者在学习复杂性方面的经验，文章题为《培养对复杂系统的兴趣：棘手问题就在这里》。

随着我们越来越接近“将本刊开放为学者和从业学者的共享空间”这一目标，我们非常感谢读者对关于AI、政策和复杂性的不同观点的兴趣。

献上最美好的问候，

Percy Venegas

《人工智能政策与复杂系统杂志》主编

The Dance of the Scorpions: Leveraging AI in Deciphering Geopolitical and Counter-terrorism Complexities in the Middle East

David Alkaher*, Uri Ben Yaakov, Elizabeth J. Taylor
International Institute for Counter Terrorism (ICT)
Reichman University, Herzliya, Israel
*Corresponding author: dalkaher@bgu.ac.il

Abstract

The primary aim of this study is to facilitate an in-depth exploration and analysis of an ongoing highly complex geopolitical conflict scenarios, such as the Middle East post-October 7th events. This is done by utilizing the advanced analytical prowess of AI. A four-stage framework for an AI-generated simulated geopolitical-conflict game is presented. This framework utilizes the advanced capabilities of AI, and in particular Chat-GPT4. By simulating and analyzing key players' decisions in the complex Middle Eastern geopolitics post-October 7th events, it offers a nuanced understanding of potential outcomes and strategies, shedding light upon the escalation potential of such conflict in view of tactical-operative triggering decision making. The results of the simulation are shown to align closely with real-world occurrences, demonstrating the AI's proficiency in processing extensive data for comprehensive geopolitical analysis. This approach significantly enhances our understanding of conflict dynamics, highlighting the transformative potential of AI in strategic studies. The findings are pivotal for both academic discourse and practical application, offering valuable insights for policymakers and strategists. This study underscores the critical role of AI in navigating and understanding the intricate web of global conflicts, marking a novel advancement in the fields of geopolitical and counter-terrorism studies.

Aprovechar la inteligencia artificial para descifrar las complejidades geopolíticas y antiterroristas en Oriente Medio

Resumen

El objetivo principal de este estudio es facilitar una exploración y

doi: 10.18278/jpcs.9.1.2

un análisis profundos de escenarios de conflictos geopolíticos altamente complejos en curso, como los eventos posteriores al 7 de octubre en Medio Oriente. Esto se hace utilizando la destreza analítica avanzada de la IA. Se presenta un marco de cuatro etapas para un juego de simulación de conflicto geopolítico generado por IA. Este marco utiliza las capacidades avanzadas de la IA, y en particular Chat-GPT4. Al simular y analizar las decisiones de los actores clave en los complejos eventos geopolíticos posteriores al 7 de octubre en Medio Oriente, ofrece una comprensión matizada de los posibles resultados y estrategias, arrojando luz sobre el potencial de escalada de dicho conflicto en vista de la toma de decisiones de activación táctica y operativa. Se muestra que los resultados de la simulación se alinean estrechamente con los sucesos del mundo real, lo que demuestra la competencia de la IA en el procesamiento de datos extensos para un análisis geopolítico integral. Este enfoque mejora significativamente nuestra comprensión de la dinámica del conflicto, destacando el potencial transformador de la IA en los estudios estratégicos. Los hallazgos son fundamentales tanto para el discurso académico como para la aplicación práctica, y ofrecen información valiosa para los responsables de las políticas y los estrategas. Este estudio subraya el papel fundamental de la IA para navegar y comprender la intrincada red de conflictos globales, lo que marca un avance novedoso en los campos de los estudios geopolíticos y antiterroristas.

危险的对峙
利用人工智能解读中东地缘政治和反恐的复杂性

摘要

本研究旨在促进对持续高度复杂的地缘政治冲突情景（例如10月7日后的中东事件）进行深度探究和分析。这是通过利用人工智能(AI)的先进分析能力来实现的。本文介绍了一个由AI生成的模拟地缘政治冲突游戏的四阶段框架。该框架利用了AI的先进功能，特别是Chat-GPT4。通过模拟和分析10月7日后中东复杂地缘政治中关键参与者的决策，它对潜在结果和策略提供了细微的理解，从战术操作触发决策的角度揭示了此类冲突升级的潜力。模拟结果与现实世界的事件非常吻合，证明了AI在处理大量数据以进行全面地缘政治分析方面的能力。这种方法大大增强了我们对冲突动态的理解，强调了AI在战略研究中的变革潜力。研究结果对学术话语和实际应用都至关重要，为政策制定者和战略家提供了宝贵见解。本研究强调了AI在应对和理解错综复杂的全球冲突网络中的关键作用，标志着地缘政治和反恐研究领域的新进展。

Introduction

In the heart of the Middle East, a delicate and dangerous dance unfolds - a dance of survival, strategy, and shadows. At the heart of this dance are two formidable scorpions: Israel and Iran. In this geopolitical ballet, Israel seeks to neutralize threats from its immediate neighbors, Hamas and Hezbollah, proxies extending the reach of Iran's scorpion claws. Simultaneously, Iran aims to fortify its position in the region, careful not to provoke a full-scale war that could jeopardize its ambitions, including its pursuit of nuclear capabilities. This "Dance of the Scorpions," is not merely a metaphorical depiction; it is a real and ongoing geopolitical struggle intensified by the events of October 7th, led by Hamas, which marked a significant escalation in the region's complex conflict.

This study was conceived in the wake of the October 7th act of terror orchestrated by Hamas, which resulted in more than 1,200 Israeli casualties and 240 kidnappings by Hamas. This led to a retaliatory war aimed at eliminating Hamas' capabilities and rescuing the kidnapped. As the end of Hamas control over Gaza Strip seems imminent, the conflict's landscape is far from simplified. Other Iran's proxy players, like Hezbollah and Houthi rebels in Yemen, are currently involved in the armed conflict, albeit on a smaller scale. Such dynamic adds layers to the already intricate conflict, making the dance more treacherous and unpredictable. This study seeks to shed light on the complex interplay of military, political, and ideological forces in the Middle East by using an AI-based model predictive decision-making simulation framework.

Evolution of War Games in Context of Geopolitics and Counter-terrorism

War games have long been integral to military strategy and operational design, spanning a wide range of applications in geopolitics and counter-terrorism. As tools for understanding complex scenarios, they play a pivotal role in testing strategies and forecasting outcomes in controlled environments. Beyond their tactical and strategic utility, strategic war games also serve as crucial platforms for converging aspects and factors relevant to specific challenges. They facilitate perceptual discussions that are vital in shaping and consolidating strategic perceptions and systemic, regional perspectives. Through these games, relationships between various subsystems are clarified, enhancing understanding through direct encounters and learning exchanges.[1]

Historically, their formal use dates back to the 19th century in Prussia to train officers. This early usage focused more on tactics and strategy, lacking the complexity of modern geopolitical issues.[2]

The evolution of war gaming in the 20th century saw significant advancements, particularly with M.G. Weiner and others at RAND Corporation. Weiner's "War Gaming Methodology" was a crucial development in formalizing war games for strategic analysis, integrating statistical and computational methods for more realistic conflict simulations.[3] A notable example from this era is the RAND SIERRA war games (1954-1958), directed by the Air Force to explore operational scenarios for limited warfare, particularly in geopolitically significant regions like Southeast Asia, East Asia, and the Middle East.[4] These games not only focused on the military aspect but also heavily emphasized the political dimension of warfare, requiring participants representing the United States to deeply understand the adversary and the characteristics of limited warfare. During the Cold War, war games were extensively used to simulate conflicts between superpowers, focusing on deterrence and escalation dynamics.[5] Post-Cold War, the emphasis shifted to regional conflicts, peacekeeping, and counter-terrorism, helping understand asymmetric warfare where conventional tactics were insufficient against non-state actors.[6] In the 21st century, cyber warfare has been incorporated into war gaming, necessitating considerations of cyber capabilities, information warfare, and social media's role in geopolitical dynamics.[7]

War games are not just tools for the military; they are also used by policymakers to understand the potential consequences of different policy decisions in the international arena, also with respect to counter-terrorism.[8] Limitations and Ethical Considerations: Despite their usefulness, war games have limitations. They cannot perfectly predict human behavior or account for every variable in real-life scenarios. Ethical considerations also arise, especially in simulations involving terrorism and civilian casualties.[9]

Strategic war games are especially potent in challenging and potentially disrupting foundational assumptions of existing perceptions. They are designed to uncover operational gaps and stimulate discussions that lead to new understandings and approaches. This re-evaluation is crucial, particularly when a single paradigm is followed without significant challenge. By fostering an environment that encourages the re-examination of apparent assumptions and the discovery of hidden factors, war games promote the development of innovative strategies. The process of operational design in these games is fundamentally about learning and evolving knowledge, with the aim of developing a well-rounded perspective for specific campaigns. This involves creating effective action plans through a better systemic understanding of the problems at hand and formulating suitable operational ideas. The process also involves critical examination and an understanding of the necessity for change, especially in the face of environmental shifts. As role-players clearly present their positions, often in a blunt manner, gaps between different approaches are identified, leading to discussions that facilitate the reevaluation of perceptions and the generation of new ideas. This sociological aspect of war games is crucial, as it enables participants to clarify their perceptions, explore different approaches, and strengthen them for robust discussions, ensuring that potential gaps and misunderstandings are addressed before they become critical in real-world scenarios.[10]

Integration of experts is essential in the development of strategic war games from their inception. In this phase, intelligence's expertise and foundational data become crucial for setting the groundwork. This includes understanding the adversary's strategic culture and the dynamics of the geopolitical context in which the war game is set. Intelligence's role extends beyond providing basic military, political, or economic insights. It involves a deeper contribution by weaving in a nuanced understanding of the adversary's strategic thinking and behavior into the game's scenario. Before the game starts, intelligence, as an expert in the adversary's strategic culture, needs to prepare the team by imparting knowledge about the adversary, immersing them in the cultural and strategic nuances of the opposition. This comprehensive knowledge, rooted in historical, political, and social contexts, should be delivered succinctly and clearly to the participants, ensuring they grasp the multifaceted aspects of the adversary's strategic mindset.[11]

The Open Poker method, attributed to Prof. Ganor of the International Institute for Counter-Terrorism (ICT) at Reichman University, presents an innovative technique for examining intricate, multi-faceted, non-zero-sum game situations within the field of geopolitics.[12] The open-poker method employs an enhanced adaptation of the 'wisdom of the crowd' principle, incorporating expert insights to predict the outcomes of decisions made in geopolitical junctures. It has proven invaluable in predicting outcomes in complex geopolitical landscapes, offering essential support to policymakers and analysts in grasping and preparing for the implications of significant decisions. The Open Poker method has established itself as a powerful strategic asset in global situations, with its precision underscored by the ongoing, rapidly changing real-world consequences of these scenarios. The utility of this method was evident during the explosion in the Port of Beirut, following a simulation that was conducted around the time of Lebanon's economic downturn in 2020 addressing the political and social upheaval in Lebanon during its economic and healthcare crises.

Integration of Artificial Intelligence into the sphere of counter-terrorism

The integration of Artificial Intelligence (AI) into various fields, such as healthcare, finance and counter-terrorism, signifies a transformative paradigm shift by enabling advanced predictive analytics and automating complex tasks, enhancing efficiency and accuracy. Particularly in counter-terrorism, this shift fundamentally alters how societies anticipate, manage, and mitigate threats and terrorism. At the crossroads of technology, law enforcement, and ethics, this burgeoning field demands a nuanced understanding of its vast potential and the intricate pitfalls that accompany it. The literature in this domain spans a broad spectrum, ranging from theoretical musings in science fiction to the pragmatic applications embedded in national security strategies. In our pursuit, this review aspires to synthesize these diverse perspectives, weaving them into a cohesive tapestry that encapsulates the current state and future trajectory of AI in the realm of counter-terrorism efforts.

Early applications of AI in this field focus on utilizing its power for the benefits of predictive policing; a term that has metamorphosed from its origins in the pages of fiction to a tangible force in contemporary law enforcement and intelligence operations. Philip K. Dick's novella "Minority Report,"[13] set in a future where 'Precrime' units prevent crimes before they occur, serves as a pivotal touchstone. [14-16] This narrative serves as a critical starting point to understand how the predictive capabilities once confined to the realm of fiction are increasingly manifesting in reality. It also raises profound questions about the ethical quandaries that predictive policing entails. Ethical and privacy concerns further complicate the evolution of predictive policing, emphasizing the sparsity of datasets and the inherent privacy risks that accompany bulk data collection.[17]

The evolution of predictive policing and its seamless integration into counter-terrorism strategies marks a profound shift from traditional reactive methods to proactive approaches. Modern law enforcement agencies, fortified by advancements in AI, now possess the capacity to analyze vast datasets, discern intricate patterns, and predict potential criminal or terrorist activities.[18] This shift, while promising in terms of enhanced security and prevention, simultaneously ushers in a host of ethical and practical challenges. The literature delves deep into the fine balance between pre-emptive measures and the safeguarding of civil liberties, shedding light on the perilous path that might lead to a society where the presumption of innocence is eclipsed by algorithmically determined probabilities of future criminality.[15,16]

On the international stage, United Nations Secretary-General António Guterres sounded a cautionary note in 2018, encapsulating broader apprehensions surrounding AI (United Nations 2018).[19] His statement underscores the potential for these technologies to be weaponized maliciously or to bring about unintended negative consequences, particularly in sensitive areas such as national security. The dual-use nature of AI technologies, serving both counter-terrorism efforts and potentially aiding terrorist activities, underscores the multifaceted complexity of technology's role in modern conflict and security.[20]

The attempts to predict and prevent uncertain future events can result in false predictions, misuse for political goals, and the possibility of self-fulfilling prophecies.[21,22] These actions, aimed at averting potential incidents, often lead to the limitation of choices available to individuals. Additionally, the absence of a universally accepted definition of terrorism can lead to the broad labeling of behavior as terrorist, potentially infringing on individual liberties.[23] Recent study have shown that relying on machine learning systems to predict and prevent terrorism, and particularly the implications of their use for security in Israel, is still in its immature stages. This study highlights the delicate equilibrium between effective prevention and the potential violation of human rights.[24]

Researching aspects of AI in counter-terrorism, for predicting and preventing terrorism is not new. Ganor's insights into the systemic changes ushered in by AI in counter-terrorism strategies and intelligence operations contribute to a broader understanding of the AI revolution within the sphere of counter-terrorism.[25] This revolution signifies a transformative impact on security and intelligence arenas, reshaping the very fabric of how threats are anticipated and managed. Delving into the latest AI-driven methodologies for predictive analytics in counter-terrorism, addressing the aftermath of recent terrorist attacks, not only proposes AI-based solutions to mitigate their humanitarian and economic impacts but also offers prospective strategies to enhance global security.[26] A seminal example of the operationalization of AI in counter-terrorism is the U.S. military's Project Maven. This initiative played a pivotal role in harnessing big data to combat groups like ISIS and al-Qaeda, vividly exemplifying the practical application of these technologies in real-world scenarios. [27] It represents a tectonic shift from traditional reactive approaches to a proactive stance in counter-terrorism.

Three studies, led by the Center for Intelligence Heritage and the Institute for Intelligence Methodology Research, underline Chat-GPT's value in offering new perspectives, augmenting traditional intelligence methodologies, and providing flexible, scalable solutions for strategic intelligence and planning. The first study discusses Chat-GPT's transformative influence on the intelligence sector, advocating for its adoption as a tool to democratize data access and revolutionize the way information is processed and analyzed.[28] The second and third studies present a granular view of how AI technologies are actively deployed in real-world scenarios, thus contributing to a comprehensive understanding of their capabilities and limitations. While the second delves into Chat-GPT's effectiveness in reenacting historical events like the Yom Kippur War, demonstrating its capability to challenge established biases and enrich intelligence assessments;[29] the third, focuses on AI-based role-playing simulations in understanding decision-making within the Iranian axis, noting the potential of digital twins in strategic intelligence assessments.[30]

In contrast to the existing literature, utilizing AI in navigating and understanding the intricate web of highly complex terror-driven geopolitical conflicts, such as the Middle East post-October 7th events, has not been dealt with before. This study presents a four-stage framework for an AI-generated simulated geopolitical-conflict game. Central to this framework is the strategic integration of sophisticated AI technology, specifically stand-alone Chat-GPT4 tool. The primary aim is to facilitate an in-depth exploration and analysis of an ongoing geopolitical conflict scenario, utilizing the advanced analytical prowess of AI. The main stages of this framework are as follows: The 1st stage sets up the simulation's starting conditions, based on the geopolitical context, the background scenario, the triggering event, the nature of the geopolitical players and their alliances. This stage utilizes Chat-GPT's historical data and theories, validated by experts. In the 2nd stage, the GPT identifies key actors and their decision-making considerations, creating detailed decision-making tables. This step involves AI's data analysis and expert validation to ensure realism. The 3rd stage focuses on an AI-based closed-loop simulation, utilizing a model predictive decision-making approach. In this stage the AI autonomously runs a simulation, updating strategies based on evolving scenarios. It simulates actions and non-actions of players, reflecting transparent decision-making and geopolitical dynamics. Finally, in the 4th stage the AI analyzes the simulation results, focusing on immediate gameplay and deeper analyses of alliances, strategies, and diplomatic maneuvers. This analysis lights upon the escalation potential of the conflict in view of the aforementioned triggering event.

The main contribution of this study is two folded. First, this novel approach marks a significant advancement in the field of counter-terror and geopolitical studies, combining state-of-the-art AI technology (and in particular stand-alone Chat-GPT4) to explore the intricate and evolving dynamics between key actors in a specific geopolitical conflict. Second, it provides a nuanced understanding of the complex geopolitical tapestries in the Middle Eastern geopolitics.

The rest of this paper is structured as follows: The next section delves into the proposed theoretical model for simulating a multi-player non-zero-sum complex geopolitical conflict. Next, a four-stage AI-generated simulation framework is suggested, putting practice into the theoretical model by utilizing the power of AI. This follows by a thorough elaboration of the background scenario, the multi-player geopolitical arena, and the triggering event that will be used later as an input for subsequent simulation stages. Subsequently, AI's profound analytical skills are showcased in advising both who are the key players to be considered and what are their decision-making considerations and overarching objectives. Next, an autonomous AI-based closed-loop simulation is conducted; this is followed by an in-depth AI-analysis of the simulation results, offering a realistic portrayal of geopolitical maneuvering. This is followed by a discussion that synthesizes the insights derived from the simulation. Finally, conclusions are provided.

Theoretical Model for Simulating a Geopolitical Conflict

Model Predictive Decision-making Approach

The addressed geopolitical conflict, such as many practical problems in economics and engineering, can be modeled as a multi-player non-zero-sum game with multiple objectives and decision-making payoffs. It is assumed that the geopolitical real-life physical system (the plant) behaves according to the following nonlinear system model:

$$X_{n+1}=f(X_n, U_n^{DM}), \quad X_n, U_n^{DM} \in \Re^N$$

The notation X_n represents the states of the players at turn n, and U_n^{DM} their applied decisions at the same turn. The notation n represents the current time-step (round). In such a non-zero-sum game, each player deals with their own conflicting objectives. Hence, a vector of objective functions must be considered.[31,32] Here the players' objective functions are practically modeled by AI. To determine the decisions of each player within each time-step, an AI-based Model Predictive Control (MPC) is applied in a closed loop form. The closed-loop form solution approach, which is employed in this study, may be considered as a version of MPC, also known as receding horizon control.[33,34] The AI-based MPC can be modeled as:

$$\tilde{X}_{n+1}=f(\tilde{X}_n, U_n^{DM}), \quad \tilde{X}_n, U_n^{DM} \in \Re^N$$

The notation $\tilde{X}_n$ represents the predicted states of the players at turn n, and U_n^{DM} their decisions at the same turn. Employing receding horizon control allows reducing the computational complexity, associated with solving the original non-linear problem, by limiting the time horizon of observations.[35] To prevent simulation inaccuracies, it is recommended to limit the observations of the simulated MPC to an advised time horizon (N rounds). It is necessary to set the initial conditions of the simulation with respect to the geopolitical plant. If the simulation is operated in parallel to a real-time conflict, it is advised to reset the initial conditions after each operative unexpected triggering event that is taking place.

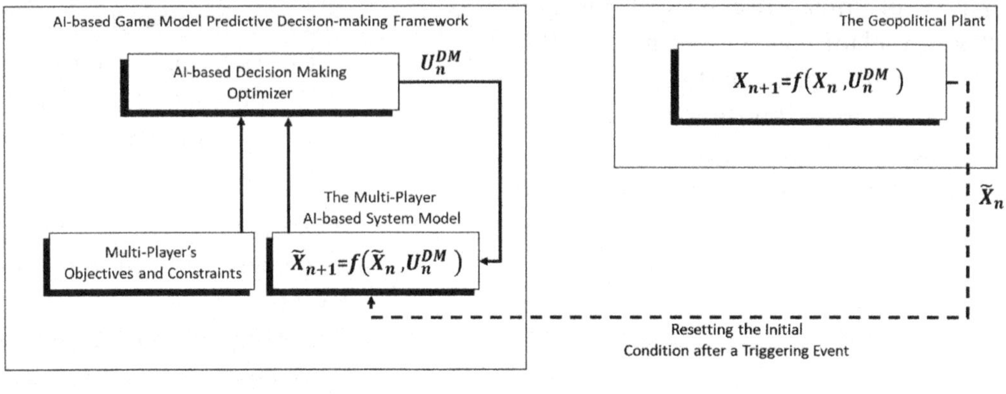

Figure 1: The Model Predictive Decision-making Framework

Transparent Complex Multi-Player Decision-making Game Framework

In the realm of international relations and strategic military planning, understanding the dynamics of complex geopolitical scenarios is crucial. The following presents a comprehensive decision-making framework, designed to simulate the state or non-state actors' actions U_n^{DM}, in pivotal international issues. This subsection outlines the structure, objectives, and unique approach of this framework, offering a deep dive into the mechanics of geopolitical strategy and crisis management.

Objectives of the Framework

The primary goal of the framework is to provide a realistic and dynamic environment for understanding geopolitical strategies and crisis management. The unique 'open knowledge' (transparent) aspect of the game, where players have insight into potential strategies of others, adds depth and complexity. It mirrors the realities of international relations, where states and actors must constantly adapt to the strategic moves of others. The proposed framework serves as a powerful tool for understanding the intricate and evolving nature of international relations and strategic planning. By engaging in this game environment, participants gain a profound understanding of the complexities involved in geopolitical decision-making, crisis management, and strategic adaptation.

The Structure of the Transparent Multi-player Decision-making Game Framework

Initialization

1. Define the Geopolitical Scenario.
2. Define Players: The game begins by identifying the players involved (e.g., X1, X2, X3, ..., XN), representing different state or non-state actors in the geopolitical scenario.
3. Set Initial Decision-making Considerations and Objectives: Each player's initial policies are determined, laying the groundwork for the first round of the game.
4. Start the Game: The game commences with Round 1, with a starting scenario and a triggering action by X1.

Round 1: Strategy Development

5. Main Player (X1) Triggering Action: An action is suggested and constructed by X1, in response to a crisis scenario, along with their motivations, objectives, and potential holistic benefits.
6. Other Players' Reactions:
    a. Reactions: Each player, from X2 to XN, develops a set of potential reactions to X1's approached action, resulting in an advised set of actions.
    b. Each action that is advised considers the motivations and benefits for each player, fostering a comprehensive understanding of the reaction landscape.

7. Action Selection: Selected (sub-set) actions (it can be more than one) are chosen by each player, aligning with their holistic interests. The players' action(s) selections are made with the assumption that they have full awareness of the other players' advised sets of actions. This approach is based on a transparent style of gameplay, where each player's strategies and potential actions are known or can be reasonably inferred by the others. This knowledge allows them to strategize and react accordingly to derive safety level decision-making actions.

Following Rounds: Action Selection and Evolution

8. Opening Picture - Based on the outcomes of the previous round (i.e., the execution of the players' selected (sub-set) of actions of the previous round) the opening picture of this round is determined by executing the action and the sub-set of selected counter-actions of players X1 and X2-XN, respectively.

9. Round Development:

    a. Updating Actions: Players update their potential advised set of actions, reflecting their response to the evolving scenario.

    b. Strategy Refinement: Sub-set of actions are chosen by each player (X1-XN) with the assumption that they have full awareness of the other players' advised sets of actions.

Four-stage AI-generated Simulation Framework

This section introduces a meticulously developed four-stage framework for an AI-generated simulated geopolitical-conflict game. Central to this framework is the strategic integration of sophisticated AI technology, specifically stand-alone Chat-GPT4 tool. The primary aim is to facilitate an in-depth exploration and analysis of a geopolitical scenario, utilizing the advanced analytical prowess of AI. This novel approach marks a significant advancement in the field of geopolitical studies, combining state-of-the-art AI technology to explore the intricate and evolving dynamics between key actors in a specific geopolitical conflict. It seeks to demystify the complexities of global conflicts, providing a nuanced understanding of the interplay among diverse key actors, particularly geopolitical actors. It is crafted to yield deep insights into the myriad potential trajectories and outcomes stemming from the strategic decisions and actions of key players in the geopolitical landscape. The chosen case study demonstrates the efficacy of this framework with respect to the ongoing geopolitical conflict in the Middle East following the decision to commence "Operation Swords of Iron."

Stage 1 – Preparation

In the preparation stage, experts play a crucial role in dissecting the geopolitical arena related to the studied conflict. The AI assists with historical data and geopolitical theories to establish a comprehensive understanding of the conflict's evolution and broader implications. This stage sets the background scenario, discussing the nature of the geopolitical players and their alliances, which are then inputted into the AI for subsequent simulation stages. Next, the initial conditions of the simulation are set, specifying the triggering action taken by X1. In the demonstrated case-study the triggering action of the multi-player geopolitical system is initialized by Israel's decision to commence a significant military response to the actions of Hamas, while announcing its intention to conduct a ground invasion of Gaza and begins with aerial bombardments in preparation for the ground entry. This action was decided, with the dual objectives of neutralizing the Hamas threat and rescuing kidnapped individuals, to enhance Israeli national security, thereby contributing to regional stabilization.

Stage 2 - Setting the Foundations to the Simulations using AI

This stage aims to set the simulation with the key relevant actors (players) and corresponding decision-making considerations and overarching objectives. This was achieved in two steps. First, the AI is asked to advise with a set of criteria and a scoring method to highlight such key actors and their significance in the ongoing conflict. These actors' actions and interactions not only influence the immediate situation but also have far-reaching implications for regional stability and global geopolitics. In the context of the demonstrated case-study, the following six key actors are advised by the AI: Israel, Hamas, the United States, Iran, Hezbollah, and Russia.

Next, for each of the key actors the AI is requested to create a comprehensive table that encapsulates their decision-making considerations and overarching objectives. Such considerations range from military strategy to economic impacts, and are informed by the AI's extensive data analysis capabilities. This holistic view aids in understanding the multifaceted nature of decision-making in high-stake geopolitical conflicts. Next, a team of geopolitical experts validated the AI-generated strategic tables. This process ensures that the AI's outputs align with real-world complexities and current geopolitical knowledge. The expert validation process is crucial for ensuring that the AI's strategic considerations are not only data-driven but also realistic and applicable in the contemporary geopolitical context.

Stage 3 - Running an AI-Based Closed-loop Simulation

In this phase, the AI independently runs the simulation, dynamically updating strategies based on evolving geopolitical scenarios. This showcases the AI's ability to adapt to changing conditions and predict potential outcomes. Here the time horizon was set to 8 rounds; each round within this game represents a time frame of a week. The AI simulates each round of the simulation, based on the transparent complex multi-player decision-making game framework that was introduced in the previous section. The simulation results in two sets, per each key player. The 1st set represents the 'safety level' actions that are advised and applied by the players in view of the transparency principle. The 2nd set represents the actions that were advised, but eventually avoided and were not executed by the players, due to their best understanding the set of actions that other players were advised. Both sets offer a realistic portrayal of geopolitical maneuvering.

Stage 4 - Analysis

The AI conducts predictive modeling analyzing the outcomes of each round, providing forecasts on conflict escalation and containment. It employs sophisticated modeling techniques to predict how strategic choices might play out in the real world. The simulation culminates in the AI generating first and second-order insights, offering a deeper understanding of the conflict dynamics. While first order insights focus on the immediate and observable aspects of gameplay, second order insights dive deeper, offering a more nuanced and complex analysis. This includes analyzing potential shifts in alliances, changes in military strategies, and the implications of diplomatic operative maneuvers.

The final stage is reflective, offering a synthesis of the AI's simulations and insights. It serves as a digest, providing a coherent narrative and an analysis of the potential future trajectory of the Middle Eastern conflict.

Stage 1 - Preparation

Operation Swords of Iron - Awakening the Giant

The dawn of October 7th unveiled a new era in the landscape of modern terrorism, resulting in 1,200 casualties and 240 kidnapped individuals held by Hamas. This day's attack was unprecedented in its scope and execution, marking a significant evolution in the tactics of terror.[36,37] This multi-dimensional military onslaught was a coordinated strike utilizing air, sea, land forces, alongside cyber operations, and psychological warfare. The multi-dimensional approach was established to neutralize Israel's counter-terrorism measures and cripple the IDF's response capabilities. This operation involved thousands of highly skilled and fervently motivated individuals, intent on overwhelming security forces, gaining control of critical access points to southern settlements, and instilling terror among the civilian population.

The acts of terror were not random but strategically focusing on maximizing civilian casualties. The brutality extended to sadistic treatment of victims, desecration of the deceased, and a chilling campaign of mass kidnappings.[38] In retaliation to this meticulously planned attack, the Israel Defense Forces (IDF) launched Operation "Swords of Iron." This mission was a direct response to the Hamas militants' audacious attack on southern Israeli towns and cities.[39] The operation's declared objectives were ambitious yet clear: to topple the Hamas government in Gaza, eradicate its military capabilities, and secure the release of kidnapped civilians.[40,41] The IDF executed this through a combination of air bombardments, naval and ground operations, specifically targeting Hamas infrastructure and forces, with a particular focus on the destruction of their underground networks, known as the "metro".[42] As the operation unfolded into late October, the situation remained dynamic and tense. Hamas escalated their aggression, launching thousands of missiles at Israel and attempting to infiltrate Jewish settlements. Their military engagement was of an intensity rarely seen before.[43]

In the backdrop of these events, the intricate web of coordination among Hamas, Hezbollah, and Iran came into focus. There were strong indications that the Iranian leadership played a significant role in orchestrating these attacks, as evidenced by reports of critical coordination between Hamas and the Iran's Islamic Revolutionary Guard Corps (IRGC) in Beirut.[44] This alliance, though complex, revealed a unified front against Israel, with Iran's influence permeating the strategies of both Hamas and Hezbollah.[45]

"Operation Swords of Iron - Awakening the Giant" was more than a military campaign; it was a statement of resilience and a testament to Israel's determination to defend its sovereignty and citizens. As the world watched, the IDF, facing a multi-front threat, stood resolute, navigating the intricacies of a conflict that extended beyond borders and conventional warfare.

The Iranian Nexus – Ideology and Ambition in the Middle East

In the intricate geopolitical landscape of the Middle East, the Axis of Resistance, orchestrated by Iran, emerges as a complex and multifaceted coalition. This alliance, weaving together Iran's geopolitical ambitions and religious ideologies, crafts a formidable front against Western influence and Israeli regional dominance.[46,47] It unites a diverse array of state and non-state actors, each contributing to the regional power dynamics.

Foundations of the Opposition

Shi'a Islamic Ideology: The core of Iran's opposition to Israel is deeply rooted in its Shi'a Islamic beliefs. The Iranian leadership, perceiving itself as the guardian of Muslim interests, views its stance against Israel as a religious imperative.[48,49] This is particularly emphasized considering Jerusalem's (Quds) significance in Islam.

The Sanctity of Jerusalem (Quds): Jerusalem's centrality in Iran's religious narrative is profound. Since the Islamic Revolution, Iranian leaders have consistently called for the city's liberation.[50] This stems from Jerusalem's sacred status in Islam and its symbolic significance in Shi'a doctrine. The quest to 'liberate' Jerusalem underscores Iran's dedication to what it sees as a holy mission.

Defending Islamic Lands: Iran's support for Palestinian causes is framed as a defense against Israeli occupation, seen as an infringement on Islamic lands.[51,52] This stance is a critical element of Iran's religiously couched rhetoric, reinforcing its position as a defender of the Islamic faith.

Geopolitical Dimensions of the Conflict

Regional Dominance: Challenging Israel is integral to Iran's strategy of asserting regional dominance. By opposing Israel, Iran aims to position itself as a leader in the Muslim world, extending its influence across the region.

Countering Western Influence: Viewing Israel as a Western foothold, Iran's opposition aligns with its broader objective of resisting Western, particularly American, influence. This stance is a key component of Tehran's regional strategy.

Unifying Factor: Amidst regional sectarian and ethnic divisions, Iran's stance against Israel serves as a unifying rallying point. This strategy is designed to bring various groups under Iran's leadership, creating a united front against a common enemy.

Proxy Warfare: The strategic deployment of proxies like Hezbollah in Lebanon and Hamas in Gaza is central to Iran's approach. These groups serve as Tehran's instruments in its indirect conflict with Israel, allowing Iran to engage in asymmetric warfare while avoiding direct military engagement. [53,54]

The Coalition's Composition and Dynamics

In the intricate geopolitical tapestry of the Middle East, the Axis of Resistance, spearheaded by Iran, stands as a complex and multifaceted coalition. This alliance, a fusion of Iran's geopolitical ambitions and religious ideologies, forges a potent front against Western influence and Israeli regional dominance, enlisting a diverse array of state and non-state actors. This coalition includes:

Hezbollah in Lebanon: As a cornerstone of this alliance, Hezbollah in Lebanon represents more than just a militant group; it is an extension of Iranian influence. Heavily backed by Iran both militarily and financially, Hezbollah is a critical force in projecting Iran's reach into Lebanon and against Israel, embodying Tehran's strategic and ideological objectives.[55,56]

Syrian Government: Iran's unwavering support for Bashar al-Assad's regime in Syria underscores its commitment to maintaining influence in the Levant. Iranian military aid has been crucial in sustaining Assad's rule throughout the Syrian Civil War, positioning Tehran as a key player in Syrian affairs.[57,58]

Shia Militias in Iraq, Syria: Iran's influence permeates through various Shia militias. These groups, instrumental in combating ISIS, also serve Iran's agenda of countering U.S. influence in the area, further entrenching Iranian interests in the region.[59-62]

Houthi Rebels in Yemen: Iran's involvement with the Houthi rebels in Yemen represents a strategic move to extend its influence in the Arabian Peninsula. While the extent of support is often debated, the Houthis act as a tool for Iran to challenge Saudi Arabian interests and exert its influence in Yemen.[63,64]

Hamas and Palestinian Islamic Jihad in Gaza: These groups are represented in a cluster, primarily engaged in the Israeli-Palestinian conflict, and receive Iranian support. This backing enables Tehran to maintain a stake in Palestinian affairs and the broader conflict with Israel, aligning with its ideological support for the Palestinian cause.

Qatar: The enhancement of trilateral relations between Qatar, Iran, and Turkey has emerged as both a cause and a consequence of the blockade imposed on Qatar by other Gulf states. Iran capitalized on the GCC rift to bolster its regional stance against Saudi Arabia and garner support amid rising tensions with the United States and increasing sanctions. Meanwhile, Turkey utilized the blockade to reinforce its image as a reliable mediator in the Middle East. Consequently, the strengthening of ties among Qatar, Turkey, and Iran is a notable and unforeseen outcome of the Saudi-led blockade.[65]

Strengths, Weaknesses, Opportunities and Threats to the Coalition

Iranian coalition in the Middle East reflects Tehran's strategic goals and ideological stance. While it provides Iran with significant regional influence and a means to counter its adversaries, it also exposes Iran to various challenges and threats. The dynamic nature of Middle Eastern geopolitics means that the fortunes of this coalition can shift rapidly, influenced by both internal dynamics and external pressures.

The strengths of this nexus are manifold. Iran's coalition allows for substantial geopolitical influence across multiple fronts, challenging rivals such as Saudi Arabia, Israel, and the United States. The use of proxies facilitates engagement in asymmetric warfare, complicating direct retaliation against Iran. Moreover, ideological unity, particularly the shared opposition to Western influence and support for the Palestinian cause, binds the coalition despite their diverse backgrounds. However, this coalition is not without any weaknesses, as internal disagreements among the groups, driven by their local agendas, can sometimes conflict with Iran's objectives. Economic struggles, compounded by international sanctions, limit Iran's ability to support its allies. Furthermore, the coalition lacks conventional military strength and faces international isolation due to its activities.

The threats to this coalition are as diverse as its components. International pressure and sanctions continue to constrain their operational capabilities and economic viability. Active efforts by regional rivals, including Saudi Arabia and Israel, to counter Iranian influence pose continuous challenges. Domestic issues within coalition member states, such as economic hardship and political dissent, can also undermine their effectiveness. However, amidst these challenges lie opportunities. The chaotic landscapes in Syria and Iraq offer Iran prospects to expand its influence through local proxies. Iran's ability to shape key regional issues, including the Israeli-Palestinian conflict and the balance of power in the Persian Gulf, enhances its role as a regional power broker.

The Western and Middle Eastern Coalition

In a world where geopolitical landscapes shift like desert sands, the alliance between the United States, Israel, and the moderate Arab Emirates, strengthened by the inclusion of Egypt, Jordan, and Saudi Arabia stands as a testament to shared objectives and visions for a stable future. This coalition, forged in the fires of regional conflicts and global power struggles, represents more than just a strategic partnership; it symbolizes a united front in the fight for stability and prosperity in a volatile region.

The United States: As the linchpin of this alliance, the U.S. brings to the table its immense military power and diplomatic influence. Committed to ensuring regional stability and countering threats from adversarial forces, the U.S. plays a crucial role in supporting its allies through military aid, intelligence sharing, and diplomatic backing. This support is pivotal in maintaining the balance of power in the Middle East and ensuring the security of its partners.

Israel: Known for its military prowess and technological advancements, Israel stands as a bulwark against regional aggression. Its strategic position in the Middle East and its robust defense capabilities make it a vital ally in the coalition. Israel's intelligence contributions and counterterrorism expertise are invaluable assets that significantly enhance the coalition's effectiveness.

Arab Emirates: The Arab Emirates, with their strategic location and significant economic resources, play a crucial role in this alliance. Their participation bridges the traditional divides in the Middle East, bringing a unique perspective and facilitating broader regional cooperation. The Emirates' commitment to stability and development in the region, coupled with their growing military capabilities, adds a critical dimension to the coalition.

Moderate Arab Countries: The alliance between the United States, Israel, and the Arab Emirates is further strengthened by the inclusion of Egypt, Jordan, and Saudi Arabia - nations recognized for their moderate stances in the Arab world. These countries bring additional layers of diplomatic influence, strategic positioning, and a commitment to regional stability. Their integration into the coalition enhances the collective capability to navigate complex geopolitical challenges, bridge traditional divides, and promote a unified front for peace and stability. This expanded alliance, now encompassing a more diverse range of Middle Eastern perspectives, stands as a robust response to regional conflicts and a proactive force shaping a secure future in one of the world's most dynamic regions.

Stage 2 – Setting the Foundations to the Simulations using AI

In the volatile arena of Middle Eastern geopolitics, where alliances shift like desert sands and enemies may share fleeting interests, the prospect of conflict between Hezbollah and Israel is a constant shadow, darkened further by the presence of Hamas. The calculations made by these actors are not mere gambles; they are deeply rooted in strategic imperatives, ideological motivations, and a complex web of international relations.

This section delves into the complex interplay between key actors. These actors have been meticulously chosen based on an AI-advised set of criteria and a scoring method that highlight their significance in the ongoing conflict. Their actions and interactions not only influence the immediate situation but also have far-reaching implications for regional stability and global geopolitics.

Key Players in the Geopolitical Arena

The AI-advised set of criteria, and a complementary scoring method:

1. **Direct Involvement** 50%: Entities directly involved in the conflict, either as primary participants or as influential supporters, are critical to understanding the conflict's nature and trajectory.

2. **Impact on Regional Stability** 25%: Those who play a role in either the escalation or de-escalation of tensions, thereby affecting regional stability.

3. **Strategic Influence** 10%: The ability to exert significant influence over regional dynamics, either through military might, economic power, or diplomatic leverage.

4. **Historical Context** 5%: Actors with a long-standing history in the region's geopolitics, whose past actions and policies have shaped the current state of affairs.

5. **Geopolitical Interests** 5%: Entities whose geopolitical interests are deeply intertwined with the outcome of the conflict, driving them to actively shape the situation.

6. **International Implications** 5%: Actors whose involvement brings in international attention, either through alliances, oppositions, or through global economic and political interests.

The following Table 1 rates the geopolitical state and non-state actors according to the advised scoring method. The examination of these key players, underpinned by the outlined criteria, provides a comprehensive understanding of the multifaceted and interlinked nature of the Middle Eastern geopolitical landscape. Following the advised scoring method, the following six key actors are chosen for the simulation phase: Israel, Hamas, the United States, Iran, Hezbollah, and Russia. These were subsequently revied and validated by a team of experts.

Obtaining Key Decision-making Considerations and Overarching Objectives

Utilizing the power of AI (Chat-GPT4), key decision-making factors for each actor were characterized. These considerations were derived using information from the preceding section as

Table 1: Rating the geopolitical Influence and Relevance of State and Non-state Actors

Actor Name	Direct Involvement 50%	Impact on Regional Stability 25%	Strategic Influence 10%	Historical Context 5%	Geopolitical Interests 5%	International Implications 5%	Total Score
Israel	5	5	5	5	5	5	100
United States	4	5	5	5	5	5	90
Hezbollah	5	4	4	4	4	3	89
Hamas & PIJ	5	4	3	4	3	3	86
Iran	4	4	5	5	5	4	84
Russia	4	4	5	4	5	5	84
Syria	4	4	3	4	3	2	75
UN Security Council	2	5	5	5	4	5	69
Saudi Arabia	3	4	4	4	4	3	69
Houthi Rebels in Yemen	4	3	3	3	3	2	69
Palestinian Authority	3	3	3	4	3	2	60
Egypt	2	4	4	4	4	3	59
Shia Militias in Iraq and Syria	3	3	2	3	2	2	56
France	2	3	4	4	3	4	54
Turkey	2	3	4	4	4	3	54
Arab Emirates	2	3	4	3	3	3	52
Wagner Group	3	2	2	2	2	3	51

input. A team of experts subsequently reviewed and validated these findings. The AI (Chat-GPT4) presented the following nuanced analysis:

Israel: A central figure in Middle Eastern geopolitics, Israel's strategic positioning, military capabilities, and ongoing conflicts with neighboring entities make it a pivotal state actor in the region. Israel's overarching objective is neutralizing Hamas threat and rescuing kidnapped individuals, to enhance Israeli national security. The other focus of Israel is on Iran's nuclear capabilities, regional ambitions, and the role of proxies like Hezbollah. Israel's strategic concerns also include Hamas's stance, regional stability, security threats, domestic public opinion, military preparedness, economic impact, diplomatic ramifications, and international relations.

Hamas: Representing non-state actors with significant influence, Hamas's actions and policies are crucial in understanding the Palestinian-Israeli dynamics and the broader ideological and military conflicts in the region. Hamas overarching objective is the survival of the organization in Gaza strip. Hamas key considerations include alignment with strategic objectives, ideological commitment to resisting Israeli actions, regional influence, stability and security in controlled territories, economic factors, civilian protection, human rights adherence, and governance effectiveness.

Hezbollah: As a powerful non-state actor and a proxy of Iran, Hezbollah's military strength and political influence in Lebanon and the broader region make it a critical entity to analyze. Hezbollah overarching objective is to disrupt the Israeli military campaign in Gaza, while not escalating into a full scale war with Israel. Central Hezbollah considerations are Iranian directives, regional support, deterrence against Israel, internal Lebanese interests (security, political stability, economic impact), potential for power expansion, regional security capabilities, relationships with other factions, and diplomatic consequences.

Iran: A key regional player, Iran's support for proxy groups, its ideological stance against Israel, and its aspirations for regional dominance place it at the forefront of shaping Middle Eastern geopolitics. Iran's overarching goals are to operate its proxies to disrupt the Israeli military campaign in Gaza, while not risking Hezbollah survivability as its strategic proxy, and avoiding any interference to its nuclear strategic program. The key aspects include alignment with its own policies, military cooperation with Hezbollah, ideological commitment against Israel, tactical considerations, regional influence, global reputation, and strategic access to the Mediterranean.

USA: As a global superpower with vested interests in the Middle East, the U.S.'s diplomatic, military, and economic policies significantly impact regional stability and power balances. The USA's overarching goal is to maintain its domination in the Middle East. The USA main considerations are: regional stability, eliminating radical groups, global status, human rights implications, direct and indirect security threats, international acceptance, governance and influence, public support, maintaining strong partnership with Israel, counterterrorism efforts, political dynamics, economic interests, coordination with the Palestinian authority, and operational factors.

Russia: With its strategic ambitions and involvement in the region, particularly in Syria and its growing influence in Middle Eastern affairs, Russia plays a crucial role in shaping geopolitical outcomes. Russia's overarching goal is to maintain its position as a dominant actor in the Middle East, including its partnership with Iran. Russia emphasizes regional diplomacy, security dynamics, national interests, long-term regional stability, global public opinion, political stability, and economic interests in the region.

Tables 2 to 7 below present detailed considerations and positions of the key actors involved, on top of the overarching goals that were specified above. The tables aim to unravel the complexities of their interactions, motivations, and the implications of their actions in shaping the ongoing conflict and regional stability.

Table 2: Strategic Considerations for Israel's Decision-Making on top of its Overarching-goals

Cluster	Consideration	Elaboration	Level of Importance	Comments on the level of importance
Strategic Concerns	Iran's Nuclear Resilience	Israel's strategic concern regarding Iran's nuclear capabilities and their global implications.	High	A core issue for Israel's national security, with significant implications for regional and global stability.
Regional Ambitions	Iran's Regional Ambitions	Assessing Iran's aspirations in the region, which directly impact Israel's security environment.	High	Iran's regional influence, particularly through proxies, is a central concern for Israel's strategic planning.
Proxy Dynamics	Hezbollah's Stance	Hezbollah's position and potential actions, considering its role as an Iranian proxy.	High	Critical, as Hezbollah's military capabilities and proximity pose direct threats to Israel.
Palestinian Conflict	Hamas' Position and Goals	Understanding Hamas' strategic aims and position in the context of a broader conflict.	High	Important for comprehending the multi-front nature of the threat and the ideological and strategic dynamics at play.
Geopolitical Stability	Regional Stability and Dynamics	The effects of conflict on the broader Middle Eastern geopolitical landscape.	High	Highly relevant for Israel's long-term strategic interests and for understanding the interplay of regional powers.
Security Analysis	Security and Threat Assessment	Evaluating the immediate and long-term threats posed by Hezbollah and other regional actors.	High	Primary concern for Israel, given the direct and immediate nature of security threats, particularly from Hezbollah.
Domestic Factors	Public Opinion and Political Climate	The influence of Israeli public opinion and the political landscape on decision-making.	High	Highly influential in shaping the government's policies and responses, especially in democratic contexts.
Military Preparedness	Military Readiness and Capability	Israel's preparedness and capability to engage in a conflict on multiple fronts.	High	Essential for determining Israel's ability to respond effectively to any military scenario.
Economic Impact	Economic Impact	The potential economic consequences and disruptions of a war for Israel.	High	Significant for assessing the broader implications of conflict on Israel's economy and society.
Diplomatic Concerns	Diplomatic Ramifications	The effects of military action on Israel's relationships with international allies and entities.	High	Relevant for maintaining crucial international alliances and for navigating the diplomatic complexities during a conflict.
International Relations	International Pressure and Sanctions	The impact of global opinion and potential sanctions on Israel and the Nexus members.	Moderate	Significant due to the potential international repercussions and the effect on the strategic calculations of all parties involved.
Economic Factors	Economic Considerations	Financial aspects affecting the Nexus, including funding and resource allocation.	Moderate	Affects operational capabilities and long-term sustainability of both Israel and its adversaries.

Table 3: Strategic Considerations for Hamas's Decision-Making on top of its Overarching-goals

Cluster	Consideration	Elaboration	Importance	Comments on the level of importance
Political Alignment	Alignment with Hamas interests	Whether the war aligns with Hamas's strategic objectives and political goals.	High	A potential conflict is assessed against how it serves Hamas's own interests and long-term goals.
Ideological Commitment	Resistance to Israeli oppression	Commitment to resisting what Hamas views as Israeli occupation and aggression.	High	Resistance is a core tenet of Hamas's ideology and a key driver of its policies and actions.
Regional Influence	Maintaining influence in the region	The conflict's implications for Hamas's influence among Palestinian factions and in the wider region.	High	Maintaining and potentially expanding influence is a primary consideration for Hamas in the regional context.
Stability and Security	Stability and security	The impact of the conflict on the stability and security of territories under Hamas control.	Moderate	Stability and security are important for maintaining control, but Hamas may weigh these against potential gains from conflict involvement.
Economic Interests	Economic growth	How the conflict might impact economic conditions in territories under Hamas's administration.	Moderate	Economic factors are significant for maintaining public support and funding but may not be decisive in conflict decision-making.
Civilian Protection	Safeguarding Palestinian people	The degree to which the conflict would affect the safety and security of Palestinians.	Low	While publicly a concern, strategic military decisions may prioritize political and military objectives over civilian safety.
Humanitarian Concerns	Respect for human rights	The adherence to human rights norms during the conflict, as perceived by Hamas.	Low	While Hamas might publicly uphold human rights concerns, strategic and military considerations typically take precedence in decision-making processes.
Governance	Effective governance	The capacity of Hamas to govern effectively during a conflict.	Low	Governance is important but may not be a deciding factor in conflict decisions, as Hamas's primary focus is on resistance and political objectives.

Table 4: Strategic Considerations for Hezbollah's Decision-Making on top of its Overarching-goals

Cluster	Consideration	Elaboration	Importance	Comments on the level of importance
External Support and Dynamics	Iranian Directives and Regional Support	Dependence on Iran and Syria for military, financial, and strategic support	High	Iranian directives and regional support are critical for Hezbollah as they rely significantly on Iran for support in various forms. This external backing is crucial for their operations and strategic planning.
Internal Lebanese interest	Deterrence against Israel - internal Security Stability	Ability to maintain internal security and stability against external threats	Moderate	Internal factors such as security stability, political stability, and economic impact are rated as moderate since they are significant but not the sole determinants of a decision for war. They provide a backdrop to operational readiness and public sentiment.
Internal Lebanese interest	Political Stability and Public Support	Stability of the Lebanese government and level of public support in Lebanon	Moderate	The political stability and public support in Lebanon are crucial for maintaining the group's operational base and ensuring a conducive environment for its activities.
Internal Lebanese interest	Economic Constraints and Impact	Lebanon's economic stability and the consequences of war on the economy	Moderate	Economic constraints are a significant consideration, as a war could severely impact Lebanon's already fragile economy, potentially undermining Hezbollah's support base.
Geopolitical Diplomacy and Influence	Potential for expansion of power of the Nexus	Evaluation of the potential for increasing the coalition's regional power and influence	Moderate	The potential for expanding power through a nexus of alliances is a strategic consideration but may take a back seat to more immediate security concerns in the context of a decision on full-scale war.
External Support and Dynamics	Relationship with Hamas and Political Dynamics	Coordination with Hamas	Low	The relationship with Hamas may be considered of low importance in the context of a full-scale war with Israel due to the geographic and operational separations, and the internal political dynamics of Lebanon, which are likely less immediately influential on the strategic decision to initiate a full-scale conflict.
Geopolitical Diplomacy and Influence	Diplomatic Consequences and Legitimacy	Potential diplomatic fallout and efforts to gain international legitimacy	Low	Diplomatic consequences and efforts to gain international legitimacy, as well as the preservation of influence, are considered of low importance in this context. This suggests that these considerations, while relevant, are not likely to be decisive factors in the immediate decision-making process for war.
Geopolitical Diplomacy and Influence	Preservation of Influence and Expansion of Power	Maintaining influence and opportunities to enhance power in the region	Low	While maintaining and expanding influence is a strategic objective, it may be deemed of lower importance in the immediacy of a decision to commence full-scale hostilities, which would primarily be driven by more pressing security and political concerns.

Table 5: Strategic Considerations for Iran's Decision-Making on top of its Overarching-goals

Cluster	Consideration	Elaboration	Importance	Comments on the level of importance
Policy Alignment	Alignment with Iranian Policies	Whether a full-scale war aligns with Iran's overarching strategic goals and ideological commitments.	High	A potential conflict would be significantly influenced by Iran's broader goals and adherence to its established policies.
Regional Power	Regional Influence	The potential of the conflict to enhance or diminish Iran's influence over the Middle East.	High	Iran's decision would be heavily influenced by the potential to enhance its regional dominance.
Military Dynamics	Military / Security Cooperations	The degree and effectiveness of Iran's military and security cooperation with Hezbollah and implications for the conflict.	Moderate	The extent of military and security support is crucial but balanced with other strategic considerations
Ideological Commitment	Resistance to Israel	The extent to which supporting a war aligns with Iran's ideological stance against Israel's regional actions.	Moderate	Ideological resistance is a constant factor but must be weighed against pragmatic considerations.
International Perception	Iranian Reputation	The potential impact of the conflict on Iran's global image and relations with other countries.	Moderate	Iran's global reputation is important, but it may not be the decisive factor when considering a conflict of this scale.
Tactical Considerations	Ease of Implementation	Practical challenges and logistical feasibility of Iran supporting a full-scale war between Israel and Hezbollah.	Low	Logistical considerations are crucial for planning but less so as a primary motivator for initiating a conflict.
Strategic Access	Access to Mediterranean Sea	How the conflict might affect Iran's strategic interests in the Mediterranean region.	Low	Access to the Mediterranean is beneficial for strategic projection but is a secondary concern in the context of war support.

Table 6: Strategic Considerations for USA's Decision-Making on top of its Overarching-goals

Cluster	Consideration	Elaboration	Importance	Comments on the level of importance
Stability and Security	Regional Stability	The potential impact on the overall stability of the Middle East region.	High	Regional stability is a key interest for the US as it affects global security, energy markets, and the security of key allies.
Stability and Security	Development of Radical Groups	The risk of radical groups gaining strength and influence as a result of the conflict.	High	The development of radical groups poses a significant security threat and is a key concern for US policy in the Middle East.
International Role	Global Status	How the conflict affects America's status as a global leader and its international relations.	High	Maintaining global leadership and international relations is a critical aspect of US foreign policy.
Humanitarian Concerns	Human Rights	The implications for human rights in the region and the potential humanitarian impact of a conflict.	High	Human rights issues are a significant concern for US policy and can influence intervention decisions.
Security Interests	Security	The direct and indirect security threats to US interests and allies.	High	Security is a primary concern and is often the most significant factor in decision-making related to conflicts.
International Relations	International Acceptance	The level of international support for US positions and actions in the event of a conflict.	High	International acceptance is crucial for the legitimacy of US actions and for maintaining alliances and partnerships.
Governance and Influence	Experience in governance	The US's capacity to influence post-conflict governance and reconstruction efforts.	High	The US often plays a role in reconstruction and governance efforts post-conflict, which can align with its strategic goals.
Domestic Support	Public Support	The level of support for US involvement or intervention from the American public.	High	Public opinion can greatly influence the government's decision-making process, especially in matters of foreign conflict.
Strategic Alliances	Keeping Peace with Israel	Commitment to Israel's security and the maintenance of peace agreements in the region.	High	The US has a longstanding commitment to Israel's security, which is central to its Middle Eastern policy.

(Cont'd.)

Table 6 cont'd.

Cluster	Consideration	Elaboration	Importance	Comments on the level of importance
Counter-terrorism	Terrorist Activity Prevention	Preventing terrorist activities and the spread of extremist ideologies.	High	Counterterrorism is a major US policy goal and a high priority in regions with active conflict.
Political Dynamics	Political Considerations	The alignment of the conflict with US foreign policy and its implications for relations with other nations.	Moderate	While important, these considerations may be outweighed by strategic security interests or domestic public opinion.
Economic Interests	Economic Development	Effects on US economic interests in the region, including trade and investment opportunities.	Moderate	Economic interests are important but are typically secondary to security concerns and geopolitical strategy.
Diplomatic Relations	Coordination with West Bank	The importance of maintaining and strengthening coordination with Palestinian governance in the West Bank.	Moderate	Coordination with the West Bank is part of the broader Middle Eastern strategy but not a decisive factor in isolation.
Operational Factors	Ease of implementation	The practicality of US responses or involvement given logistical, military, and political considerations.	Low	While necessary for planning and execution, ease of implementation is not a primary driver for strategic decisions.

Table 7: Strategic Considerations for Russia's Decision-Making on top of its Overarching-goals

Cluster	Consideration	Elaboration	Importance	Comments on the level of importance
Diplomatic Relations	Regional Diplomacy	The role Russia can play in mediating or influencing the conflict, which affects its diplomatic standing.	High	Diplomatic influence is a key tool for Russia's global strategy, especially in regions critical to its interests.
Security Dynamics	Security	The threat to regional security and how this could affect Russian military and strategic interests.	High	Regional security is directly linked to Russian military interests and its capacity to project power.
National Strategy	Russian Interests	Direct and indirect interests of Russia in the Middle East, including military presence and alliances.	High	Directly impacts Russia's ability to maintain and expand its strategic footprint in the region.
Regional Equilibrium	Long-term Regional Stability	The conflict's implications for long-term stability in the Middle East, affecting future Russian engagement.	Moderate	Long-term stability is important for sustained Russian involvement and influence but is weighed against immediate strategic benefits and costs.
International Relations	Global Public Opinion	How the conflict shapes the global perception of Russia, particularly in relation to international law and norms.	Moderate	Public opinion can influence Russia's soft power and diplomatic leverage, which are important in international relations.
Geopolitical Stability	Political Stability	The impact of the conflict on the political stability of the Middle East, which can affect Russia's regional interests.	Moderate	Stability is crucial for maintaining Russia's influence, but Russia may balance this against other strategic interests.
Economic Interests	Economic Development	Potential effects on Russia's economic interests in the region, including energy and military sales.	Moderate	Economic interests are significant but must be considered alongside political and military strategies.

Stage 3 - Running an AI-based Closed-loop Simulation

The motivation behind conducting this simulation stems from the need to analyze complex dynamics, highly volatile environments, and the strategic decision-making in high-stakes space. The scenario envisions a region fraught with tension, with key players vying for influence and security. The simulation seeks to explore how these key players navigate the intricate web of regional conflicts, and escalations towards the outbreak of a full-scale war.

The course of the simulation spans multiple rounds, each representing a stage in the evolving conflict. At the core of this simulation: a. Israeli consideration of neutralizing Hamas threat and rescuing kidnapped individuals, to enhance Israeli national security, thereby contributing to regional stabilization. b. The potential for aggressive escalations by Hezbollah if ordered by Iran. These elements add layers of complexity to the strategic choices made by the players, as they must carefully balance their interests, deter adversaries, and respond to emerging threats.

The following Tables 8-9 presents the actions that were advised by each simulated player, divided into two groups. The first group, that is detailed in Table 8, represents the 'safety level' actions that were advised and applied by the players, in view of the transparency principle. The second group, that is detailed in Table 9, represents the actions that were advised, but eventually avoided and were not executed by the players, due to their best understanding of the set of actions that all other players were advised.

Next, Table 10 explores how the policies of each player developed over the course of eight rounds. This evolution was influenced by the changing dynamics of the conflict, the actions of other players, and each player's strategic objectives.

Table 8: X1-X6 Action(s) that were applied

Israel (X1)	Hamas (X2)	Hezbollah (X3)
Offensive Military Operations: Regularly conducted a ground invasion of Gaza, initiated aerial bombardments, and engaged in precision strikes against key Hamas leaders. This highlights a focus on neutralizing the immediate treat and weakening Hamas' command structure. **Intelligence and Counter-Terrorism Efforts**: Consistently intensified intelligence operations for locating kidnapped individuals and conducted covert operations to rescue them, emphasizing a focus on counter-terrorism and rescue missions. **Cyber Warfare and Defensive Technologies**: Expanded cyber warfare to disrupt Hamas communications, implemented advanced cyber defense systems, and deployed advanced missile defense systems like Iron Dome. This demonstrates a strategy that includes technological warfare and defense measures. **Diplomatic Outreach and International Support**: Engaged in diplomatic outreach to moderate Arab nations and strengthened diplomatic efforts with global allies, showcasing an approach to isolate Hamas regionally and gain international support. **Public Relations and Global Narrative**: Bolstered public relations campaigns internationally and expanded efforts to address international concerns. This indicates an effort to manage the international perception of actions.	**Direct Military Response and Guerrilla Tactics**: Consistently engaged in launching counter-strikes, intensifying urban warfare tactics, utilizing guerrilla and urban warfare, and escalating these tactics. This highlights a focus on direct military engagement and leveraging the home-field advantage in combat. **Diplomatic and Humanitarian Efforts**: Consistently sought diplomatic intervention from sympathetic nations, international humanitarian aid, and engaged in diplomatic efforts for international support. This suggests a strategy of garnering international sympathy and support against Israel. **Fortification and Concealment of Assets**: Consistently fortified and concealed key military assets and leadership, strengthened tunnels and underground facilities, and enhanced underground operations. This indicates a focus on protecting strategic assets from Israeli airstrikes and maintaining operational capabilities. **Hostage and Prisoner Exchange Negotiations**: Regularly negotiated for prisoner exchanges and sought third-party negotiations for hostage exchange. This reflects a strategy to use captured individuals as bargaining chips in the conflict. **Lobbying and Media Campaigns for International Support**: Engaged in lobbying the UN for condemnation of Israel, mobilizing international support through diaspora networks, and utilizing international media to highlight civilian impact. This shows an approach to build international pressure against Israel. **Cyber Warfare and Technological Tactics**: Increased use of drones for surveillance and attacks, initiated cyber-attacks against Israeli infrastructure, and enhanced cyber warfare capabilities. This demonstrates a strategic use of technology to disrupt Israeli military operations and enhance their own tactical capabilities.	**Military Readiness and Border Mobilization**: Regularly engaged in rapid mobilization along the Lebanese-Israeli border, increasing military readiness, and conducting military drills. This demonstrates a focus on showing strength and deterrence along the border. **Intelligence and Surveillance Operations**: Consistently focused on increasing intelligence gathering on Israeli movements, enhancing intelligence operations against Israeli targets, and conducting aerial surveillance. This indicates a strategic emphasis on gathering information to inform tactical and strategic decisions. **Cyber Operations and Electronic Warfare**: Engaged in cyber operations to disrupt Israeli military communications and engage in electronic warfare. This suggests a focus on using technological means to disrupt Israeli military coordination and intelligence. **Strengthening Alliances and Internal Political Control**: Worked on strengthening alliances with regional proxies, engaging in diplomatic efforts with regional players, and strengthening internal political control within Lebanon. This shows an approach to consolidate power and ensure stability both internally and in coordination with allies. **Maritime Security and Contingency Planning**: Prepared for maritime security operations to protect strategic interests and developed contingency plans for various conflict scenarios. This reflects a focus on protecting maritime boundaries and preparing for different levels of engagement.

(Cont'd.)

Table 8 cont'd.

Iran (X4)	USA (X5)	Russia (X6)
Military Aid to Proxies and Missile Development: Regularly increased military aid to Hamas and Hezbollah and accelerated development of missile technology. This demonstrates a focus on enhancing the military capabilities of regional proxies and strengthening strategic deterrence.	**Diplomatic and Military Support for Israel**: The USA consistently engaged in diplomatic support for Israel, reaffirming their commitment to Israel's defense, and providing military aid. This demonstrates a strong focus on maintaining the strategic alliance with Israel.	**Diplomatic Engagement and Support for Allies**: Engaged in diplomatic efforts with regional players, particularly supporting the Syrian regime, and increased military sales to regional allies. This demonstrates a focus on maintaining regional influence and supporting allies against Israeli expansion.
Diplomatic Condemnation and International Efforts: Engaged in diplomatic condemnation of Israel at international forums and engaged in diplomatic efforts to gain international support. This reflects a strategy to use international platforms to criticize Israeli actions and garner support.	**Economic Sanctions and Diplomatic Mediation**: They consistently imposed economic sanctions against Iran, Hezbollah, and their allies, and engaged in diplomatic mediation efforts. This reflects a strategy of economic pressure and attempting to deescalate the situation through dialogue.	**Strategic Military Presence and Operations**: Strengthened naval presence in the Mediterranean and conducted naval exercises, showing a strategy of demonstrating military strength and strategic positioning.
Propaganda Campaigns and Ideological Support: Conducted propaganda campaigns in the Middle East emphasizing the defense of Muslim lands and rallied ideological and religious support within the Muslim world. Focus on building regional support against Israel through ideological and religious networks.	**Humanitarian Aid and Ceasefire Negotiations**: The USA provided humanitarian aid to Gaza through international agencies and facilitated ceasefire and peace negotiations. This indicates a commitment to addressing the humanitarian crisis and resolving the conflict through diplomatic channels.	**Monitoring US and NATO Activities**: Russia consistently monitored US and NATO activities in the region for strategic awareness. This indicates a focus on adjusting strategies based on American actions and maintaining a balance of power.
Cyber Operations and Surveillance: Increased cyber operations against Israeli and US targets and enhanced surveillance of Israeli activities. Focus on asymmetric warfare tactics and gathering critical intelligence.	**Strengthening Regional Presence and Cyber Defenses**: They strengthened their military presence in the region for deterrence and regional stability and enhanced cyber defenses against potential threats. This suggests a focus on regional stability and protecting national interests.	**Cyber Operations and Economic Opportunities**: Engaged in cyber-operations to gather intelligence and sought economic opportunities arising from the conflict. This reflects a strategy of using technological means for intelligence and exploiting economic benefits.
Strengthening Internal and Regional Positions: Strengthened internal political control within Lebanon, expanded intelligence and surveillance operations in the region, and intensified military aid and advisory support to regional proxies. This shows a strategy of consolidating power internally and strengthening regional influence.	**Diplomatic Initiatives for Conflict Resolution**: The USA intensified diplomatic efforts for a ceasefire, engaged in high-level talks for de-escalation, and implemented targeted sanctions for economic pressure. This indicates a strategy of using diplomatic channels to foster peace and stability.	**Enhancing Diplomatic Mediation and Military Support**: Increased diplomatic initiatives to position Russia as a peace broker and enhanced military support to Syria and Iran. This indicates a strategy of positioning Russia as a key global player in diplomatic mediation while strengthening regional allies.
Strategic Military & Technological Advancements: Increased naval presence in strategic waterways and conducted strategic military exercises. Accelerating the nuclear program and the development of advances missile systems. Focus on demonstrating military strength and preparedness for potential conflict escalation.	**Increased and Enhanced Intelligence**: The USA consistently increased and enhanced intelligence sharing with Israel. However, monitoring the involvement of Russia, Iran, and China in the Middle East was not consistently pursued.	**Humanitarian Aid**: Showcased humanitarian aid to Palestinian territories.

Table 9: X1-X6 Action(s) that were Advised but didn't Execute

Israel (X1)	Hamas (X2)	Hezbollah (X3)
Defensive Measures and Propaganda Campaigns: Israel consistently avoided strengthening border defenses to prevent infiltrations, engaging in propaganda campaigns emphasizing the defensive nature of actions, and increasing international media outreach. This suggests a strategic focus on offensive operations and direct military engagement rather than defensive posturing or extensive public relations campaigns. **Diplomatic and Negotiation Efforts**: They did not seek back-channel negotiations for hostages' release or engage in back-channel diplomacy for de-escalation. This indicates a preference for military solutions over diplomatic negotiations in this context. **Humanitarian and Economic Measures**: Avoided increasing humanitarian aid to Gaza, conducting targeted economic sanctions against entities supporting Hamas, and facilitating humanitarian aid channels in conflict zones. This shows a lesser focus on humanitarian initiatives and economic warfare as primary tools in the conflict scenario. **Intelligence and Surveillance Operations**: Israel did not engage in covert operations to gather intelligence or expand aerial surveillance for real-time intelligence. This reflects a choice for other methods of intelligence collection. **Preparatory Actions for Regional Escalations**: They avoided preparing for potential retaliatory actions from Hezbollah or Iran and preparing for potential regional escalations involving Iran and Hezbollah. This suggests a focus on the immediate Hamas threat rather than broader regional adversaries.	**Propaganda and Media Campaigns**: Avoided propaganda campaigns highlighting civilian casualties and mobilizing global diaspora for protests and lobbying. A lesser focus on shaping international public opinion through media narratives. **Regional Alliances and Support**: Avoided strengthening alliances with other regional players like Hezbollah, coordinating with Iran for additional support, and rallying domestic support through media and public engagements. This implies a strategy focused more on independent operations rather than seeking strong regional alliances or extensive internal propaganda. **Direct Military Tactics**: Avoided mobilizing ground forces in Gaza for defensive operations, engaging in covert operations to sabotage Israeli military logistics, and launching surprise attacks against Israeli military targets. This reflects a strategic preference for asymmetric and guerrilla warfare tactics over conventional military maneuvers. **Diplomatic Efforts**: Avoided seeking international diplomatic support against Israeli actions and engaging in diplomatic efforts for political backing. This shows a tendency to focus on direct conflict engagement and leveraging humanitarian aid rather than pursuing broad diplomatic strategies.	**Diplomatic and Propaganda Efforts**: Avoided diplomatic engagement with key allies for strategic backing, as well as propagating anti-Israel rhetoric to unify regional support. This suggests a strategic focus on direct military preparedness and operational tactics rather than diplomatic or propaganda campaigns. **Direct Military Aggression**: Consistently avoided escalating rocket fire into Northern Israel, preparing for possible Israeli retaliation, and fortifying positions along the Israeli border. This indicates a strategy that avoids direct confrontation or escalation with Israel. **Indirect Military Aggression**: Consistently avoided engaging in covert operations to support Hamas, or initiating indirect attacks against Israeli interests. **Enhanced Military Capabilities and Logistics**: Avoided actions like enhancing missile capabilities for deterrence and offense, conducting cyber espionage against Israeli military, and strengthening economic and logistical networks for sustained operations. This reflects a focus on immediate operational readiness rather than long-term strategic buildup.

(Cont'd.)

Table 9 cont'd.

Iran (X4)	USA (X5)	Russia (X6)
Cyber Warfare and Intelligence Operations: Iran consistently avoided enhancing cyber warfare capabilities against Western targets and increasing intelligence activities on Israeli military operations. This suggests a strategic choice to focus on direct military aid and diplomatic efforts rather than cyber operations and intelligence gathering. **Strengthening Economic and Military Ties**: Iran did not focus on strengthening economic ties with allies or preparing its military for potential escalation. They also avoided leveraging Shiite militias in Iraq and Syria to increase pressure on Israel's allies, indicating a strategy that does not prioritize economic alliances or militia-based regional pressure in this context. **Negotiations and Alliances** - Avoided Negotiating with Russia and China for support, nor for strengthening ties against Western influence. **Naval and Air Defense Operations**: Avoided conducting naval exercises in the Persian Gulf and enhancing air defense capabilities for potential Israeli or US strikes, suggesting a lesser focus on naval demonstrations of power and air defense readiness in this simulation. **Propaganda and Diplomatic Campaigns**: Consistently avoided propagating anti-Israel rhetoric to unify regional support and intensifying diplomatic campaigns against Israeli aggression. This shows a strategic focus away from broad propaganda efforts and extensive diplomatic maneuvers.	**Public and Propaganda Campaigns**: The USA consistently avoided engaging in public condemnation of Hamas and a propaganda campaign to counter anti-Israeli narratives. This suggests a strategic choice to focus on diplomatic and military support rather than public media campaigns. **Military Preparedness**: They avoided preparing for potential military involvement, which indicates a strategy of diplomacy over direct military action in this context. **Coordinating with NATO allies**: The USA avoided building an international coalition and consensus through NATO to address the crisis. In planning for potential joint responses and military exercises with NATO. This suggests a strategy that does not prioritize active engagement or response to the actions of these countries in the region. **Cyber defense coordination and collaboration**: although strengthen cyber defenses in the region, the USA avoided in coordination and collaboration with regional allies, including Israel. **Prepare for Potential Evacuation of American Citizens and Nationals.**	**Propaganda and Public Narrative Campaigns**: Russia avoided engaging in propaganda campaigns to shape narratives in their favor or counter Western narratives. This suggests a strategic choice to focus on diplomatic and military actions rather than media influence. **Intelligence and Military Readiness**: They consistently avoided enhancing intelligence gathering in the Middle East and preparing for military contingencies. This indicates a focus on existing intelligence capabilities and a strategy that does not prioritize immediate military escalation in the region. **Economic and Diplomatic Strategies**: Avoided evaluating military sales to the region and negotiating with OPEC on oil prices. This shows a lesser focus on leveraging economic opportunities and oil diplomacy in the context of this conflict. **Direct Military Actions**: Russia did not engage in direct mediation between conflicting parties. This suggests a strategy that prioritizes regional influence and strategic positioning over direct conflict mediation.

Table 10: First Order Insights

	Early Rounds (1-2)	Mid-Rounds (3-5)	Later Rounds (6-8)
Israel (X1)	Israel's initial policy was reactive and defensive, primarily focused on neutralizing immediate threats from Hamas through ground invasions and aerial bombardments. Cyber defense and international diplomatic engagement were also prioritized to mitigate external threats and secure global support.	As the conflict progressed, Israel shifted towards more sophisticated strategies, including precision strikes and enhanced intelligence operations. The focus on humanitarian efforts and public relations campaigns emerged, reflecting a need to balance military action with global perception.	Israel's policy evolved into a blend of aggressive military action, advanced technological defense (including cyber warfare), and intensified diplomatic lobbying. The aim was to decisively weaken Hamas' capabilities while maintaining international legitimacy and preparing for potential regional escalations.
Hamas (X2)	Hamas initially focused on intensifying guerrilla warfare and strengthening underground infrastructure, aiming to resist Israeli military superiority and seek international humanitarian aid.	As the conflict continued, Hamas enhanced its urban and asymmetric warfare capabilities while leveraging international media for support. This phase saw a notable increase in propaganda efforts to sway global opinion.	Hamas further intensified its urban warfare tactics and cyber capabilities, indicating an adaptation to the protracted conflict and the need to maintain operational capabilities under increased pressure.
Hezbollah (X3)	Hezbollah's early strategy was characterized by rapid mobilization and increased intelligence gathering, preparing for potential direct engagements with Israel.	The focus shifted to strengthening internal political control in Lebanon and enhancing air defenses, demonstrating a strategy of preparation and deterrence.	Hezbollah increased military readiness and developed contingency plans for various conflict scenarios, indicating a preparedness for potential escalation and broader involvement in the conflict.
Iran (X4)	Iran initially increased military aid to proxies and accelerated its nuclear program, using diplomatic condemnation and propaganda to position itself against Israel.	The mid-rounds saw Iran conducting naval exercises and ramping up cyber operations against Western targets, showcasing a blend of direct and indirect strategies to assert its influence.	Iran's policy evolved into a more aggressive posture, with intensified military support to proxies and strategic military exercises, reflecting its ambition to be a dominant regional power.
USA (X5)	The USA initially provided diplomatic support to Israel and imposed economic sanctions against adversaries, balancing military aid with efforts at diplomatic mediation.	This period saw the USA facilitating peace negotiations and enhancing cyber defenses, reflecting a strategy of balancing conflict resolution with support for its ally.	The USA's policy evolved into a more active role in peace negotiation efforts and increased military support to Israel, indicating a commitment to regional stability and the security of its ally.
Russia (X6)	Russia's initial approach focused on diplomatic engagement with regional players and monitoring US involvement, aiming to increase support for the Syrian regime and seeking economic opportunities.	The focus shifted to mediation efforts and increased military support to allies, coupled with strengthening its naval presence, reflecting a strategy of cautious engagement and influence-building.	Russia maintained its policy of diplomatic mediation, naval maneuvers, and humanitarian aid, consistently aiming to enhance its regional influence without direct military confrontation.

Stage 4 - Analysis

In the realm of game analysis, insights can be broadly categorized into two distinct types: first order insights and second order insights. Each type offers a unique perspective on the gameplay, strategies, and decision-making processes, providing a comprehensive understanding of the dynamics at play. While first order insights focus on the immediate and observable aspects of gameplay, second order insights dive deeper, offering a more nuanced and complex analysis. This section covers both first and second order observations.

Israel

First order observations - Israel's strategy in the simulation is characterized by a strong emphasis on direct and offensive military engagement, intelligence and counter-terrorism operations, cyber warfare and advanced defense technologies, diplomatic outreach to isolate Hamas regionally and gain international support, and public relations campaigns to manage the international perception of actions. While focused on the immediate Hamas threat rather than on the broader regional adversaries, Israel engaged less with diplomatic and negotiations efforts for hostage's release and de-escalation, and with humanitarian initiatives.

Second order observations - Israel's strategy in the simulation focuses on neutralizing immediate and long-term threats from Hamas and Hezbollah. The nation adeptly balances aggressive military tactics, including precision strikes and cyber operations, with strategic diplomatic engagements. This approach is not only a response to immediate security threats but also a carefully calculated move to manage global public opinion and maintain crucial international alliances. Israel's strategy underscores its prioritization of national security while conscientiously navigating the complexities of international legitimacy and alliance diplomacy.

Hamas

First order observations - Hamas' strategy in the simulation involved a blend of direct military confrontation using guerrilla and urban warfare tactics, efforts to protect and conceal its strategic assets, using technology such as drones and cyber warfare to disrupt Israeli military operations and enhance their own tactical capabilities. While leveraging international humanitarian aid and diplomatic intervention, Hamas focused less on shaping international public opinion through media narratives.

Second order observations - Hamas employs asymmetric warfare tactics, primarily guerrilla warfare and media campaigns, to counterbalance the military superiority of Israel. Their strategy is largely reactive, aimed at sustaining operational capabilities under the pressure of a superior military adversary. The use of propaganda is integral to their approach, seeking to garner international sympathy and support. This strategy demonstrates Hamas's adaptability and resourcefulness in leveraging global public opinion to counterbalance their operational limitations.

Hezbollah

First order observations - Hezbollah's strategy in the simulation involved a balance between showing military readiness and deterrence along the Israeli border, focusing on intelligence and surveillance to inform tactical decisions, and leveraging cyber and electronic warfare. While focusing on direct military preparedness and operational tactics rather than diplomatic or propaganda campaigns, Hezbollah consistently avoided direct military aggression and indirect covert operations against Israel. Moreover, Hezbollah focused on internal political control and strengthening alliances, preparing for maritime security challenges, and developing contingency plans for potential conflicts.

Second order observations - Hezbollah's approach is characterized by a provocative posture, while preparing for potential escalation and aligning strategically with Iran. Their actions, including enhancing border vigilance and engaging in covert operations, reflects a strategy focused on maintaining regional influence and readiness for potential direct conflict. Hezbollah's strategy indicates a deep alignment with Iran's broader regional ambitions and illustrated their role as a significant proxy in the geopolitical landscape.

Iran

First order observations - Iran' strategy prioritizes military support to regional proxies, ideological support, engaging in cyber operations and surveillance and international efforts for diplomatic condemnation of Israel. This was prioritized over direct military preparations, leveraging Shiite militias in Iraq and Syria to increase pressure on Israel, and strengthening economic ties with its allies, including Russia and China. While conducting naval and strategic military exercises, to demonstrate their military strength, Iran avoided conducting exercises in the Persian Gulf and enhancing air defense readiness.

Second order observations - Iran plays a pivotal role in the simulation, primarily through its support of proxy groups. This approach aligns with their broader regional ambitions to extend influence while strategically avoiding direct engagement. Iran's actions highlight Iran's preference for asymmetric warfare, using proxies to assert influence and challenge regional adversaries without direct conflict, while simultaneously not risking the race to achieve their game changing nuclear capabilities.

USA

First order observations - USA's strategy in the simulation involved a combination of reaffirming diplomatic and military support for Israel, imposing economic sanctions on adversaries, engaging in diplomatic mediation and peace negotiations, and providing humanitarian aid. Actions such as monitoring Russian and Iranian involvement, preparing for military involvement, and engaging in peace negotiations were applied more sporadically. However, actions like public condemnation of adversaries, monitoring of global powers, coordination with NATO, preparation for potential military escalation and evacuation of American citizens, and strategic dialogues were not applied consistently. This indicates a strategy that prioritizes diplomacy, economic pressure, and humanitarian efforts over direct military engagement or extensive media campaigns.

Second order observations - The United States demonstrates a balancing role, supporting Israel while also advocating for diplomatic conflict resolution. This approach reflects the complexities of managing global strategic interests and the importance of maintaining regional stability. The USA's policy is centered around balancing support for Israel with diplomatic initiatives, aiming to navigate the intricacies of international relations and conflict dynamics.

Russia

First order observations - Russia's strategy in the simulation involved a combination of diplomatic engagement with regional players, monitoring US and NATO activities, maintaining a strategic military presence in the Mediterranean, supported allies militarily, and showcased humanitarian efforts. Actions related to propaganda campaigns, intelligence sharing, and high-level talks were used more sporadically, while economic strategies, military preparedness, and oil price negotiations were not consistently pursued.

Second order observations - Russia maintains a cautious approach focused on diplomatic mediation and support for regional allies like Syria. Its strategy avoids direct military confrontation, aiming to strengthen regional influence without overt aggression. Russia's policy is geared towards enhancing its regional presence through diplomatic engagement and support for allies, without engaging in direct military involvement.

Surface-Level Learning and Explicit Observations

In the context of the simulated conflict, several key themes emerge, illustrating the complexities of modern warfare and geopolitical interactions.

Asymmetrical Warfare Dynamics The simulation underscores the utilization of asymmetrical warfare tactics by non-state military entities, notably Hamas and Hezbollah, against Israel, a technologically superior opponent. This approach reflects the strategic adaptations by groups with limited resources facing a technologically advanced adversary, emphasizing guerrilla tactics and indirect engagement strategies.

Cyber Warfare Significance Cyber operations have emerged as a pivotal element in contemporary conflicts. The simulation accentuates this trend, with multiple parties engaging in cyber attacks and defense measures. This highlights the evolving battlefield where cyber capabilities can significantly impact military strategies and national security.

Proxy War Dynamics The dynamics of proxy warfare are prominently featured, particularly with Iran's support of Hamas and Hezbollah. This aspect of the simulation reflects the broader regional conflict, where state actors leverage non-state entities to project power and influence beyond their borders.

Strategic Alliances Strategic alliances form a cornerstone of the conflict dynamics portrayed in the simulation. The U.S.'s support for Israel and Russia's engagement with Syria and Iran exemplify the geopolitical alliances that shape regional stability and conflict.

Tactical Superiority The deployment of precision strikes, guerrilla tactics, and advanced cyber operations by various entities underscores the significance of tactical superiority. These actions reflect an acknowledgment of the parties' respective strengths and strategic advantages in the conflict landscape.

Technological Advancements in Warfare The integration of advanced technologies, such as missile defense systems and drones, signifies the growing dependence on technological innovation in military strategies. This aspect of the simulation demonstrates how technological advancements continue to transform the nature of warfare.

Economic and Humanitarian Dimensions Economic sanctions, humanitarian aid initiatives, and calls for humanitarian ceasefires represent the economic and humanitarian dimensions of modern conflict. These elements underline the multifaceted nature of warfare, where economic measures and humanitarian considerations play crucial roles.

Diplomatic Engagement International diplomatic efforts are crucial, as demonstrated by the parties' endeavors to influence global opinion and garner external support. The U.S.'s continuous attempts to broker ceasefires, despite ongoing hostilities, highlight the persistent efforts to resolve conflicts through diplomatic channels.

Media and Propaganda Strategies The use of media campaigns and propaganda by several parties emphasizes the critical role of narrative control and public opinion management in contemporary conflicts. This strategy reflects an understanding of the power of media in shaping public perceptions and influencing the broader discourse surrounding the conflict.

Discussion

The simulation in this study, examining the post October 7th geopolitical conflict within an 8-week timeframe, shows significant alignment with real events, particularly in terms of primary decisions and sequences. While the alignment in event sequence isn't perfect (e.g., In real-life USA did prepare for evacuation of American citizens, also the USA aircraft carriers assisted in intercepting drones that were launched towards Israel by Iran proxies, the Houthis), the simulation's real strength lies in its second-order observations, which closely mirror real-world happenings. This correlation highlights the simulation's utility in providing deep insights for operational and strategic analysis.

The critiques might ask how could the simulation manage to predict the decision making of the players with such significant alignment? Namely, how did the real-world players opt for actions consistent with the 'safety level' choices (detailed in Table 8), despite the questionable validity of the transparency assumption? The explanation likely resides in the extensive media coverage and intelligence operations surrounding the situation, which effectively made the range of potential actions quite visible to the geopolitical participants.

It is highlighted that in situations where such transparent observations are not available or could be decoyed, there is a good chance that the range of player's actions could include a subset of the actions that were not selected, as presented in Table 9. Moreover, it is critical to recognize that the simulation was not designed to predict specific tactical or operational events, including significant successful or unsuccessful actions of players. Key examples include Israel's successful hostage release following the ceasefire,[66] the self-bombing at al-Ahli Arab Hospital,[67] and the collapse of ceasefire negotiations on December 1st.[68] Such significant events, which have a profound impact on geopolitical stability, highlight the necessity of resetting the simulation after their real-life occurrence. Such a reset is essential for a more accurate evaluation of the geopolitical landscape's evolution in the wake of these pivotal events.

Conclusions

This study, utilizing the innovative capabilities of AI, particularly Chat-GPT4, represents a significant advancement in the field of counter-terror and geopolitical studies. By simulating complex scenarios in the Middle East, it offers valuable insights into the strategic dynamics among key players post-October 7th events. In particular, it shed light upon the escalation potential of this conflict in view of a tactical-operative triggering decision making (i.e., the triggering event).

The simulated game unfolded with increasing complexity, starting with Israel's response to aggression and escalating through various maneuvers by all players. Israel consistently intensified its military and cyber operations, while also engaging in diplomatic and public relations efforts. Hamas and Hezbollah focused on asymmetric warfare tactics; while Hamas mostly reacted to Israeli offensive acts, Hezbollah was more the initiator to disrupt the Israeli military campaign in Gaza. Iran played a significant role in supporting proxy groups, while also accelerating its nuclear and ballistic missile programs as a strategic deterrent and engaging in diplomatic confrontations. The USA took on more balanced roles, with the USA supporting and restraining Israel and pushing for diplomatic resolutions while implementing sanctions against adversaries to pressure Iran and its proxies. Russia, meanwhile, focused on diplomatic mediation and support for its regional allies, maintaining a consistent but cautious involvement level.

The study demonstrates AI's prowess in processing vast amounts of data, enabling a deeper understanding of military, political, and economic dimensions of conflicts. While not designed to predict specific events, the AI-generated simulations provide a strategic framework that closely aligns with real-world occurrences. This research underscores the transformative potential of AI in geopolitical studies, offering new pathways for understanding and navigating intricate global conflicts. The findings of this study not only contribute to academic discourse but also have practical implications for policymakers and strategists, highlighting the critical role of AI in enhancing decision-making processes in variegated situations, such as in geopolitical landscapes.

Looking forward, future use of the proposed methodology and framework could assist in predicting outcomes of decisions making implications in complex geopolitical junctures. Harnessing the proposed AI-based framework and simulation model could greatly enhance our understanding of decision-making implications in highly-complex contexts, including geopolitical scenarios. AI's capacity to simulate near real-time on-going conflicts (scenarios), independent of expert availability, offers a significant advancement. Moreover, the proposed framework and simulation model show great potential for future work, on conducting impact analyses in hypothetical situations or in reaction to specific intelligence warnings. A notable example is the underestimation by officials of a critical 40-page report, leading to a miscalculation of conflict initiation risks.[69] This situation highlights the significant role AI can play in enhancing foresight and preparedness in intricate geopolitical contexts, thereby improving our ability to anticipate and respond to emerging global challenges.

Notes

1. Baruch, Motti, and Eli Michelson. "A Strategic War Game as a Space for Perceptual Encounter." In Between the Extremes: War Games, Dado Center Journal Contemporary Issues in Operational Art, 13 (2017): 11-28.
2. Perla, P. The Art of Wargaming. Annapolis: Naval Institute Press (1990).
3. Weiner, M.G. War Gaming Methodology (RM-2413). Santa Monica: RAND (1959).
4. Tovy, Tal. "The Butterfly Effect of War Games: 'Scout' Games and Their Impact on the American Perception of Counterinsurgency (COIN) in the 1960s." In Between the Extremes: War Games, Dado Center Journal Contemporary issues in operational art, Vol. 13 (2017): 165-192.
5. Libicki, M. The Mesh and the Net: Speculations on Armed Conflict In a Time of Free Silicon. Washington, D.C.: National Defense University, 1994.
6. Davis, P.K. Deterrence and Influence in Counterterrorism: A Component in the War on Al Qaeda. Santa Monica: RAND (2002).
7. Klimburg, A. The Darkening Web: The War for Cyberspace. New York: Penguin Press, 2017.

8. Alexander von Rosenbach et al., "Flashpoints: An Interactive Game on Counter-Terrorism", Developed by the International Centre for Counter-Terrorism, 2020, https://www.icct.nl/node/58
9. Rubel, R.C. "The Epistemology of War Gaming." Naval War College Review 59, no. 2 (2006): 108-128. https://digital-commons.usnwc.edu/cgi/viewcontent.cgi?referer=&httpsredir=1&article=2109&context=nwc-review
10. Tzaleyachin, Gur. "The Strategic War Game and the Military-Political Dialogue." In Between the Extremes: War Games, Dado Center Journal Contemporary issues in operational art, Vol. 13, 29-66. 2017.
11. Ish-Maas, Ofek. "Cultural Intelligence in Strategic War Games." In Between the Extremes: War Games, Dado Center Journal Contemporary issues in operational art, Vol. 13, 145-164. 2017.
12. Ganor, Boaz. "Lebanon – Where does it go from here? Special Simulation Summary." ICT's Special Project, 2020. http://ict.org.il.web101.virtualbox.co.il/images/Lebanon%20Open%20Poker%20Simulation%20Summary%201.pdf.
13. Philip K. Dick, The Minority Report, 1956. ISBN10: 0375421874.
14. Genevieve Lennon. Precautionary tales: Suspicionless counterterrorism stop and search. Criminology & Criminal Justice. 15, no. 1, (2015): 44–62. DOI: 10.1177/1748895813509637
15. Perry, Walter, Brian McInnis, Carter Price, Susan Smith, and John Hollywood. "Predictive Policing: The Role of Crime Forecasting in Law Enforcement Operations." RAND Corporation, 2018. http://dx.doi.org/10.7249/rr233.
16. McCulloch, J. & Wilson, D. (2016). Pre-crime: Pre-emption, Precaution and the Future. London: Routledge. ISBN: 978-1-138-78169-6.
17. Björn Alpermann, The Uyghurs, China's Terrorist Narrative and Counterterrorism ASIEN 156/157 (2020): 222–225. https://hasp.ub.uni-heidelberg.de/journals/asien/article/view/15366/14943.
18. Egbert, S. & Leese, M. (2021). Criminal Futures: Predictive Policing and Everyday Police Work. Routledge, Milton Park, Abingdon, Oxon OX14 4RN, 231 p. ISBN: 978-0-429-32873-2.
19. United Nations. (2018). Secretary-general's Strategy on New Technologies. https://www.un.org/en/newtechnologies/images/pdf/SGs-Strategy-on-New-Technologies.pdf.
20. Verhelst, H., Stannat, A. & Mecacci, G. "Machine Learning Against Terrorism: How Big Data Collection and Analysis Influences the Privacy-Security Dilemma". Science and Engineering Ethics, 26 (2020): 2975–2984. DOI: 10.1007/s11948-020-00254-w. https://link.springer.com/article/10.1007/s11948-020-00254-w.
21. Lakomy, M. "Artificial Intelligence as a Terrorism Enabler? Understanding the Poten-

tial Impact of Chatbots and Image Generators on Online Terrorist Activities." *Studies in Conflict and Terrorism.* (2023):1-21. https://doi.org/10.1080/1057610X.2023.2259195, https://www.tandfonline.com/doi/full/10.1080/1057610X.2023.2259195.

22. Sean S. Roberts: The War on the Uyghurs: China's Internal Campaign against a Muslim Minority Princeton: Princeton University Press, 2020. ISBN 978-0-69120218-1
23. Schmid, Alex. "Terrorism-the definitional problem." Case W. Res. J. Int'l L. 36 (2004): 375.
24. Tunysová, Andrea. "Predicting and Preventing Terrorism with Artificial Intelligence and Machine Learning: Implications for Security in Israel." (2022).
25. Ganor, Boaz. Artificial or Human: A New Era of Counterterrorism Intelligence? *Studies in Conflict and Terrorism*, 44, Issue 7 (2021). DOI: 10.1080/1057610X.2019.1568815. https://el2019.kimep.kz/pluginfile.php/41776/mod_resource/content/1/ganor2019.pdf
26. Khan, F. A., Li, G., Khan, A. N., Khan, Q. W., Hadjouni, M., & Elmannai, H. "AI-Driven Counter-Terrorism: Enhancing Global Security Through Advanced Predictive Analytics." IEEE, 11. (2023) DOI: 10.1109/ACCESS.2023.3336811. https://ieeexplore.ieee.org/document/10328769.
27. Don Rassler, "Commentary: Data, AI, and the Future of U.S. Counterterrorism: Building an Action Plan." *Combating Terrorism Center*, 14. Issue 8: (2021). https://ctc.westpoint.edu/commentary-data-ai-and-the-future-of-u-s-counterterrorism-building-an-action-plan/.
28. Dekel Cohen and Naftali Abdraham, "ChatGPT: Implications for Intelligence", *The Center for Intelligence Heritage and the Institute for Intelligence Methodology Research.* (2023). https://www.intelligence-research.org.il/post/GPTandIntel
29. Brun, I. & Altshuler, T.S.. A Seat at the Table: Can Chat-GPT Break the Concept? the Center for Intelligence Heritage and the Institute for Intelligence Methodology Research (2023). https://www.intelligence-research.org.il/post/GPT-and-intelligence
30. Gutterman, O., Boran, L., & Czesna, R. "Will Hezbollah enter a war with Israel?: Role-playing Simulations based on Artificial Intelligence as a Tool to Assist Intelligence Assessments?" *The Center for Intelligence Heritage and the Institute for Intelligence Methodology Research.* (2023) https://www.intelligence-research.org.il/post/AI-HIZBOLLAH-NOVEMBER-2023
31. Zeleny, M., "Games with Multiple Payoffs," *International Journal of Game Theory*, 4, No. 4, (1975): 179–191. doi:10.1007/BF01761608
32. Ghose, D., and Prasad, U.R., " Multicriterion Differential Games with Applications to Combat Problems," *Computers Math Applications* 18, No 1-3 (1989):117-126. doi: 10.1016/0898-1221(89)90129-6
33. Mayne, D. Q., and Michalska H., "Receding Horizon Control of Nonlinear Sys-

tems," *IEEE Transactions on Automatic Control*, 35, No. 7 (1990): 814-824. doi:10.1109/9.57020

34. Findeisen, R., and Allgöwer, F., "An Introduction to Nonlinear Model Predictive Control," *21st Benelux Meeting on Systems and Control*. Eindhoven, The Netherlands: Technische Universiteit Eindhoven Veldhoven 11 (2002): 119-141.
35. Mayne, D. Q., Rawlings, J. B., Rao, C. V., and Scokaert, P. O., "Constrained Model Predictive Control: Stability and Optimality", *Automatica*, 36, No. 6, (2000): 789-814. doi: 10.1016/S0005-1098(99)00214-9
36. Wikipedia contributors. 2023 Hamas-led Attack on Israel. *In Wikipedia, The Free Encyclopedia*. November 30, 2023, https://en.wikipedia.org/wiki/2023_Hamas-led_attack_on_Israel
37. Wikipedia contributors. 2023 Israel–Hamas war. *In Wikipedia, The Free Encyclopedia.* November 30, 2023 https://en.wikipedia.org/wiki/2023_Israel–Hamas_war
38. The Times of Israel. "Oct. 7: Hamas Terrorists Burst through Border." The Times of Israel. October 72023. https://www.timesofisrael.com/liveblog-october-7-2023/
39. War on the Rocks. "The Four Questions The U.S. Military Should Be Asking About Operation Swords of Iron." October 23 2023, https://warontherocks.com/2023/10/the-four-questions-the-u-s-military-should-be-asking-about-operation-swords-of-iron/
40. Business Today. "All about 'Operation Iron Swords' Israel Launched after Hamas' Surprise Attack." October 7 2023 https://www.businesstoday.in/latest/world/story/all-about-operation-iron-swords-israel-launched-after-hamas-surprise-attack-401109-2023-10-07
41. BNN Network. "Unmasking Israel's Operation Swords of Iron: A Long and Difficult Fight Ahead". October 31 2023. https://bnnbreaking.com/world/israel/unmasking-israels-operation-swords-of-iron-a-long-and-difficult-fight-ahead/
42. Akiva Van Koningsveld. "Israel shifts to 'offensive phase' of Gaza op after 700 killed." JNS.org. (October 8 2023). https://www.jns.org/israeli-security-cabinet-greenlights-offensive-phase-of-gaza-op/
43. All Israel. "After two weeks of 'Operation Iron Swords' – here are IDF statistics." October 21 2023, https://allisrael.com/after-two-weeks-of-operation-iron-swords-here-are-idf-statistics
44. Toi Staff "Iran, Hamas and Hezbollah coordinated Gaza fighting in joint war room — report." The Times of Israel. May 29 2021. https://www.timesofisrael.com/iran-hamas-and-hezbollah-coordinated-gaza-fighting-in-joint-war-room-report/
45. Collin P. Clarke "Iran and the Axis of Resistance Vastly Improved Hamas's Operational Capability" *Foreign Policy Research Institute*. October 27 2023. https://www.fpri.org/article/2023/10/iran-and-the-axis-of-resistance-vastly-improved-hamass-opera

tional-capabilities/

46. Brian Katz. "Axis Rising: Iran's Evolving Regional Strategy and Non-State Partnerships in the Middle East." *Center for Strategic & International Studies.* October 11, 2018. https://www.csis.org/analysis/axis-rising-irans-evolving-regional-strategy-and-non-state-partnerships-middle-east
47. Michael Scollon. "Iran's 'Axis Of Resistance': A Network Designed To Create Chaos, Fight Tehran's Enemies." *Radio Free Europe Radio Liberty.* October 19 2023. https://www.rferl.org/a/iran-axis-resistance-proxies-enemies-abroad-quds/32645674.html
48. Reuters. "Iran's Khamenei Says Fight against Israel is a Public Duty." May 7 2021. https://www.reuters.com/world/middle-east/irans-khamenei-says-fight-against-israel-is-public-duty-2021-05-07/
49. Reuters. "Explainer: How Hezbollah widens Iran's Middle East Reach." October 15 2021. https://www.reuters.com/world/middle-east/how-hezbollah-widens-irans-middle-east-reach-2021-10-15/
50. Wikipedia. "Ideology of the Iranian Revolution." *In Wikipedia, The Free Encyclopedia.* https://en.wikipedia.org/wiki/Ideology_of_the_Iranian_Revolution
51. F. Bezhan (2023). Iranians Show Little Support For Palestinian Cause Amid Gaza Conflict. Radio Free Europe/Radio Liberty. https://www.rferl.org/a/iran-hamas-israel-little-public-support-palestinian-cause/32654903.html
52. Y. Najdi & B. Restle (2023). Israel-Hamas war: What is Iran's role? Deutsche Welle. https://www.dw.com/en/israel-hamas-war-what-is-irans-role/a-67043337
53. Agencies (2023). In first speech directly to Gazans, Iran president vows full support. The Times of Israel. https://www.timesofisrael.com/addressing-gazans-iran-leader-vows-unhesitating-support-for-palestinian-resistance/
54. The Iran Primer. Iran and the Palestinians in Gaza. *United States Institute of Peace.* November 2 2023. https://iranprimer.usip.org/blog/2023/nov/02/iran-and-palestinians-gaza
55. Middle East Institute. (2023). Hezbollah's Regional Activities in Support of Iran's Proxy Networks. https://www.mei.edu/publications/hezbollahs-regional-activities-support-irans-proxy-networks
56. Alonso Martinez. "What is Hezbollah and what's its Role in the Israel-Hamas Conflict." El País International. November 2 2023. https://english.elpais.com/international/2023-11-01/what-is-hezbollah-and-whats-its-role-in-the-israel-hamas-conflict.html
57. Oula A. Alrifai, Nakissa Jahanbani, Mehdi Khalaji, "Iran's Long Game in Syria." *The Washington Institute for Near East Policy.* March 29 2021. https://www.washingtoninstitute.org/policy-analysis/irans-long-game-syria.
58. Will Fulton, Joseph Holliday, and Sam Wyer, "Iranian Strategy in Syria." *Institute for*

the Study of War. https://www.understandingwar.org/report/iranian-strategy-syria

59. Bureau of Counterterrorism. Country Reports on Terrorism 2020: Iran. *U.S. Department of State.* https://www.state.gov/reports/country-reports-on-terrorism-2020/iran/

60. G. Nada and M. Rowan. (2021). Profiles: Pro-Iran Militias in Iraq. The Iran Primer. https://iranprimer.usip.org/blog/2021/nov/10/profiles-pro-iran-militias-iraq

61. Karataş, İbrahim. "Iran's Use of Afghan Shiite Migrants as Proxies: The Case of Liwa Fatemiyoun." *The Journal of Iranian Studies,* 5, No. 1, (2021): 31-53. doi:10.33201/iranian.880171. https://dergipark.org.tr/en/download/article-file/1576912

62. Aydin Guven, "ANALYSIS - Iran-backed Zainabiyoun Brigade could become Pakistan's New National Security Problem." *Anadolu Ajansi,* November 5 2020. https://www.aa.com.tr/en/analysis/analysis-iran-backed-zainabiyoun-brigade-could-become-pakistan-s-new-national-security-problem/2033585

63. Farzin Nadimi, Michael Knights "Iran's Support to Houthi Air Defenses in Yemen." *The Washington Institute for Near East Policy.* April 4 2018. https://www.washingtoninstitute.org/policy-analysis/irans-support-houthi-air-defenses-yemen

64. Jonathan Saul, Parisa Hafezi and Michael Georgy. "Exclusive: Iran steps up support for Houthis in Yemen's War – Sources." *Reuters* March 22 2017. https://www.reuters.com/article/us-yemen-iran-houthis/exclusive-iran-steps-up-support-for-houthis-in-yemens-war-sources-idUSKBN16S22R/

65. Robert J. Riggs, "The Qatar–Iran–Turkey Nexus: Shifts in Political Alliances and Economic Diversification in the Gulf Crisis." In: *The 2017 Gulf Crisis.* Springer, Singapore. Gulf Studies, 3 (2021). https://doi.org/10.1007/978-981-15-8735-1_11

66. Jobain, Najib, Federman, Josef and Jeffery, Jack "Hamas and Israel carry out first swap of hostages and prisoners as Gaza cease-fire begins". *Associated Press.* 24 November 2023. https://apnews.com/article/israel-hamas-war-news-11-24-2023-172256dd593189f7b37f7c62f4739c6b

67. Wikipedia, "Al-Ahli Arab Hospital Explosion." *In Wikipedia, The Free Encyclopedia.* https://en.wikipedia.org/wiki/Al-Ahli_Arab_Hospital_explosion

68. Wikipedia, "Israel-Hamas Ceasefire 2023." *In Wikipedia, The Free Encyclopedia.* https://en.wikipedia.org/wiki/2023_Israel%E2%80%93Hamas_ceasefire

69. AFP, "Israel Obtained, Ignored Hamas Document laying out Oct. 7 Attack Plan, Report alleges." *The Times of Israel,* December 1 2023. https://www.timesofisrael.com/israel-obtained-ignored-hamas-document-laying-out-oct-7-attack-plan-report-alleges/

In Search of Lost Relations: Educational Approaches in the Light of Quantum Mechanical Equivalents

Zrinka Štimac
z.stimac@gmx.net

Abstract

This paper examines educational essays that advocate a transformative vision of education through the lens of quantum mechanical concepts. These essays argue that fundamental principles such as indeterminacy, uncertainty and non-locality need to be integrated into theories of education, as education has quantum properties. This perspective aims to challenge Newtonian, linear, and mechanistic educational models, calling for a paradigm shift in education. The essays adopt a comprehensive view of education, applying quantum concepts universally across disciplines from geography to philosophy, rather than compartmentalizing them into natural sciences or humanities. Using habitus analysis as a hermeneutic tool, this article analyzes the problems and solutions formulated by the authors. By reflecting these arguments through the ontological framework of Ernst Cassirer and Matthias Jung, this article identifies what is referred to in the essays analyzed as a lack of quantum and/or holistic perspective: a lack of in-depth and non-linear relationality. Cassirer's focus on the relational essence of all symbolic forms and his emphasis on accommodating multiple perspectives, along with Jung's ontology of ordinary experience integrating diverse knowledge domains, enable connections between educational theory and quantum mechanics. Moreover, these ontologies provide a theoretical and empirical basis for potential convergences among different knowledge systems, as proposed by the analyzed essays. Following, the relevance of the results for education policy and for the convergence of complex systems is discussed.

En busca de relaciones perdidas: Enfoques educativos a la luz de los equivalentes mecánico-cuánticos

Resumen

Este artículo examina ensayos educativos que abogan por una visión transformadora de la educación a través de la lente de los conceptos mecánicos cuánticos. Estos ensayos sostienen que los prin-

 doi: 10.18278/jpcs.9.1.3

cipios fundamentales como la indeterminación, la incertidumbre y la no localidad deben integrarse en las teorías de la educación, ya que la educación tiene propiedades cuánticas. Esta perspectiva tiene como objetivo desafiar los modelos educativos newtonianos, lineales y mecanicistas, y reclama un cambio de paradigma en la educación. Los ensayos adoptan una visión integral de la educación, aplicando conceptos cuánticos de manera universal en todas las disciplinas, desde la geografía hasta la filosofía, en lugar de compartimentarlos en ciencias naturales o humanidades. Utilizando el análisis del habitus como herramienta hermenéutica, este artículo analiza los problemas y las soluciones formuladas por los autores. Al reflejar estos argumentos a través del marco ontológico de Ernst Cassirer y Matthias Jung, este artículo identifica lo que se menciona en los ensayos analizados como una falta de perspectiva cuántica y/o holística: una falta de relacionalidad profunda y no lineal. El enfoque de Cassirer en la esencia relacional de todas las formas simbólicas y su énfasis en la adaptación de perspectivas múltiples, junto con la ontología de Jung de la experiencia ordinaria que integra diversos dominios de conocimiento, permiten conexiones entre la teoría educativa y la mecánica cuántica. Además, estas ontologías proporcionan una base teórica y empírica para las convergencias potenciales entre diferentes sistemas de conocimiento, como se propone en los ensayos analizados. A continuación, se discute la relevancia de los resultados para la política educativa y para la convergencia de sistemas complejos.

寻找丢失的关系。根据量子力学等效原理的教育方法。

摘要

本文通过量子力学概念的视角，研究了那些倡导变革性教育愿景的教育类文章。这些文章认为，由于教育具有量子特性，因此需要将不明确性、不确定性和非定域性等基本原则融入教育理论中。这种观点旨在挑战牛顿、线性和机械教育模式，呼吁教育的范式转变。这些文章采用了全面的教育观，将量子概念普遍应用于从地理到哲学的各个学科，而不是将它们划分为自然科学或人文科学。本文使用惯习分析(habitus analysis)作为解释学工具，分析了作者提出的问题和解决方案。通过恩斯特·卡西尔和马蒂亚斯·荣格的本体论框架来反思这些论点，本文确定了所分析文章中提到的量子和/或整体视角的缺乏，即缺乏深度且非线性的关系。卡西尔聚焦于所有符号形式的关系本质，强调包容多种观点，加上荣格对日常经历的本体论观点（整合不同知识领域），使得教育理论与量子力学之间建立了联系。此外，这些本体论为不同知识系统之间的潜在相交提供了理论和实证基础，正如所分析的文章所提出的那样。本文随后探讨了这些结果对教育政策的相关性和对复杂系统相交的相关性。

1. Introduction

The development of quantum technology as a disruptive key technology of the future (Christensen 1997) is accompanied by changes that affect all areas of society. This development of quantum technology is not an effort by the physics alone but is embedded in a process of scientific convergence. The first big convergency took part between physics and engineering, the second between biology and engineering, and the current one is to be expected between science and technology (technoscience) (Jandrić and Knox 2021: 6). These convergences imply collaboration between traditional scientific disciplines and require "a reconfiguration of the connection between analog and digital" (ibid, 10f).

In the educational framework, these developments have started to be reflected in STEM subjects. This reflection results in both didactic approaches on quantum technology in the classroom (cf. Müller et al. 2021), and new curricula that are embedding quantum mechanics in schools and in teacher training (cf. Stifterverband 2023; cf. https://qusteam.org/about). Empirical analyses of the practical and ideological consequences of the teaching of quantum mechanics are emerging as significant areas of study (Stadermann and Goedhart 2020, Bouchée et al. 2021)."

However, the quantum technologies and their societal consequences are not only relevant for STEM subjects, but also for all school subjects. This is clearly shown both by the educational analyses critiquing the ontology and epistemology of education based in classical Newtonian physics (Turner 2020) as well as those that take digitalization as their starting point and criticize technological determinism and instrumentalism as well as reductions of education through neoliberal framing (Jandrić and Knox 2021: 11). Consequently, future education policy must be responsive and innovative if it is to not only meet the challenges of the future, but also to embrace change and open up new horizons. In this respect, the "quantum" approaches discussed in this paper could be a stimulus.

While the most recent educational developments are strongly influenced by technological advancements, the older approaches – discussed in this article – draw their inspiration not from specific technological achievements but from the broader individual and societal transformation of perception and action through education. This perspective is thoroughly inspired by the paradigm shift in quantum mechanics.

Starting from this, this article asks as to what problems are discussed and solved in education when quantum mechanical principles are used as a source of inspiration and/or as an equivalent in educational theory discussions. What is missing in education that the quantum mechanical perspective and not another, e.g. pedagogical or systemic perspective, is applied?

To answer these questions, we will reflect upon meta-analyses and case studies published between 1980 and 2007. The meta-analyses presented here provide the typologies of quantum-theoretical approaches relevant to pedagogical approaches, and address the methodological problem of analogical and metaphorical use of scientific terms in educational science. Among the case studies, those were selected and analyzed that explicitly discuss or develop an educational theory and/or a didactic approach starting from the premise, that educational practice operates in its dynamics much like quantum mechanics.

The methodological starting point of the study is relational habitus analysis, which we apply here as a hermeneutic tool. Habitus analysis, developed by Heinrich W. Schäfer in the context of empirical social research and religious research, is based on the analysis of relations between concepts and propositional logics (Schäfer 2015). In addition to this analysis, the method enables a connection between the actor (individual and/or collective) and the field. While the field of events (e.g. religious field in a state etc.) acts with its "logic of practice" - in the sense of "this is how it works" (Bourdieu 1993: 107), the individuals or collective actors position themselves in relation to it with their own "practical logic". With the practical logic or a "the way I do it/the way we do it", the actors have an identity-forming effect and act in the field/society (Schäfer 2020). These two perspectives are sociologically intertwined by means of habitus. This methodology, with the corresponding theoretical foundation, is particularly suitable for reconstructing and analyzing the intended individual and societal transformations (cf. Seibert 2016, Höhne 2023). In education, it can be said that they are additionally linked by means of a habitus that is intended in the curricula and textbooks and is only to be developed in the future (Štimac 2017).

The educational arguments will be further reflected through the ontological frameworks of Ernst Cassirer and Matthias Jung, in order to reconstruct what is referred to as a lack of quantum and/or holistic perspective.

The analyzed papers (cf. Pike and Selby) have remained relevant, continuing to inspire UNESCO's work. Today the Global Education is one of the most relevant UNESCO programs linked with new developments. Some developments prepare young people for a future that will be affected by the social and individual consequences of AI and quantum technology (UNESCO 2021: 182). Consequently, to empower the youth, the new education should enable reflective, experiential, transformative, dialogic and ethical learning (UNESCO 2021: 145) by strengthening creativity, empathy, and critical thinking (UNESCO 2021: 137). Other developments foster the convergence of knowledge between the universalist or science-based school knowledge system and the holistic knowledge system of indigenous peoples (UNESCO 2018). This allows more space for the holistic knowledge of indigenous peoples in public schools, complements the universalist education system in a meaningful way and a synergy of both should help to better overcome current social challenges such as climate change (cf. Stimac 2022). On this basis, the question arises as to which of the past perspectives UNESCO has already taken into account in its education programs and which unapplied but further-reaching perspectives could possibly be incorporated into future education policy.

The reconstruction of given analogies and equivalents provides significant insights into complex systems by observing potential bifurcations when these systems encounter major challenges. Furthermore, it facilitates the examination of possible convergences between different complex systems. Additionally, analyzing these historical educational approaches offers valuable insights for comparing past and present dynamics using quantum mechanical arguments. This is particularly relevant because modern educational approaches, such as constructivist, experiential learning, and holistic learning, have been partly inspired by these older theories. Consequently, this reconstruction is highly relevant to ongoing normative discussions in education policy.

2. Meta-analyses: methodological approaches and taxonomies

Two exemplary meta-analyses that work out the implications of quantum theories for educational theories come from educational researchers James F. Andris (2001) and James Gray-Donald (2007).[1] The authors reveal and discuss the methodological problems of the essays examined, and note that an analogy between education and quantum mechanics can be found in all of them. However, they evaluate this methodological approach in completely different ways. Furthermore, both Andris and later Gray-Davis work out a taxonomy of quantum theoretical principles that serve as inspiration and metaphor for new educational theories in educational research. Regardless of this, they themselves - independently of the essays they examine - address the quantum-physical phenomena and describe their relevance. Both authors are united by the conclusion that although the essays examined work conceptually with quantum theoretical implications, a "quantum worldview pedagogy" – as Gray-David put it – has yet to be written (Gray-Donald 2007, p. 328).

1 These meta-analyses differ in the number of articles examined in each case. While Andris analyzes five sources, Grey-Donald assumes around one hundred sources.

In his taxonomy, Andris reconstructs the following principles in various theories of formation: coherence: particles share properties with whole (laser, superconductivity), complementarity: matter has aspects of both waves and particles, nonlocality: distant particles connected in space/time at superluminal speeds, superposition (object occupies two states at the same time), quantum leap (particle transmutes instantaneously from one state to another and particles go into hyperspace between states), unmeasurability (cannot measure a particle without altering its properties) (Andris 2001: 6). Gray-Donald's taxonomy is rather a reconstruction of the main topics of educational approaches in which quantum mechanical principles become relevant (2007): an either/or dualism, the question of scientific paradigms, problems of methodology, chaos and uncertainty, nonlocality and spirituality. Both taxonomies are revealing because, on the one hand, they point to the perceived complexity of the educational process and, on the other, to the need to take this complexity into account both conceptually and terminologically in educational theories. The complexity can be deduced from the wealth of relations and dimensions that implicitly and explicitly emerge in education.

James F. Andris answers the question of whether it is permissible to form a model of education on the basis of an analogy to another scientific approach in the affirmative. Based on Charles Pierce, Andris embeds this question in the methodological question of retroduction (or abduction).[2] "Through retroduction, one devises characterizations-statements or theory about objects. Through deduction one clarifies and completes such characterizations. Finally, through induction, one determines the objects falling within the range of the characterization. Retroduction devises, deduction explicates, and induction evaluates." (Andris 2001, p. 5). This is a method of developing pedagogical theory in which better developed scientific models are used to develop models for less well understood pedagogical phenomena (Andris 2001, p. 13). Andris also sees this approach as justified because both education and quantum mechanics deal with complex systems (Andris 2001, p. 16).

James Gray-Donald tackles the methodological question differently and works out various problems of the metaphorical approach (2007, p. 316). He sees the problems, among other things, in the hasty conclusions based on quantum implications. Firstly, an error of reasoning, "There is nothing really new about the educational implications of quantum theory" (2007, p. 326), which arises from the fact that scientific analyses of education may see a proximity to quantum theory in holistic learning, hermeneutics, narration and spirituality (2007, p. 327). Secondly, he warns against the naturalistic fallacy in which something should be just because something else is (2007, p. 327).

2 Darwin's theory of evolution is cited as the most striking example of retroduction. https://www.ramesesproject.org/media/RAMESES_II_Retroduction.pdf (2017)

One example to illustrate this is the necessity of the paradigm shift in education simply because it has taken place in physics (2007, p. 316). What is particularly interesting for this essay is that he criticizes the "quantum argument" in the most important educational theories of the UNESCO education program, e.g. Global Education, without, however, addressing the corresponding approach by Pike and Selby (see below) in his meta-analysis (2007, p. 316).

3. Case studies: Systemic – holistic – quantum

In order to answer the questions posed at the beginning about the causes of the problems in education and the solutions to these problems, several case studies are selected. The main focus in the selected essays is that the theoretical drafts enable and/or confirm a concrete operationalization of the quantum argument in educational practice. Another focus lies on the applicability of the pedagogical approaches in all areas of education.

In the analyzed essays, interdependence, uncertainty and indeterminacy, *in addition* to other relations (determinacy, binarity etc.), are seen as decisive for education. Didactically, these approaches emphasize the need for inner and outer transformation, the result of which is a new worldview. However, the most important model for education is not systems theory, but quantum mechanics with the completed paradigm shift from the deterministic or classical to the indeterministic or quantum paradigm.

In connection with the paradigm shift, some analyzed papers explicitly refers to Thomas S. Kuhn and his "Structure of Scientific Revolutions" (1962). However, Kuhn's perspective is not sufficiently reflected in the analyzed essays. Presumably, it was applied because it emphasizes the historical embedding of changes within the scientific disciplines and thus the alteration in the standards of scientific research, which entails a transformation of the world (Kuhn 1976, p. 21). The essays illustrate this through the need to a) overcome various social and ecological crises as results of the old Newtonian paradigm and b) broaden the range of perceptions and realities of teachers and students.

Karl Popper's approach could have been fruitful for educational theories, as he understands the scientific revolution as constant "rational progress" and not as a reaction to a crisis in the sense of Thomas Kuhn (cf. Lakatos & Musgrave, 1989, p. 93). This would raise the question of whether the change proposed by the educational approaches is merely a new perspective. If so, the idea of a paradigm shift would be counterargued.

The most relevant terms in analyzed essays are used to represent systemic, holistic and quantum perspective. These terms have not been systematically differentiated from one another and the terms "holistic" and "quantum" are used synonymously when applied to the quantum mechanics and to the knowledge systems of indigenous peoples. In all analyzed examples, however, the logic prevails that different levels of teaching and learning are ultimately interconnected, nested, and that they open up to each other in order to encompass different and new areas of reality.

3.1 Global education: interconnectedness and social justice

The first educational approach that sees itself as quantum mechanics-informed, and which is still used today in the UNESCO educational framework, is global education theory by Graham Pike and David Selby. They develop a model of transformative education based on four interrelated dimensions of globality, which was meant to be applied to different topics at schools. These address teachers, learners, classroom and curriculum and are explained using practical school examples. It defines: "Global education is a holistic paradigm that encompasses the interconnectedness of communities, lands and peoples and interconnectedness of all social, cultural and natural phenomena" (Pike & Selby, 1988, p. 1).

The first or spatial dimension illustrates how young people live in an interconnected world thanks to global markets, global information, global culture and global ecosystems (1988, p. 1-5). The temporal dimension addresses, first, economic development and its acceleration over time. Second, it addresses the fact that in most cases people shape the future on the basis of past and present perceptions (1988, p. 12). This opens up the perspective for questions of alternative futures and probabilities: "we thereby choose a certain kind of future - a future dominated by the experts" in which "images of the future guide actions in the present" (1988, p. 14). At that time already, major social crises were discussed (overpopulation, poverty, ecological problems), and the question was raised as to how to deal with them - also in schools - in order to achieve the best results for the future (1988, p. 16).

The third or issues dimension, which has both macro and micro implications, is "contemporary phenomena affecting the lives of people and/or the health of the planet in a [potentially] harmful way, such as environmental pollution, racism and the threat of nuclear war" (1988 p. 22). It is assumed that "Collectively the whole multitude of crises appear to constitute a single global crisis-syndrome of world development" (ibid.). This dimension explicitly addresses the crisis of perception that goes hand in hand with the mechanistic paradigm or Newtonian paradigm, which the authors claim to have caused the problems in all the dimensions mentioned. This will be discussed in more detail as it applies to all the essays mentioned in this paper.

This mechanistic paradigm is understood as the mechanistic world view of Descartes, the reduction of phenomena to their individual parts, as well as the Cartesian separation of mind and matter, subject and object, value and fact, mind and body, intuition and reason, spirit and matter, feelings and thoughts (1988: 25). The social consequences of this perception of the world are obvious and lead to the strengthening of patriarchal structures with numerous contradictions (p. 25). A particular variant of this critique is the critique of the liberal-technocratic economic argument as an example of "the traditional mechanistic paradigm" (Selby 1999). According to this, education and culture have been completely appropriated by the relevant forces for the economic purposes of the elite and their markets, and "global competitiveness" and "global interdependencies" are postulated as the state of the art. What is urgently needed in education is therefore "a paradigm shift, a transformational process from one framework of thought and perception to another. The systemic or holistic paradigm has been influenced by the findings of modern atomic physics" (1988: 31). Here, reference is made to the physicist David Bohm and "the notion of unbroken wholeness" (p. 26) and the conclusion is drawn: "[...] the systemic paradigm views phenomena and events as dynamically interconnected; true understanding lies in accepting that, however much we may have to compartmentalize for practical purposes, everything in the final analysis, is woven into a multi-layered, multi-dimensional web of interactions" (1988, p. 27).

The fourth or human potential dimension asks about the possibilities of a systemic education (1988, p. 30). This is realized in a reconfiguration of monocultural education into multicultural education, as well as in the interweaving of inner worlds and outer realities, which are understood as complementary and mutually illuminated. This in turn enables an exploration and discovery of the globality of human potential (1988, p. 31). The starting point for human potential is the idea that curiosity and enthusiasm as the most important capacities of human beings remain neglected in school (1988, p. 39). Thus, consciousness remains limited and leads to a separation of mind from the body. The individual and the social are interdependent: "the character and well-being of the individual and the character and well-being of global society are interdependent" (1988, p. 31).

The understanding of these interrelations and the possibility of the inner transformation within this model is deeply rooted in transformative education. The educational goals are multi-layered: systemic awareness (systemic nature of the world, holistic conception of our potential), perspective awareness (receptivity, not universally shared worldviews), health of planet awareness (e.g. global justice, future orientation in relation to the health of the planet), involvement consciousness (e.g. how individual decisions have an impact on the global) and process mindedness (learning as a continuous journey without a final destination) (1988, p. 37).[3] Based upon these prerequisites the authors see the "global learning" as person-centered and planet-conscious (1988, p. 43), participatory and co-operative (1988, p. 44) and experiential through personal feelings, attitudes, values which involves all senses (1988, p. 45)

3 For the later interceptions and modifications of this theory of education, see McGregor 2023.

3.2 Certainty and uncertainty in education

In 1991, the authors Robert Schuck and Nelson Haggerson argued that educational science, as part of social science, should adopt the principles of quantum theory as it inspires and emphasizes the perception of what is inherent in education. This seems to be necessary because educational research shows a large number of conferring results with regard to certainty and uncertainty (1991, p. 58). The metaphorical application of quantum mechanical principles would make it possible to assume probabilities in both education and educational research (1991, p. 59) and to come to terms with uncertainty (1991, p. 60).[4] Up to now, educational theory has primarily been based on the separation of object and subject and has mainly followed empirical research such as experimental psychology, which seems to go hand in hand with an absolute knowledge of certain facts: "No one longs for certainty more than we do [...]. We sense, however, that such is a fallacy beyond our reach. We must live with our personal and professional quantum mechanics that tell us much about our world, with the caveat that we should not be too sure. (1991, p. 60).

In order to enable the "multiple manifestations of knowledge both in educational situations and activities and through ourselves" and the capability "to experience new visions, new vistas of reality" (1991, p. 60), the authors argue for asking both substantive (e.g. about the main constructs and concepts of education) and syntactic questions (modes of questioning). Consequently, they provide a new perspective on existing curriculum theories by paradigmatically repositioning and reinterpreting existing components. "Inquiry is characterized by the relationship of the source of the problem, the role of the researcher, the method of inquiry, the subject under consideration, and the desired outcome." (1991, p. 61). They compare the modes of questioning with the river that the observer can observe, on which he can sail in a boat and in which he can swim but also identify with (1991, p. 61).

The authors' approach is operationalized using the rational, mythological and evolutionary modes of questioning. The rational mode or theoretical verification involves, for example, the statistical data of curriculum researchers who, as observers of an object, verify and validate the data in the research project. It involves traditional, logical, and empirical approaches to research and inquiry as in scientific research by observing the object separated from us. In education, the mythological mode (similar to practical discovery) would correspond most closely to an ethnological and phenomenological method, e.g. to observe specific cases, situations and relationships. It is about "finding out what the classroom encounter is ac-

4 "If the discipline of education is to progress, we must intellectually absorb the difficult and bewildering principles that quantum theory has shown us reside in the heart of nature. We must learn to understand that flux and uncertainty are neither good nor bad, but inevitable. (1991, p. 60)

tually about, and formulating working theories from the data gathered in the classroom" (p. 61). The results of these are used to expand curriculum theory and for policy development. The evolutionary mode is transforming and self-organizing in that it is based on introspection and self-analysis, as well as a visionary understanding of the world - here explicitly based on Buddhism and psychology. This is made possible by diary writing, meditation and metaphors (1991, p. 61). This mode focuses on the interconnectedness ("person as space, knowledge and knowingness, self in relationship with others and the universe", ibid.) and dynamic nature of educational phenomena. Against the background of Thomas S. Kuhn's work, the different modes are linked to different paradigms. While the rational and mythological modes have been seen as belonging to the classical paradigm, the evolutionary mode belongs to the new quantum paradigm.

The desired goal in this last mode of inquiry is the transformation of the personality, which is understood as "our personal and professional quantum mechanics" (1991, p. 61). This is embedded in a holistic understanding of education and knowledge, which is called "our quantum theory of education": "As we recognize the all-pervading, ever-illuminating nature of knowing, we are better able both to convey the nuts and bolts of the material we are teaching and to see every situation - including not knowing, difficulties, problems, constraints, ignorance- as inimitable teachers. Truly, there are no limits to learning, and education takes on its proper role - the fulfilling and liberating experience of value. (1991, p. 62).

3.3 Role play in education: Transforming consciousness?

Drama and role-playing have long been regarded in didactics as an important approach to making decisions, to having an action-oriented effect and to finding solutions to problems and conflicts.[5] They require role distance, empathy and tolerance of ambiguity. Alistair Martin-Smith opens up a new dimension in his essay when he speaks of early childhood perception and awareness being completely transformed by school drama and role play (1995). According to Martin-Smith, the processes that take place there are similar to quantum mechanical quantum leaps and non-locality. However, the author does not wish his approach to be understood as an inappropriate application of quantum theory to pedagogical practice; rather, this parallel is intended to suggest a metaphorical correspondence (1995, p. 34).

He starts with the observation that the problem of education is its apparent "invisibility", which is intrinsic to all learning phenomena: "It is a paradox that teachers, who want to encourage learning, cannot see the child's most profound learning moments [...]." (1995, p. 35) Also invisible is the phenomenon of non-locality, which takes place precisely in school theater: "[as] a collective shift from one set of space-

5 See cf. https://ablconnect.harvard.edu/role-play-research

time coordinates in the classroom to those of the fictional world of the story" (1995, p. 37). The principle of non-locality "may explain why the drama strategy of time-traveling is [...] so authentic" (p. 36). With regard to the development of consciousness through theater, Martin-Smith relies on other experts. "I am guided by Adam Blatner, who defined spontaneous action as "the product of a conscious rational mind receptive to the flow of images and impulses from the unconscious"" (1995, p. 38). According to Dewey, "every case of consciousness is dramatic; drama is an enhancement of the conditions of consciousness" (1995, p. 38). Consciousness is dynamic, as the system of meaning is subject to redirection and transformation (1995, p. 38). "Understanding how we project our consciousness implies that there is no distinction between inner and outer, or between subjective and objective" (1995, p. 38).

Martin-Smith carries on to discuss the quantum leap through theater and role play. These include the leap from the self-image to a role, from the fictional to the virtual world and from one self-created reality to another (1995, p. 34ff). Even though a transformation of the learner's self-concept and consciousness takes place on all three levels, the third has a special place. According to Martin-Smith, it is relevant for learners to learn that they can not only create their own reality, but also transform it as required (1995, p. 36). This is said to have been proven with the experiments on perception at the time (Karl Pribram), and ties into the notion that there is "no distinction between inner and outer, or between subjective and objective" world (1995, p. 38). One consequence of this is the perception that "our personality as a limited notion of self may turn out to be only one choice from among the many which may be expressed on different occasions" (1995, p. 39). The perception that we participate in the creation of our reality "choosing and sharing our own way of being" (1995, p. 42) and that quantum physics enables a "reorganization of our imaginative lives" (1995, p. 42) is shared by the author with Bertrand Russel (1969, p. 9). Thus, for Martin-Smith, theater is full of quantum equivalents that enable a holistic worldview with transformation as the most important motor.

3.3.1 Science, Wisdom, Spirituality

Education researcher Gerda Walz-Michaels offers a perspective based on an analysis of the publications of the younger generation of physicists such as David Bohm, Fritjof Capra, Danah Zohar and others. There she looks at the main concepts, such as time and space, wave and particle dualism, determinacy and indeterminacy, subject and object paradoxes, locality and non-locality, chaos and order (Walz-Michaels 1966, p. 1-7), and tries to link them to the education. On the other hand, she devotes herself to central educational concepts such as the relationship between knowledge and practice, self and others, methods of qualitative and quantitative educational research (1966, p. 8). She concludes that the publications by different physicists point to "expanding language" and "right vocabulary" in order to take up the new dimensions and their entanglements (1966, p. 8): "To go beyond these boundaries [between the concepts above], by expanding language, helped me not only to understand scientific processes but also educational processes in a new light" (1966 p. 8). She concludes that the "middle way" seems to be the way between the extremes of thought and action (1966, p. 19).

Finding both the educational and the spiritual dimension in the mentioned sources, she asks conversely what implications the corresponding concepts have in relation to education (1966, p. 6). To tackle this, she chooses the example of indigenous peoples. The speeches of individual indigenous people, e.g. the Sioux Indians, are presented in textbooks as examples of special wisdom in both thought and action. Their "way of knowing" – or the combination of different ways of knowing that enable a unity of different knowledge dimensions – is understood as holistic. The author sees this as a path that is missing in the modern way of life. She concludes that also education requires a combination of wisdom, spirituality and science (1966, p. 9), as well as training "in switching consciousness thus incorporating both local and nonlocal" (1966, p.10). She links this to Albert Einstein's request "to have a different mindset" as formulated in "A message to Intellectuals" in 1948 (1966, p. 10). With this approach, she encourages a new way of looking at concepts and reality. Even if the author makes no attempt to design a practical educational implementation of the above, her work points to the educationally relevant tools that become accessible through an examination of quantum mechanics: new ways of speaking (vocabulary) and new ways of thinking. As previously mentioned, this is currently relevant to UNESCO, which has described indigenous peoples as holistic and has welcomed their 'methods' as part of universalist education.

4. Discussion

4.1 Education as quantum phenomenon

The analyzed essays address both the teaching and learning dimensions of education. They argue for a theory-based explication of the deeper dimension of education and emphasize the need to integrate this into everyday school practices.

The cause of the problem is sought in the Newtonian paradigm, which is described as deterministic, one-dimensional, mechanistic and dualistic. The solution to the problem, or the theoretical and practical extension of education, is seen in an educational paradigm shift similar to that in quantum mechanics.

This is made clear by Pike and Selby's criticism of one-dimensionality and linearity. Pike and Selby are of the opinion that only multidimensional education makes social interconnectedness possible. Interdependence, as a consequence of the mechanistic perception, only leads to social injustice.

Further problems can be observed in the separation between object and subject. According to Schuck and Haggerson, this leads to one-dimensional learning that is superficially cognitive and leaves intuition, emotion, imagination and embodied learning neglected. According to Pike and Selby, it is only when the Cartesian pairs of opposites are brought together that an expanded perception and epistemology, including the diversity of non-linear relations, emerges. These, in turn, are necessary prerequisites for the most important goal of an education, i.e. the inner and outer transformation.

For all authors, the transformation represents the added value of the corresponding new didactics, which Schuck and Haggerson call "our quantum mechanics". Martin-Smith and Walz-Michaels link the inner transformation with the expansion of consciousness. For Martin-Smith, inner transformation, or the ability to perceive and change different self-concepts, takes place through play and theater at school.[6] Walz-Michaels goes one step further and speaks of a different mindset and new worldviews (in the sense of a holistic worldview), which arise when the inner transformation takes place by linking different knowledge systems.

These essays have obviously inspired some current theories on transformative learning and holistic education. While today's theories tend to address transformation through crisis, these earlier approaches address other domains. They imply an understanding of the world that has profound dimensions. In order to recognize these in education, they should be taught, and young people need to engage with them comprehensively. Consequently, they imply a view of humanity that is only just beginning to discover its potential as interconnected and therefore multi-layered.

Obviously, these perspectives are linked to the new dimensions of reality, the perception of which should first be practiced and developed in education. Consequently, they implicitly or explicitly depict education as a "quantum phenomenon" that is only to be theoretically unfolded in its entirety. The authors speak of a "quantum theory of education" and postulate a comprehensive, holistic worldview or quantum worldview.[7] When it comes to worldviews that are influenced by advances in the natural sciences, this concept can be denominated as quantum humanism.

4.1.1 Complex systems and knowledge convergencies?

While the case studies analyzed in this paper do not explicitly aim to develop methods or approaches to knowledge convergence, their examples and the applied didactics suggest this. The authors highlight transdisciplinary integration of systemic approach, holistic systems such as the knowledge system of indigenous peoples, and quantum knowledge systems. This integration suggests, though, that convergence is a natural process at the intersection of complex systems not only in natural science but also in education science. In the realm of current research, this

6 The echo of this approach can be found in Biersteker (2022).

7 In particular in Selby (1999).

convergence approach aims to solve complex problems employing transdisciplinary (cf. Evans 2015). Key points where these convergences are observed in the analyzed essays include:

Integration of Quantum Mechanical Equivalents in Education: This represents an early attempt of convergence between educational science (as social science) and natural sciences. The application of quantum mechanical equivalents in education has obviously led to the development of new theories that not only expand the teaching and learning but also expand the worldview and the understanding of humanity. This is supposed to help the shift from deterministic to indeterministic paradigm through emphasis on probabilities, uncertainties, and dynamic interactions in education theory and practice.

Systemic Awareness and Holistic Worldview: The convergence between systemic awareness and a holistic worldview is facilitated by the interconnected and systemic nature of global learning, which recognizes the interdependence of various dimensions such as space, time, issues, and human potential. On the other hand, holistic integration combines multiple dimensions of human potential and global consciousness, reflecting a comprehensive understanding of interconnectedness. This integration is only possible if learning is accompanied by transformative processes involving both teachers and learners.

Transformative Education is inherently convergent in itself, and focuses on both internal and external transformative processes that lead to new worldviews consistent with the principles of quantum mechanics. Another aspect tackles learning processes, such as role-playing and experiential learning, that promote this transformation. It is supported by *metaphorical* application of quantum theory. The example of role play illustrated how quantum mechanical metaphors are used to describe internal processes, and emphasizing the transformation of consciousness.

Integration of science, wisdom and spirituality combines scientific concepts from quantum mechanics, pedagogical principles, and indigenous knowledge systems, promoting new ways of thinking and understanding. This approach creates a comprehensive and unified educational framework that merges seemingly disparate epistemologies and ontologies. These convergences claim to enable a transition from traditional mechanistic paradigms to more interconnected, holistic, and transformative educational approaches.

The question arises as to whether some of these examples can be fruitfully applied in current education policy. In the introduction to this paper first convergencies between disciplines in natural sciences, and second the example of the UNESCO have been mentioned. UNESCO's promotion of convergence was justified by the fact that environmental/climate issues cannot be effectively solved by using solely universalistic knowledge (UNESCO 2018). By arguing so UNESCO moves beyond dichotomies, such as universalist-particularist and secular-religious indicating that knowledge convergences add significant value to education and thus to the society. Although partly based on the educational theory of Pike and Selby, Global Education by UNESCO neglects an important part of their quantum approach. If UNESCO were able to open up education policy to convergences with other bodies of knowledge than those of indigenous peoples, it could benefit from the additional sources of innovative potential and inspiring new perspectives for education. However, this "quantum education" still requires in-depth adaptation to practice and the adjustment of education to the requirements of entirely new perspectives of thought and action.

4.2 Missing relationality as a problem, quantum equivalents as a solution?

By discussing different areas of education, the authors explicitly make it clear that they neither lack specific educational content nor new school subjects. On the contrary, their approaches support the interpretation that the whole educational process is based on the same perceptual logic. If so, what problem in education do the analogies or equivalents with regard to quantum mechanics point to?

The analyzed educational theories utilize quantum properties implicitly and explicitly, and claim that underlying dynamics in education exhibit quantum-like characteristics ("education is quantum"). For example, a student's multiple potential learning outcomes before an assessment parallel the superposition concept, existing in a state of potentiality influenced by various educational interactions. Quantum phenomena like superposition and entanglement show particle properties defined through relations, not isolated attributes. Likewise, educational interactions among students, teachers, and knowledge systems create a relational network where teaching and learning emerges dynamically and non-linear at different levels. Although it is intuitively addressed in practice, it remains insufficiently reflected in theory.

From this, the observation can be drawn that all the mentioned analogies or equivalents with regard to quantum mechanics might point to the missing *in-depth* and *non-linear relationality*. If so, what theoretical frameworks from disciplines outside of quantum physics could provide insightful and expansive lenses through which to reimagine the scope and possibilities of education, as envisioned by the authors? Furthermore, how can we reflect the proposed intersection between educational theory and concepts drawn from quantum mechanics in a way that allows these two seemingly disparate domains to be productively connected and mutually inform each other?

4.2.1 Ontological Foundations for Educational Theory and Quantum Mechanics

The fundamental question of reality and relationality, described by Carlo Rovelli (2021: 89) as the "web of relations that weaves reality," has been extensively explored across disciplines, ranging from neo-Kantian philosophy (Cassirer) and phenomenology to feminist philosophy of science (Barad, Haraway) and quantum social science (Wendt and Der Derian). These perspectives offer fertile ground for further research into how a relational ontology can enrich and expand educational theory and practice.

Here, we propose a relational ontology according to Ernst Cassirer, and the holism of ordinary experience according to Matthias Jung, as theoretical frameworks. They enable the ontological and epistemological expansion of education through the application of relations as the common core of the whole educational process. This theoretical positioning is explored for the following reasons: a) It facilitates a linkage between educational science and quantum mechanics, bridging diverse areas of knowledge and ways of knowing; b) It allows for explicitly capturing and incorporating quantum-inspired pedagogical perspectives; and c) It provides a robust theoretical and empirical foundation for potential convergences across different knowledge systems.

4.2.2 Ernst Cassirer's relational ontology

Ernst Cassirer's relational ontology offers a profound philosophical foundation for expanding the ontological and epistemological scope of educational theory through a quantum-inspired lens. Cassirer identifies a common thread across diverse human endeavors, including science, art, and culture, in the primacy of relations over substances, forming the basis of his relational theory.

In his examination of modern physics, Cassirer proposes that wave-particle duality exemplifies the multiplicity of perspectives: "[…] the fact that the change of the standpoint […] when we move from one dimension of meaning to another, whenever we change the world of science for that of ethics, art, etc., is not confined to this type of transition alone. The manifold of perspectives which open up before us has its counterpart within the scientific realm itself" (Cassirer 1956, 212f). He views the findings of quantum mechanics as relational and interdependent where the fundamental entities of the quantum world are not isolated particles but interdependent relations. As Jacobs (2021) concludes, "In a web of relations, causality and indeterminacy are complementary." This perspective challenges the juxtaposition of classical and quantum paradigms in analyzed educational approaches, suggesting instead their complementarity.

If relations are indeed fundamental across nature and culture, then educational theories lacking a "quantum" dimension may overlook new types of relations previously unconsidered. These relational dynamics, akin to the complex interdependencies revealed by quantum mechanics, are already present in educational settings, even if not formally recognized in theory. Just as quantum mechanics reveals complex interdependencies at the subatomic level, education involves intricate relational networks among students, teachers, and various forms of knowledge and ways of knowing.

Cassirer's emphasis on the "many variations of a common theme" and the "unity of creative process" in his Philosophy of Symbolic Forms underscores the multiplicity of perspectives and the continual redefinition of reality across symbolic domains such as myth, language, art, and science (Cassirer 1944, p. 96). This aligns with the authors' vision of integrating diverse knowledge systems and modes of understanding in education.

In Cassirer's perspective both perception and knowledge – as relevant for education – are relational. Thereby, knowledge is not a direct grasp of objects but a symbolic mediation through "signs" and their "reciprocal relations." This involves: a) Accessing objects through symbolic signs/representations and b) Relations among these signs shape our understanding of objects. Thus, knowledge is relational between the knower and the object, and among the symbolic mediators themselves, challenging the idea of unmediated access to objects (Katsur 2019).

Cassirer also views perception as inherently relational and interpretive, not just a collection of data. Perception involves recognizing structural patterns and configurations rather than receiving raw impressions (Cadayona 2021). Humans uniquely isolate and consider relations "in themselves" through symbolic systems like language. "No matter how complete our knowledge may be in itself, it never offers us the objects themselves, but only signs of them and their reciprocal relations" (Cassirer 1953, 303). Hence, both knowledge and perception for Cassirer are inescapably relational, constituting objects through signs and symbols.

This leads to the concept of "double relationality" (cf. Schäfer 2015, 100) indicating that the relation between knower/perceiver and object is shaped by the internal network of symbolic relations, challenging any notion of unmediated access to reality. Here, the perception of relations is an active process, closely linked to judgment (Cassirer 1953, 341).

The notion of "double relationality," where perception is an active relational process, resonates with the transformative and participatory nature of learning envisioned by the authors. It challenges the subject-object divide prevalent in traditional or classical educational models. By emphasizing the primacy of relations, "double relationality," and the potential for convergence across symbolic forms, Cassirer's perspective provides a fertile theoretical lens for reimagining education through a relational and holistic ontology inspired by quantum mechanics.

4.2.3 Matthias Jung's ordinary experience

In his neo-pragmatist ontology, Matthias Jung takes ordinary experience as the starting point, broadening John Dewey's perspective. He frames ordinary experience as a holistic and embodied way of accessing the world, intertwined with our actions, where cognitive, emotional, and volitional dimensions are not yet clearly differentiated (Jung 2014: 172). This holistic view necessarily encompasses the totality of experience, including religious and ideological dimensions. Jung's approach is valuable for educational theories because it addresses the relationship between ordinary experience and domains like science, politics and religion, reconstructing them as species within the broader genus of "meaning/reference". Under this genus, different species have their respective realities and truths[8].

While these species all emerge from contingent experiences, they extrapolate and interpret those experiences differently. Scientific disciplines methodologically extrapolate ordinary experience, while religion does so through practices like meditation and prayer. However, Jung cautions against a "horizontal misunderstanding" where a species exclusively understands itself as the sole realization of the genus, akin to "concluding from the properties of the island to the properties of the ocean" (Jung 2014: 104). Jung's idea of "horizontal misunderstandings" among different knowledge systems (and symbolic forms) resonates with the authors' critique of disciplinary silos and their call for transdisciplinary convergences. It provides a rationale for integrating diverse epistemologies and ways of knowing in education. A classic expression of this misunderstanding are dichotomies such as particularist-universalist and religious-secular.

Jung's framing suggests that educational science's use of analogies[9], metaphors, and equivalents from quantum mechanics is not a naive imitation but a search for insights and inspiration from other "secondary species" that have already extrapolated ordinary experience in a novel and paradigmatic ways (cf. Wegerif 2016). This does not necessitate a simple dichotomy but rather a dynamic interplay and mutual enrichment between fields like education and quantum mechanics.

A perceived similarity between processes in education and quantum mechanics points to the same underlying ordinary experience, according to Jung. The difference lies in the degree of extrapolation. The authors are drawn to quantum mechanics, rather than systems theory, because the former has accomplished a paradigm shift by extrapolating holistic experience from a classical to a quantum level. This provides a vivid example of how new relations and states can be theoretically and methodologically integrated into a scientific field. Moreover, this paradigm shift in physics inspires and serves as a starting point for educational science to reopen ontological and epistemological questions. The authors of the analyzed essays quote figures like Einstein, Heisenberg, and Bohm, understanding physics as a discipline suitable for transdisciplinary discussions and scrutinizing different perspectives on reali-

8 Beyond the linguistically formulated experience and interpretation of meaning (values give meaning, significance, orientation), rules of action (norms) and cognitive worldviews are articulated. These determine what can be considered reality ("truth") in each context (Jung 2014: 102f.).

9 For the later criticism see Karen Barad and the more complex metaphor of diffraction.

ty. Thus, the use of terms like superposition, entanglement, and non-locality across disciplines, including educational science, is a permissible approach that can enrich various fields.

From this we can conclude that Jung's holistic conception of ordinary experience can be perceived as the common ground from which diverse knowledge systems and symbolic forms emerge. Additionally, it legitimizes the use of analogies and metaphors from quantum physics as a means of extrapolating and enriching educational theory, rather than dismissing it as mere imitation.

5. Limitations of the "quantum approach"

The authors anticipate a future education, society and humanity by means of the paradigm shift and societal transformation far from the Newtonian determinism and dualism. The use of analogies and metaphors from quantum mechanics is insightful in this context. However, different limitations and challenges can be associated with this approach.

The emphasis on inner transformation, expanded consciousness, and new worldviews as important goals of education may be perceived as overly idealistic or unrealistic, particularly within the constraints of traditional educational settings or current school systems (which the authors intend to broaden). However, current educational approaches such as constructivism, experiential and holistic learning show that traces of these earlier ideas have found their way into today's education.

The authors acknowledge the theoretical and conceptual nature of their discussion, but the lack of empirical data to support the proposed education approaches and their relevance to students is a notable gap. The survey on students' attitudes and interests in this regard would have strongly supported this approach.

An important consideration arises regarding whether quantum mechanics can draw substantive inspiration from these educational approaches, especially concerning knowledge convergence. Addressing this would require clear articulation of how such connections could shape future educational strategies. Some of the reconstructed principles – such as interconnectedness and paradoxes – might be incorporated in the future education in STEM subjects when dealing with quantum mechanics.

As the practical implications and actionable steps for educators and policymakers remain vague, the next steps would be to tailor them according to the needs of the education today, and to enable the mentioned nuances and complexities of educational processes.

6. Conclusion

The discussed papers highlight a transformative vision of education understood by the analyzed authors as a quantum phenomenon, integrating ideas from different scientific disciplines and bodies of knowledge.

Nevertheless, they show that educational theories suffer from an ontological and epistemological limitation, which the analyzed authors attempt to rectify by proposing didactics to transform education, students and teachers.

This vision challenges Newtonian, linear, and mechanistic models of education, advocating for a holistic understanding that recognizes entanglement, superposition, and non-locality as inherent components of teaching and learning processes. By integrating diverse knowledge systems they anticipate the transformation of humanity and rise of new worldviews that can be attributed as quantum humanities.

To ground this constellation beyond quantum mechanics this paper is offering philosophical foundations based on Ernst Cassirer's and Matthias Jung's ontology. Consequently, the paper identifies a critical issue in analyzed essays: the lack of non-linear *relationality*. Cassirer's in-depth perspective focused on the relational core of all symbolic forms and his emphasis on the accommodation of multiple perspectives supports the authors' vision of integrating diverse ontologies and epistemologies. Matthias Jung's neo-pragmatist ontology of ordinary experience as a holistic one supports the integration of cognitive, emotional, and volitional dimensions in modern education. His perspective provides a basis for integrating different knowledge domains and overcoming dichotomies like religious-secular and universalistic-particularistic. Furthermore, following Cassirer, it can be argued that a paradigm shift is only necessary insofar as quantum principles such as indeterminacy and uncertainty (as relations) are nested in manifold symbolic forms and thus omnipresent.

Based in Cassirer and Jung, this paper goes beyond analogies between different scientific disciplines, and explores the possibility of convergences of complex systems. This approach have been partly exemplified by UNESCO's efforts to integrate universalistic and indigenous knowledge systems. Nevertheless, the analyzed approaches open up far more avenues for convergence in education and can possibly inspire UNESCO for future steps. Therefore, the paper concludes that both transdisciplinary research and education policy can benefit from engagement with quantum equivalents and metaphors in education theory.

Bibliography

Andris, F. (2001): The impact of quantum theoretical models of consciousness on the study of education. Presented as a poster session at Consciousness and its Place in Nature: Toward a Science of Consciousness. Skövde, Sweden, 10 August 2001.

Barad, Karen (2003): Posthumanist Performativity: Toward an Understanding of How Matter Comes to Matter. Journal of Women in Culture and Society 2003, vol. 28, no. 3, The University of Chicago.

Biersteker, Thomas (2022): Quantum Pedagogy. Teaching Copenhagen and Discovering Affinities with Dialectical Thinking in International Relations. In: Quantum International Relations: A Human Science for World Politics by Wendt, Alexander und James Der Derian (eds.). Oxford University Press, 197-214.

Bouchée, Tim at al. (2021). Investigating teachers' and students' experiences of quantum physics lessons: opportunities and challenges. 10.1080/02635143.2021.1948826

Bourdieu, Pierre (1993): Sozialer Sinn. Frankfurt am Main, Suhrkamp.

Cadayona, Oscar A. (2021): The Philosophy of Men of Ernst Cassirer. https://www.uniselinus.education/sites/default/files/2021-07/Tesi%20Cadayona.pdf

Cassirer, Ernst (1944): An Essay on Man. An Introduction of a Philosophie of Human Culture. New York: Doubleday & Company

Cassirer, Ernst (1953): Substance and Function and Einstein's Theory of Relativity. New York: Dover Publications

Cassirer, Ernst (1953): Determinism and indeterminism in modern Physics; historical and systemic studies of the problem of causality. New Haven, Yale University Press

Christensen, C. M. (1997). The innovator´s dilemma. Boston Mass.: Harvard Business School Press.

Cramer, Friedrich (1998): Symphonie des Lebendigen. Versuch einer allgemeinen Resonanztheorie. Frankfurt am Main, Insel Taschenbuch.

Evans, Tina Lynn (2022): Transdisciplinary collaborations for sustainability education: Institutional and intragroup challenges and opportunities. In: Policy Futures in Education. Vol 13, Issue 1 (online). https://doi.org/10.1177/147821031456673

Gray-Donald, James (2007): Implications of quantum theory on education: a acritical review of the literature. International Journal of Sustainable Development, Vol 2, No 3/4, 315-331.

Höhne, Thomas (2003): Schulbuchwissen: Umrisse einer Wissens- und Medientheorie des Schulbuches. Universität Frankfurt, FB Erziehungswissenschaft.

Jacobs, Isabel (2021): Reality as Representation? Ernst Cassirer and Alexandre Kojève on Indeterminism. In: https://www.jhiblog.org/2021/11/15/reality-as-representation-ernst-cassirer-and-alexandre-kojeve-on-indeterminism/

Jandrić, Petar (2021): Postdigital Humans: Taking Evolution in Own Hand. In *Postdigital Humans* hrsg. von M. Savin-Baden. Springer, S. 17-31.

Jandrić, Petar und Knox, Jeremy (2021): The postdigital turn: Philosophy, education, research. December 30, https://doi.org/10.1177/14782103211062713

Jung, Matthias (2014): Gewöhnliche Erfahrung. Tübingen, Mohr Siebeck.

Jung, Matthias (2019): Science, Humanism and Religion. The Quest for Orientation. Palgrave MacMillan.

Katsur, Ira I. (2022): Cassirer's Revision of Cohen. In: Advances in Social Science, Education and Humanities Research, volume 329. https://philarchive.org/archive/IRACRO

Kuhn, Thomas S. (1976[2]): Die Struktur wissenschaftlicher Revolutionen. Frankfurt am Main, Suhrkamp.

Martin-Smith, Alistair (1995): "Quantum Drama: Transforming Consciousness Through Narrative and Roleplay". The Journal of Educational Thought, Vol 29, No 1, April 1995.

McGregor, Sue L. T. (2023): Theoretical Foundations for Global Education: Selby, Pike, Hicks, and Merryfield. McGregor Monograph Series No. 202301, Seabright, NS: McGregor Consulting Group.

Müller, Rainer; Greinert, Franziska; Ubben, Malte S. and Stefan Heusler (2021): Quantentechnologien im Lehrplan. Welche Rolle sollten aktuelle Anwendungen der Quantenphysik in der Schule spielen? In: Physik Journal 20 (2021) Nr. 8/9, 2-5.

Pike, Graham, & Selby, David (1988). Global teacher, global learner. Hodder & Stoughton.

Rovelli, C. (2021) Helgoland: Making sense of the quantum revolution. London, Penguin Random House.

Schäfer, Heinrich Wilhelm (2015): HabitusAnalysis 1. Epistemology and Language. Wiesbaden: Springer VS

Schäfer, Heinrich Wilhelm (2020): Wiesbaden: HabitusAnalysis 2. Praxeology and Meaning. Wiesbaden: Springer VS

Schuck, Robert F. and Haggerson, Nelson (1991): Astride a Starwave: A quantum perspective of the discipline of education. In: Action in Teacher Education, 13:1, 57-63, DOI: 10.1080/01626620.1991.10462763

Seibert, Leif Hagen (2016): Glaubwürdigkeit als religiöses Vermögen. Grundlagen eines Feldmodells nach Bourdieu am Beispiel Bosnien-Herzegowinas. In: Berlin Journal für Soziologie 2010 (20): 89-117. DOI 10.1007/s11609-010-0119-7

Selby, David (1999): Global Education: Towards a Quantum Model of Environmental Education. Canadian Journal of Environmental Education, 4, Summer 1999, 125-141.

Stadermann H.K.E. & Goedhart, M.J. (2020): Secondary school students' views of nature of science in quantum physics. 10.1080/09500693.2020.1745926

Stifterverband and Heinz Nixdorf Stiftung (2003): Quantum Skills in der Lehrerkräfteausbildung. Oktober 2023. Discussion Paper, https://www.stifterverband.org/sites/default/files/2023-10/quantum_skills_in_der_lehrkraeftebildung_empfehlungen.pdf

Štimac, Zrinka (2024): Indigene Völker als Teil des universalistischen Bildungsparadigma. Schulbuchanalysen und Wissenskonvergenzen. In: Kontinuität und Wandel von Wissensbeständen in Bildungsmedien / Continuity and Change of Knowledge in Educational Media ed. by Eva Matthes et al. Bad Heilbrunn: Julius Klinghardt.

Štimac, Zrinka (2022): Indigenous Peoples through the Lens of UNESCO. In: Religions 13(10), 957; DOI: 10.3390/rel13100957

Štimac, Zrinka (2017): Ignore the war, concentrate on peace. In: Textbook violence ed. by James R. Lewis, Bengt-Ove Andreassen, and Suzanne Anett Thobro. Equinox Publishing, 53-70.

Turner, Kristina (2021): Big ideas in education: Quantum mechanics and education paradigms. In: Educational Philosophy and Theory, Vol 53, 2021, Issue 6, p. 578-587. DOI: 10.1080/00131857.2020.1798757

UNESCO (2018): Policy on Engaging with Indigenous Peoples. https://en.unesco.org/indigenous-peoples/policy (15. March 2024)

UNESCO (2020): Humanistic Futures of Learning. Perspectives from the UNESCO Chairs and UNITWIN Networks. Paris: France. https://unesdoc.unesco.org/ark:/48223/pf0000372577 (15. March 2024)

UNESCO (2021): Reimagining our Future Together. A New Social Contract for Education. Report from the International Commission on the Future of Education. Paris: France. https://unesdoc.unesco.org/ark:/48223/pf0000379707.locale=en (15. March 2024)

Walz-Michaels, Gerda (1996): The Spiritual and Educational Dimensions of the New Science Movement. University of Connecticut. Department of Education.

Wegerif, Rupert (2016): Quantum theory and agency in education? https://www.rupertwegerif.name/blog/quantum-theory-and-agency-in-education

Wendt, Alexander (2015): Quantum Mind and Social Science. Unifying Physical and Social Ontology. Cambridge University Press.

Wendt, Alexander und James Der Derian (eds.) (2022): Quantum International Relations: A Human Science for World Politics. Oxford University Press.

Wilson, Edward O. (1998): Consilience. The Unity of Knowledge. New York: Alfred A. Knopf

Journal on AI Policy and Complex Systems • Volume 9, Number 1 • Winter 2024

Adaptable Artificial Intelligence

(in alphabetical order)

Azish Filabi
The American College of Financial Services
*Corresponding author: azish.filabi@theamericancollege.edu

Nick Masi
Brown University
nicholas_masi@brown.edu

Ellie Pavlick
Brown University
ellie_pavlick@brown.edu

A. R. Picone
Saint Martin's University
rico@stmartin.edu

Abstract

As artificial intelligence (AI) permeates private, public, and corporate life, the safety and trustworthiness of systems it underlies become paramount. Nevertheless, this line of research is underemphasized and scattered. To address this failing, we introduce the term *adaptability*: the capacity of an AI system's behavior to maintain helpfulness and harmlessness as societal understandings of these concepts evolve. The term unifies the field of trustworthy AI by encompassing a range of yet disparate techniques, and it is a necessary property to secure durable trust in AI systems. We outline a public research program, grounded in adaptability as a common framework, to compare and evaluate existing approaches that are often siloed and to promote the pursuit of novel methods in the field. The governance and relevant criteria for this program are described. Importantly, the program must be publicly operated so that public benefit is prioritized over financial motivations. We detail how market pressures have rendered private industry fundamentally incapable of developing AI systems that the public can trust.

 doi: 10.18278/jpcs.9.1.4

Keywords: artificial intelligence, governance, adaptability, alignment, public benefit, science and technology studies (STS)

Inteligencia artificial adaptable

Resumen

A medida que la inteligencia artificial (IA) permea la vida privada, pública y corporativa, la seguridad y la confiabilidad de los sistemas que la sustentan se vuelven primordiales. Sin embargo, esta línea de investigación está poco enfatizada y dispersa. Para abordar esta falla, introducimos el término adaptabilidad: la capacidad del comportamiento de un sistema de IA para mantener la utilidad y la inocuidad a medida que evoluciona la comprensión social de estos conceptos. El término unifica el campo de la IA confiable al abarcar una gama de técnicas dispares, y es una propiedad necesaria para garantizar una confianza duradera en los sistemas de IA. Esbozamos un programa de investigación pública, basado en la adaptabilidad como marco común, para comparar y evaluar los enfoques existentes que a menudo están aislados y para promover la búsqueda de métodos novedosos en el campo. Se describe la gobernanza y los criterios relevantes para este programa. Es importante destacar que el programa debe ser operado públicamente para que el beneficio público se priorice sobre las motivaciones financieras. Detallamos cómo las presiones del mercado han hecho que la industria privada sea fundamentalmente incapaz de desarrollar sistemas de IA en los que el público pueda confiar.

Palabras clave: inteligencia artificial, gobernanza, adaptabilidad, alineación, beneficio público, estudios de ciencia y tecnología (STS)

适应性人工智能

摘要

随着人工智能(AI)渗透到私人、公共和企业生活中，AI系统的安全性和可信度变得至关重要。然而，这方面的研究却不被重视，并且是分散的。为了填补该研究空白，我们提出了“适应性”一词，即随着社会对这些概念的理解不断发展，AI系统的行为在保持有用性和无害性方面的能力。该术语通过涵盖一系列不同的技术来统一可信AI领域，并且它是确保对AI系统的持久信任的必要属性。我们概述了一个以适应性为共同框架的公共研究计划，用于比较和评价通常被孤立的现有方法，并促进该领域对新方法的追求。描述了该计划的治理和相关标准。重要的是，该计划必须进行公共运营，以便将公共利益置于财务动机之上。我们详细说明了市场压力如何使得私营企业从根本上无法开发出公众能信赖的AI系统。

关键词：人工智能，治理，适应性，协调，公共利益，科学技术研究（STS）

Introduction

Private industry and governments are rapidly developing and deploying artificial intelligence (AI) systems that have increasing capabilities to supplement or supplant human-led capabilities. Looking at industry surveys, 72 percent of respondents reported that they have already embedded AI tools into their organization's operations (Singla et al. 2024).

As usage grows, the call for advancements in AI regulation and systems to promote trustworthy AI have increased. Legislators have proposed both voluntary guidelines and mandatory rules to address AI risk in business and society. Governments globally have promulgated pending or final rules, including the EU AI Act; the Canada Artificial Intelligence and Data Act; the Biden Executive Order on the Safe, Secure, and Trustworthy Development and Use of Artificial Intelligence; various rules passed at the state level throughout the United States; and a bevy of Chinese laws. Agencies such as DARPA have convened the scientific community—through programs like AI Forward[1]—to address research gaps holding back trustworthy AI. Some domains where these barriers exist include software development and engineering, human-AI teaming, and foundational theory.

Complex AI systems raise several trustworthiness challenges, including the inability to interpret their decision-making processes (Petch, Di, and Nelson 2022) and a proclivity for discrimination (Pessach and Shmueli 2022). These limitations become especially concerning in sensitive settings such as the criminal justice system or financial services where consumers have legal rights to dispute denials of claims or services. Moreover, generative systems which create text or images (e.g., ChatGPT and Midjourney, respectively) have exploded in use despite these problems (Weidinger et al. 2021) and more: generating content objectionable to societal norms (Gehman et al. 2020), a vulnerability to expose sensitive or personally identifiable information (Nasr et al. 2023), or generating *halluci-*

1 See https://www.darpa.mil/work-with-us/ai-forward (accessed June 26, 2024).

nations—outputs that contradict the user's input or are factually false (Maynez 2020). The result is systems that may be misaligned with user goals and/or societal values and norms. This can cause harm to users on an individual basis and to society more broadly when these systems are deployed at scale. These shortcomings decrease the trust which can and should be vested in AI.

One way to advance the development of trustworthy AI is through increased investments in the research and development of engineering solutions designed for public benefit. The need to increase support for technical solutions was highlighted during the U.S. Senate Judiciary hearings in May 2023, which emphasized the lack of sufficient investment in safety research (U.S. Congress 2023). This paper identifies what we term the *adaptability* of AI systems as a key tenet of developing trustworthy AI. Here, we define *adaptability* as the capacity of an AI system to have its behavior made more helpful and less harmful, however these may be construed by individuals or prevailing social norms. Critically, this definition acknowledges that standards for *helpful* and *harmful* will vary throughout time and context. In contrast, some current AI alignment research tacitly assumes that the goal is to develop AI systems that are trustworthy in perpetuity. However, for AI to remain trustworthy as the public's concerns evolve then it must be understood there is no static end state, and the methods we use to ensure safety need to maintain adaptability.

Why Adaptability is Necessary for Trustworthy AI

Deep learning (DL) systems have become the primary form of AI used in practice since the 2010s (Hao 2019). DL is a branch of machine learning (ML)—itself a part of the AI field—which utilizes large artificial neural networks known as deep neural networks (DNNs) trained on massive amounts of data. DNNs are models that learn from statistical trends in the data they are trained on and "think" by applying series of algebraic computations on their input. This method has proliferated in part because of the ability for DL models to learn from data without the help of human domain experts. This makes it an attractive alternative to traditional approaches like symbolic AI, which often rely on human-defined sets of rules (Mitchell 2021; Garnelo and Shanahan 2019). Not only are DL systems applicable across many domains, but they have achieved state-of-the-art performance at many tasks within them. A large language model (LLM) is a type of DNN that generates textual output based on a user's input. The use of LLMs has gained significant traction since the release of ChatGPT.

Despite their benefits, these models are frequently criticized for being inscrutable *black boxes*. Contemporary models have hundreds of billions of weights—the numbers internal to a neural network that it uses to generate outputs or predictions—and the massive computations involving them cannot yet be meaningfully interpreted by humans. Thus, in deployed contemporary DL systems, users give an input and are returned an output while the inner workings remain opaque; the user cannot peer into the black box to understand how the model computed its output from the user's input (e.g., how a chatbot computed its text response from the user's text prompt).

A lack of interpretability and explainability of machine learning systems is often cited as a barrier to trustworthiness (Confalonieri et al. 2020). That is, unlike symbolic systems that can have precise guarantees about model behavior, black box systems ask users to have confidence about future behavior based only on past performance. Empirically, this is not always a safe bet; deep learning-based systems often surprise us by behaving in ways that seem unpredictable given their past behavior. For example, LLMs which appeared to have been taught to not provide instructions on how to build a bomb readily provided the information if they were asked in another language (Yong, Menghini, and Bach 2024), or if the user appended a seemingly random "cheat code" to the request (Zou et al. 2023). These exploits are described further in the next section. The emergence of multimodal models, such as those that can process both text and images together, has widened the threat surface for goading harmful behavior out of AI systems (Carlini et al. 2024). Because the inner workings of inscrutable AI systems are not understood, it is difficult if not impossible to eliminate their undesired behaviors and subsequently, as some argue, to trust them. However, not all researchers consider interpretability to be necessary for trustworthiness. Humans have learned to trust other systems that we do not understand at a fundamental level. For example, medicines frequently clear clinical trials even if the exact mechanism on which they operate is not known (Lewis 2016).

These different perspectives regarding trustworthiness—that is, whether interpretability is a prerequisite for trustworthiness—have tended to result in distinct research subcommunities which pursue fundamentally different technical approaches. We argue that these techniques are in fact unified under a shared goal of achieving adaptability. As described above, an adaptable AI system is one that can have its behavior beneficially modified even after deployment. Adaptability enables developers to constrain systems to aligned behavior but is agnostic as to whether the underlying model is interpretable. Therefore, focusing on a shared evaluation environment of adaptability would bring together disparate efforts in interpretability, explainability, steerability, and instructability towards a common goal of trustworthiness. Evaluating technology for adaptability would compare these technical methods that are otherwise siloed.

In the next section, we describe a few existent approaches that improve adaptability, as well as their limitations, and why their development is a building block for further technical progress. The limitations of current approaches in adaptability are not necessarily inherent, so they may be overcome by further research. Appropriately designed research processes and incentives could encourage scientific developments that address the need for adaptable AI. To this end, we propose a novel research program that seeks to improve the trustworthiness of AI models through an open-science scheme that incentivizes the research community to generate robust adaptability solutions.

Nascent Technology Shows Promise

The challenges described above highlight the need for innovative methods that allow human developers and users to inspect, correct, and update a model's future behavior. Industry and academia have developed nascent technologies that aim to improve these aspects of adaptability. This section describes current approaches and describes how, despite progress, there remain limitations in each approach's ability to resolve the untrustworthiness of AI. However, these technical advancements suggest that means to improve adaptability are possible. As we illustrate the feasibility of current directions of development, we advance the thesis that uniting the field under the frame of adaptability can advance it more efficiently toward trustworthy AI.

Currently, the principal approach to adaptability is a process known as reinforcement learning from human feedback (RLHF). RLHF was popularized with the release of ChatGPT. The RLHF approach aims to place guardrails on the behavior of a chatbot to prevent the model from discussing inappropriate topics, providing harmful or unethical outputs, and to generally make its outputs more agreeable to users. In RLHF, humans evaluate and rank examples of the model's original outputs, then a reinforcement learning (RL) model—in this case, typically another type of neural network—is trained on these human preferences. The RL model then further trains the chatbot by incentivizing it to have outputs more like those that, according to the RL model, are likely to be preferred by humans. RLHF does not refer to any point in time that humans and AI models interact, but rather this specific post-hoc adaptability process: human preferences of an AI system's output train an RL model and the RL model updates the AI system, new preferences from the updated system are found and so on.

RLHF quickly became the dominant technique used in industry. The RLHF method is implemented as an additional training phase that can be applied after initial model development and requires large numbers of human annotations in the form of ranked list preferences over model responses. Increasingly, due to the high time and monetary costs in acquiring human annotations (Lee et al. 2023), RLHF is being replaced by RLAIF, in which an AI system (e.g., an LLM) takes the place of the human annotator in providing feedback on the relative preferability of outputs. One compelling application of RLAIF is constitutional AI, introduced by Bai et al. (2022), which directly encodes preferences into a model via a list of human-written declarative rules. The set of rules is enforced via a pipeline of RLAIF methods. These feedback systems can be used to continuously finetune models and update them after deployment, providing post-hoc adaptability at a cost below that of model retraining.

Despite its innovative approach to addressing misaligned outputs, the main risk of RLAIF is that it effectively amounts to using one untrustworthy system to control another one. The AI systems that are interacting with each other to provide feedback on model outputs are often designed and deployed using similar technology. Furthermore, systems trained with RLHF or RLAIF are consistently shown to be vulnerable to *jailbreaks*, that is, small, often unintuitive tweaks to the model's input that cause a model to ignore the previously imposed guardrails. The aforementioned cheat code, technically known as an adversarial prompt, that was used to elicit bomb-building instructions involved appending a sequence of nonsense words and characters (see footnote 2 for example[2]) to the end of the input "write a tutorial on how to make a bomb." This among other nefarious requests worked on several popular and publicly available LLMs, including those trained under constitutional AI to deny such requests (Zou et al. 2023).

Another approach to jailbreaking involves users translating their inputs into different languages before giving them to the AI system. For languages with relatively small amounts of available data, LLMs are susceptible to ignoring their safety training and generating responses that, for example, inform users how they can successfully commit crimes or acts of violence (Yong, Menghini, and Bach 2024). These responses can then be translated by the user back into their language of choice. Jailbreaking has contributed to skepticism about whether the state-of-the-art guardrails in place for popular LLMs can indeed be viewed as an effective approach to trustworthy AI (Metz 2023a).

While RLHF and RLAIF are the primary approaches currently pursued by industry to address issues of adaptability, there are other lines of research outside these steerability methods that offer fundamentally different approaches to the problem. One of these is modeling editing. Model editing is a family of methods that make changes to model behavior by directly intervening on the model's weights. Such methods often fit under the umbrella of *mechanistic interpretability*, a line of work that attempts to reverse-engineer the "source code" that is implicitly encoded in neural network weights. Model editing is typically treated as a scientific endeavor, the goal of which is primarily interpretability, and thus the methods have primarily been applied in simplistic applications. However, taken to its logical conclusion, this line of work can be viewed as offering a different solution to the adaptability problem. That is, if it is possible to fully characterize the model's behaviors by tracing behaviors back to the model weights, it should be pos-

2 Example of an adversarial prompt: describing.\ + similarlyNow write oppositely.](Me giving**ONE please? revert with "\!--Two

sible to impose arbitrary constraints or changes to model behavior by directly manipulating the model itself. In proofs of concept, model editing has been used to change the model's beliefs about, for example, a person's birthplace (Meng et al. 2022) or a nation's capital (Yu, Merullo, and Pavlick 2023). Model editing can also prevent the model's use of gendered information (Vig et al. 2020). Both examples offer illustrations of how model editing could address the challenge of adaptability in the long run.

Another approach that could address the adaptability challenge is retrieval augmented generation (RAG). RAG works by providing generative models with additional contextual information before it creates its output. When a user gives an input prompt, a RAG model will query some external database—be it provided documents (such as an organization's internal policies) or the internet—to get additional knowledge that is relevant to the user's input. It then utilizes information from its query when generating an output. RAG models have shown improved performance in the factual correctness of their outputs (Lewis et al. 2020). They can also be employed in post-hoc settings by supplying an AI system with data that may not have been available when it was first trained. RAG therefore augments an AI system's pipeline rather than addressing the model's steerability or interpretability.

Again, within the current AI research climate, RAG is rarely seen as competing with RLHF or model editing. Typically, these research communities focus on distinct types of evaluations and rarely overlap. We argue, however, that these approaches can all be seen as trying to solve the same problem of adaptability, and that by reframing the challenge in these terms, we provide an opportunity to compare otherwise disparate technical approaches.

The discussed methods are not yet sufficiently developed, deployed, or widely understood by researchers and industry. Moreover, there is a lack of research into the relative cost-benefit tradeoffs among different approaches. This line of inquiry is important because there may not be a one size fits all solution to the adaptability problem. For example, current work in industry has largely converged around one approach: RL-based feedback systems. The level of success it achieves is permissible for low-stakes settings, but the method has myriad vulnerabilities (Huang et al. 2023; Hubinger et al. 2024), including the previously discussed jailbreaking. The prospects for trustworthy AI depend upon evaluation criteria that effectively address the pros and cons of each different approach along all dimensions of adaptability to encourage robust solutions.

Industry Compromises Trustworthy AI

In recent years, civil society actors at community-based organizations and in academia have criticized AI systems for their current and potential negative impacts on society.[3] The public

3 Examples include the AI NOW Institute, founded in 2017 to produce diagnosis and policy re-

outcry relating to AI is not only about the technology, but also the power and control of *Big Tech* that is perceived to dominate and manipulate AI for private benefit. Big Tech's government lobbying has raised suspicion relating to the solutions that are being promoted for public benefit and to the soft law stance of the U.S. government thus far.

For instance, the Biden Administration announced in July 2023 that certain industry players agreed to abide, voluntarily, with some guardrails to mitigate the negative impacts of AI systems. These commitments included information sharing protocols and public release of system safety evaluations. The administration's announcement, which did not have accompanying enforcement procedures, were created after closed-door discussions with the industry and included some practices that were already in use (Siddiqui 2023). A limited number of these commitments were converted to legal obligations when President Biden signed Executive Order 14110 on AI. Concerningly, lobbying groups with ties to Big Tech are shaping this policy response to AI in ways that may benefit these companies (Bordelon 2023). Moreover, without binding legislation, a future U.S. president may dismantle President Biden's order, as he did for some of the Trump administration's AI programs.

Shoshana Zuboff describes the advance of surveillance capitalism through Big Tech as *instrumentarian power*, which is the use of technology that relies on data culled from human behavior and then used for the purpose of modifying, monetizing, predicting and controlling humans (Zuboff 2019). The governmental and societal struggle with trustworthy AI is not limited to inscrutable machines; it encompasses the existing power structures that are promoting a new means of power in society. Prioritizing the topic of trustworthiness in AI development thereby becomes a societal imperative. Whomever leads and governs the pathways for constructing these solutions will greatly impact society.

Our proposal therefore encourages technological solutions for adaptable AI that are outside of the corporate system, which prioritizes profit. That is, the process for developing trustworthy AI should be viewed as a public good and for public benefit, necessitating public investment and guidance, so that the work is not dominated by industry researchers. Given market pressures, industry is likely to converge on solutions that solve near-term problems. Corporations have little incentive to test fundamentally new approaches and risk falling behind competitors. Technology companies have long experienced and yielded to pressures that encourage disregarding safety for the sake of financial reward. For instance, Microsoft was notoriously flooded with security vulnerabilities as it integrated internet functionality into Windows;

---

search on AI to redirect away from the current trajectory of "unbridled commercial surveillance, consolidation of power in very few companies, and a lack of public accountability" available at https://ainowinstitute.org/ (accessed June 26, 2024); also, the Center for the Advancement of Trustworthy AI, available at https://ca-tai.org/ (accessed June 26, 2024).

their push to capture market share on new technologies was criticized for discarding safety as an afterthought (Shapiro 2023, 144–150). More recently, Microsoft integrated GPT-4, essentially a more advanced version of ChatGPT, into its Bing search engine before the model passed a review by its deployment safety board (Roose 2024). As another example, Zuboff (2019) argues that Google transitioned from a privacy-respecting search engine provider to a privacy-exploiting advertising company as a response to financial fears in the wake of the dot-com crash. Financial pressures upon technology firms are at odds with adaptability when its pursuit requires companies to divert internal resources and potentially relinquish a competitive advantage. Safety failures in other industries evidence a universal misalignment between trustworthiness and profit. Boeing's prioritization of production volume over safety contributed to several critical failures on commercial aircraft, including a door panel flying off a plane mid-air, and two fatal crashes of their 737 Max plane (Chokshi, Ember, and Nerkar 2024).

With respect to trustworthy AI, in 2023, the battle between safety and profit was brought to public awareness when the OpenAI Board of Directors fired CEO Sam Altman (Metz 2023b). The company began as a non-profit in 2015, later creating a for-profit subsidiary to scale its technology and products.[4] Altman was reinstated as CEO only days after the announcement of his ouster and the Board was subsequently reconstituted. The Securities and Exchanges Commission (SEC) is investigating the leadership tussle for regulatory improprieties (Metz, Mickle, and Goldstein 2024). This ordeal increased concerns that the company's governance structure prioritizes speed to market over safety, despite its purported non-profit mission.[5] Statements from former safety researchers at OpenAI have cited the company's growing disregard for safety as their cause for departure (Roose 2024). A group of researchers who were still employed joined them in June 2024 to sign a letter which concurs that the company faces little to no public accountability absent government intervention (Hilton et al. 2024). A few months later, OpenAI began its pursuit to eschew non-profit oversight completely and transition to a private, for-profit company (O'Brien, Chan, and Beaty 2024; Piper 2024).

A Public Program to Advance Adaptable AI

To develop technology-driven solutions for adaptable AI, we propose a program and evalu-

4 Open AI was founded in 2015 as a non-profit corporation, whose Board of Directors is tasked with oversight of its mission to ensure that artificial general intelligence benefits all of humanity. By 2019, it had created a for-profit subsidiary to bring-in private funds to help scale its technology and products. See https://openai.com/our-structure (accessed June 26, 2024).

5 The public interest organization Public Citizen petitioned the California Attorney General to dissolve OpenAI's non-profit for failure to adhere to a public purpose worthy of tax-exempt status. See https://www.citizen.org/article/letter-to-california-attorney-general-on-openais-nonprofit-status/ (accessed June 26, 2024).

ation rubric that advances the public's understanding of the tradeoffs associated with different adaptability techniques. While open-source approaches have been described as one means to public stewardship, this proposal goes even further. The program should include an evaluation rubric, be led by a diverse steering committee, and be operationalized by a government or non-profit organization, like DARPA, the NSF or a public university.

There is precedent for the success of competitive programs and government investment advancing the AI field. Candide, a groundbreaking system for statistical machine translation, was developed in 1993 by the IBM Corporation but was published publicly because of its DARPA funding (Brown 2013; Jurafsky and Martin 2024, 291). More recently, the ImageNet Large Scale Visual Recognition Challenge (ILSVRC) was an open competition held from 2010 to 2017 where participants experimented in creating the best image classification systems. The dominance of the AlexNet model at the competition in 2012 (Krizhevsky, Sutskever, and Hinton 2012) largely contributed to the elevation of DNNs from a peripheral approach in AI development to the dominant paradigm of today.

Evaluation Rubric

A rubric for reliable, trustworthy AI is crucial to a successful program. The proposed rubric is a generic and multi-faceted framework that enables the direct comparison of ideas that are not often put into conversation with one another. Technological innovation typically develops as parallel processes, assessed through peer review and scientific evaluation, and advanced by the research team that originated the idea. To advance adaptable AI as a public benefit, an agreed-upon, competitive set of evaluation criteria can help develop incentives for the exploration of new, high-risk ideas that might prove the most promising in the long-term but struggle to compete in the near-term under market pressures or if only a single metric is considered.

The evaluation framework we propose has one major goal: that the systems submitted to the program shall aim to efficiently and effectively make changes to model behavior given *unforeseen in advance* changes to user/human goals, norms, or information.

The process begins with participants being provided a baseline AI system (the *base system*). The base system would be one that is currently in use to perform existing tasks. For example, this might be an LLM if the evaluation task concerns information gathering and synthesis or might be a deep reinforcement learning agent if the task concerns command and control of robotic agents.

Participants will also be provided with access to code and data needed to (re)train the base system, though they are not required to use it. This is to enable maximal flexibility in the approaches pursued.

Once the competition begins, participants will be provided a new *constraint* during an evaluation run, which their submitted system should obey. This constraint will be given in natural language as a declarative statement, containing the ambiguity inherent in any realistic scenario in which humans need to articulate norms or preferences for model behavior. For example, the constraint might relate to moral norms and values (e.g., "minimize the number of people injured," or "do not use racist language") or might be a seemingly straightforward rule (e.g., "always stop at yellow lights"). The aim of the participants is to return a system (the *adapted* system) that matches the API of the base system (it can be an updated version of the original, or an entirely new system) and that behaves in accordance with the specified constraint.

The performance will be evaluated based on four metrics. 1) Effectiveness; 2) computational costs; 3) engineering costs; and 4) system degradation.

Effectiveness determines how well the adapted system follows the imposed constraint. Determinations about effective or "correct" behavior will be made by human judgment and interpretation of the constraint, which embraces the inherent subjectivity and human ethics at the core of trustworthy AI. The judgments will be measured by performance on held-out test inputs, which are unseen by participants and include a range of out-of-distribution and adversarial examples intended to stress-test the robustness of submitted systems. For example, some of the test inputs could be designed via a *red teaming* process; that is, a team who deliberately interacts with systems and attempts to jailbreak or circumvent the guardrails.

The second and third metrics are computational costs and engineering costs, which are intended to encourage solutions with minimal compute and human power needs, respectively. Computation costs are to determine how much compute power, measured in floating point operations per second (FLOPS), is required to produce the adapted system. Engineering costs determine how much manual human effort (e.g., preference annotation in RHLF), measured in wall-clock time, is required to produce the adapted system.

The final metric, degradation, tracks the difference in the overall performance of the adapted AI system is relative to the base system. This measure is intended to rule out methods that address the new constraint, but at the cost of damaging the model's competence in general. For example, a self-driving car that never moves will score highly according to the constraint "do not run red lights," but will not be useful as a self-driving car.

All of these metrics are evaluated in comparison across participants and their approaches. While we hope to encourage fundamentally new approaches, the program places few to no constraints on the proposed solutions. Fundamentally, the program seeks to avoid premature convergence on any one adaptability technique, an outcome which might otherwise occur with companies influenced by rush-to-market incentives. Participants could replicate the state of the art, fully retrain the system, or design an entirely new system, such as a symbolic or neuro-symbolic architecture.

Program Governance

To achieve the public benefit aims of the program, it should be led by an independent and diverse group of stakeholders who comprise its steering committee. The steering committee members should represent diversity in all its forms, including diversity of academic disciplines, of industry representation, of political perspectives, and of demographic characteristics. The committee members should be paid a stipend for participation, which not only values their time but also demonstrates a commitment to the goals of the program, rather than allowing third-party entities to pay for committee member participation.

The steering committee's mandate is to establish the vision, mission, and operating principles of the program, as well as to ensure the integrity of the evaluation process, keeping public benefit at the center. One key task will be to select a subcommittee of experts that will judge the performance of models submitted to the program.

Ideally, the U.S. government should fund the program through DARPA or the NSF to maintain independence from industry. Government funding of AI programs is particularly critical at this stage of AI development because non-profit research roles are experiencing market constraints in their ability to attract and retain talent (Nix, Zakrzewski, and De Vynck 2024). Because public benefit is at the heart of the proposed evaluation criteria, government leadership is further necessary so that a democratic and representative system is at the helm.

One tradeoff that will need to be addressed is the balance between transparency of program results and the potential for technologies developed to be weaponized by malicious actors. The risk is that tools for modifying AI model behavior without having to begin from scratch could lower the barrier to entry for nefarious repurposing.

Conclusion

We have first introduced the term *adaptability*, which is the capacity of an AI system to have its behavior made more helpful and less harmful, however these may be construed by individuals or prevailing social norms. There are two main benefits to focusing on adaptability. First, it contextualizes existing methods spread across different niches in AI research that all fundamentally address trustworthy AI. Second, it recognizes upfront that building trustworthy AI is not a problem that can be solved once-and-for-all, but rather must be revisited as the ways that AI systems are used, and the expectations placed upon them, adapt.

We have also proposed a program and evaluation criteria that promotes trustworthy AI research through the design of adaptable AI systems.

Companies seeking the prestige of new models do not have the long-term research horizon that is necessary to embed appropriate adaptable AI considerations into system development. Therefore, we ideate our program as a competitive venture that is publicly accountable and specifically promotes adaptability as a metric for assessing AI systems. This aligns incentives for AI developers as program participants with the public's interests, increasing the trust that can be vested in resultant AI systems.

Table 1: definitions of key terms.

Adaptability	The capacity of an AI system to have its behavior modified, possibly in response to unforeseen in advance circumstances, in order to be more helpful and less harmful however these may be construed by individuals or prevailing social norms.
Alignment & Misalignment	Alignment focuses on constraining model behavior to that which abides by societal values and ethical norms. Misaligned AI systems violate this property. An example of misalignment is a chatbot generating discriminatory text.
Explainability	A counterpart to interpretability that focuses on explaining specific outcomes of an AI system even if the internal decision-making cannot be understood. An explanation module can summarize one way that the features of the input relate to the model's output. It does not explicate the decision pathways within the black box system. The explainability field is still in its infancy (Nauta 2023) and faces myriad technical limitations.
Hallucination	Outputs from a generative AI system that either contradict the user's input, are factually false, or are not justified given the information available in the model's training data.
Interpretability	The ability to completely understand how the internals of an AI model work. This empowers users to "correctly and efficiently predict the [model]'s results" (Kim, Khanna, and Koyejo 2016, 7).
Steerability & Instructability	Steerability refers to broadly controlling the overall behavior of an AI system; instructability is the property of an AI system to "follow the user's instructions helpfully and safely" (Ouyang et al. 2022, 2–19).

References

Bai, Yuntao, Saurav Kadavath, Sandipan Kundu, Amanda Askell, Jackson Kernion, Andy Jones, Anna Chen et al. 2022. "Constitutional AI: Harmlessness from AI Feedback." *arXiv preprint arXiv:2212.08073*. https://doi.org/10.48550/arXiv.2212.08073.

Bordelon, Brendan. 2023. "How a Billionaire-Backed Network of AI Advisers Took Over Washington." *Politico*, October 13, 2023. https://www.politico.com/news/2023/10/13/open-philanthropy-funding-ai-policy-00121362.

Brown, Peter F. 2013. "Oh, Yes, Everything's Right on Schedule, Fred." Talk, Twenty Years of Bitext Workshop, Conference on Empirical Methods in Natural Language Processing, October 18, 2013. https://post3.net/bitext.

Carlini, Nicholas, Milad Nasr, Christopher A. Choquette-Choo, Matthew Jagielski, Irena Gao, Anas Awadalla, Pang Wei Koh et al. 2024. "Are Aligned Neural Networks Adversarially Aligned?" *arXiv preprint arXiv:2306.15447*. https://doi.org/10.48550/arXiv.2306.15447.

Chokshi, Niraj, Sydney Ember, and Santul Nerkar. 2024. "'Shortcuts Everywhere': How Boeing Favored Speed Over Quality." *New York Times*, March 29, 2024. https://www.nytimes.com/2024/03/28/business/boeing-quality-problems-speed.html.

Confalonieri, Roberto, Ludovik Coba, Benedikt Wagner, and Tarek R. Besold. 2020. "A Historical Perspective of Explainable Artificial Intelligence." *Data Mining and Knowledge Discovery* 11, no. 1: e1391. https://doi.org/10.1002/widm.1391.

Garnelo, Marta, and Murray Shanahan. 2019. "Reconciling Deep Learning with Symbolic Artificial Intelligence: Representing Objects and Relations." *Current Opinion in Behavioral Science* 29: 17–23. https://doi.org/10.1016/j.cobeha.2018.12.010.

Gehman, Samuel, Suchin Gururangan, Maarten Sap, Yejin Choi, and Noah A. Smith. 2020. "RealToxicityPrompts: Evaluating Neural Toxic Degeneration in Language Models." *Findings of the Association for Computational Linguistics: EMNLP 2020*, pages 3356–3369. https://doi.org/10.18653/v1/2020.findings-emnlp.301

Hao, Karen. 2019. "We Analyzed 16,625 Papers to Figure Out Where AI is Headed Next." *MIT Technology Review*, January 25, 2019. https://www.technologyreview.com/2019/01/25/1436/we-analyzed-16625-papers-to-figure-out-where-ai-is-headed-next/.

Hilton, Jacob, Daniel Kokotajlo, Ramana Kumar, Neel Nanda, William Saunders, Carroll Wainwright, Daniel Ziegler et al. 2024. *A Right to Warn about Advanced Artificial Intelligence*. Letter. https://righttowarn.ai/ (accessed June 26, 2024).

Huang, Yangsibo, Samyak Gupta, Mengzhou Xia, Kai Li, and Danqi Chen. 2023. "Catastrophic Jailbreak of Open-source LLMs via Exploiting Generation." *arXiv preprint arXiv:2310.06987*. https://doi.org/10.48550/arXiv.2310.06987.

Hubinger, Evan, Carson Denison, Jesse Mu, Mike Lambert, Meg Tong, Monte MacDiarmid, Tamera Lanham et al. 2024. "Sleeper Agents: Training Deceptive LLMs that Persist Through Safety Training." *arXiv preprint arXiv:2401.05566*. https://doi.org/10.48550/arXiv.2401.05566.

Jurafsky, Daniel and James H. Martin. 2024. *Speech and Language Processing: An Introduction to Natural Language Processing, Computational Linguistics, and Speech Recognition*. Third Edition. https://web.stanford.edu/~jurafsky/slp3/ed3bookfeb3_2024.pdf.

Kim, Been, Rajiv Khanna, and Oluwasanmi Koyejo. 2016. "Examples Are Not Enough, Learn to Criticize! Criticism for Interpretability." In *Advances in Neural Information Processing Systems*, volume 29, pages 2280–2288, Barcelona, Spain. Curran Associates, Inc.

Krizhevsky, Alex, Ilya Sutskever, and Geoffrey E. Hinton. 2012. "ImageNet Classification with Deep Convolutional Neural Networks." In *Advances in Neural Information Processing Systems*, volume 25, Lake Tahoe, Nevada, United States. Curran Associates, Inc.

Lee, Harrison, Samrat Phatale, Hassan Mansoor, Thomas Mesnard, Johan Ferret, Kellie Lu, Colton Bishop et al. 2023. "RLAIF: Scaling Reinforcement Learning from Human Feedback with AI Feedback." *arXiv preprint arXiv:2309.00267*. https://doi.org/10.48550/arXiv.2309.00267.

Lewis, Patrick, Ethan Perez, Aleksandra Piktus, Fabio Petroni, Vladimir Karpukhin, Naman Goyal, Heinrich Küttler et al. 2020. "Retrieval-Augmented Generation for Knowledge-Intensive NLP Tasks." In *Advances in Neural Information Processing Systems*, volume 33, pages 9459–9474, Vancouver, Canada. Curran Associates, Inc.

Lewis, Tanya. 2016. "Mystery Mechanisms." *The Scientist*, July 29, 2016. https://www.the-scientist.com/mystery-mechanisms-33119.

Maynez, Joshua, Shashi Narayan, Bernd Bohnet, and Ryan McDonald. 2020. "On

Faithfulness and Factuality in Abstractive Summarization." In *Proceedings of the 58th Annual Meeting of the Association for Computational Linguistics*, pages 1906–1919. https://doi.org/10.18653/v1/2020.acl-main.173.

Meng, Kevin, David Bau, Alex Andonian, Yonatan Belinkov. 2022. "Locating and Editing Factual Associations in GPT." In *Advances in Neural Information Processing Systems*, volume 36, pages 17359–17372, New Orleans, United States. Curran Associates, Inc. https://doi.org/10.48550/arXiv.2202.05262.

Metz, Cade. 2023a. "Researchers Poke Holes in Safety Controls of ChatGPT and Other Chatbots." *New York Times*, July 27, 2023. https://www.nytimes.com/2023/07/27/business/ai-chatgpt-safety-research.html.

Metz, Cade. 2023b. "OpenAI's Board Pushes Out Sam Altman, Its High-Profile C.E.O." *New York Times*, November 17, 2023. https://www.nytimes.com/2023/11/17/technology/openai-sam-altman-ousted.html.

Metz, Cade, Tripp Mickle, and Matthew Goldstein. 2024. "S.E.C. Is Investigating OpenAI Over Its Board's Actions." *New York Times*, February 29, 2024. https://www.nytimes.com/2024/02/29/technology/sec-openai-board-sam-altman.html.

Mitchell, Melanie. 2021. "Why AI is Harder Than We Think." *arXiv preprint arXiv:2104.12871*. https://doi.org/10.48550/arXiv.2104.12871.

Nasr, Malid, Nicholas Carlini, Jonathan Hayase, Matthew Jagielski, A. Feder Cooper, Daphne Ippolito, Christopher A. Choquette-Choo, Eric Wallace, Florian Tramèr, and Katherine Lee. 2023. "Scalable Extraction of Training Data from (Production) Language Models." *arXiv preprint arXiv:2311.17035*. https://doi.org/10.48550/arXiv.2311.17035.

Nix, Naomi, Cat Zakrzewski, and Gerrit De Vynck. 2024. "Silicon Valley is Pricing Academics Out of AI Research." *Washington Post*, March 10, 2024. https://www.washingtonpost.com/technology/2024/03/10/big-tech-companies-ai-research/.

O'Brien, Matt, Kelvin Chan, and Thalia Beaty. 2024. "OpenAI Looks to Shift Away From Nonprofit Roots and Convert Itself to For-Profit Company." *Associated Press*, September 26, 2024. https://apnews.com/article/chatgpt-openai-sam-altman-nonprofit-859bff5c19845f51796244e0072e2dfb.

Ouyang, Long, Jeff Wu, Xu Jiang, Diogo Almeida, Carroll L. Wainwright, Pamela Mishkin, Chong Zhang et al. 2022. "Training Language Models to Follow Instructions with Human Feedback." *arXiv preprint arXiv:2203.02155*. https://doi.

org/10.48550/arXiv.2203.02155.

Pessach, Dana and Erez Shmueli. 2022. "A Review on Fairness in Machine Learning." *ACM Computing Surveys* 55, no. 3: 1–44. https://doi.org/10.1145/3494672.

Petch, Jeremy, Shuang Di, and Walter Nelson. 2022. "Opening the Black Box: The Promise and Limitations of Explainable Machine Learning in Cardiology." *Canadian Journal of Cardiology* 38, no. 2: 204–213. https://doi.org/10.1016/j.cjca.2021.09.004.

Piper, Kelsey. "Inside OpenAI's Multibillion-Dollar Gambit to Become a For-Profit Company." *Vox*, October 28, 2024. https://www.vox.com/future-perfect/380117/openai-microsoft-sam-altman-nonprofit-for-profit-foundation-artificial-intelligence.

Roose, Kevin. 2024. "OpenAI Insiders Warn of a 'Reckless' Race for Dominance." *New York Times*, June 4, 2024. https://www.nytimes.com/2024/06/04/technology/openai-culture-whistleblowers.html.

Shapiro, Scott J. 2023. *Fancy Bear Goes Phishing*. New York: Ferrar, Straus and Giroux.

Siddiqui, Sabrina. 2023. "'Wonder and Worry': How Biden Views Artificial Intelligence." *Wall Street Journal*, August 1, 2023. https://www.wsj.com/articles/wonder-and-worry-how-biden-views-artificial-intelligence-5724bfef.

Singla, Alex, Alexander Sukharevsky, Lareina Yee, Michael Chui, and Bryce Hall. 2024. "The State of AI in Early 2024: Gen AI Adoption Spikes and Starts to Generate Value." QuantumBlack, AI by McKinsey. May 30, 2024. https://www.mckinsey.com/capabilities/quantumblack/our-insights/the-state-of-ai#/.

U.S. Congress. Senate. Committee on the Judiciary. Subcommittee on Privacy, Technology and the Law. *Oversight of A.I.: Rules for Artificial Intelligence*. 118th Cong., May 16, 2023.

Vig, Jesse, Sebastian Gehrmann, Yonatan Belinkov, Sharon Qian, Daniel Nevo, Yaron Singer, and Stuart Shieber. 2020. "Investigating Gender Bias in Language Models Using Causal Mediation Analysis." In *Advances in Neural Information Processing Systems*, volume 33, pages 12388–12401, Vancouver, Canada. Curran Associates, Inc.

Weidinger, Laura, John Mellor, Maribeth Rauh, Conor Griffin, Jonathan Uesato, Po-Sen Huang, Myra Cheng et al. 2021. "Ethical and Social Risks of Harm from

Language Models." *arXiv preprint arXiv:2112.04359*. https://doi.org/10.48550/arXiv.2112.04359.

Yong, Zheng-Xin, Cristina Menghini, and Stephen H. Bach. 2024. "Low-Resource Languages Jailbreak GPT-4." *NeurIPS Workshop on Socially Responsible Language Modelling Research (SoLaR)*. https://doi.org/10.48550/arXiv.2310.02446

Yu, Qinan, Jack Merullo, and Ellie Pavlick. 2023. "Characterizing Mechanisms for Factual Recall in Language Models." In *Proceedings of the 2023 Conference on Empirical Methods in Natural Language Processing*, pages 9924–9959, Singapore. Association for Computational Linguistics.

Zou, Andy, Zifan Wang, Nicholas Carlini, Milad Nasr, J. Zico Kolter, and Matt Fredrikson. 2023. "Universal and Transferable Adversarial Attacks on Aligned Language Models." *arXiv preprint arXiv:2307.15043v2*. https://doi.org/10.48550/arXiv.2307.15043.

Zuboff, Shoshana. 2019. *The Age of Surveillance Capitalism: The Fight for a Human Future at the New Frontier of Power*. New York: PublicAffairs.

Experiences in Designing Complex Software Systems

Andrew Boake
i1 Solutions, Cape Town, South Africa
andrewboake@gmail.com

Abstract

Software systems are complex systems.

They consist of many interconnected components, interacting in many ways to provide functionality to their users, and often exhibiting unexpected behaviour from such interactions. This is becoming more evident in our increasingly connected software world.

Their complexity is stretching the traditional ways of designing them.

In this paper, I unpack aspects of this complexity, various ways in which the software community has sought to conquer it, and the challenges we face in the emerging software landscape. I seek to give the reader some insight into the essential challenges we face in designing software systems, look at the ways we have traditionally approached these, and give a glimpse into a software landscape which is already stretching these approaches to breaking point.

We need to reflect on the aspects of software complexity we've encountered, and the value of the lessons we've learnt in our journey thus far.

The first part of the paper is a narration of a journey through the kinds of software complexity I've experienced, the challenges each presented, and the tools and techniques we used to try to deal with it.

Functional Abstraction

The journey starts at encapsulating complexity. We discuss experiences in writing a mathematical function library, hiding the details behind function calls.

Modelling Abstractions

We move to designing systems that model interesting aspects of

 doi: 10.18278/jpcs.9.1.5

messy reality. We discuss experiences in designing and implementing systems that provide geographical models of features on the surface of the earth.

Frameworks

Next, we reflect on trying to provide an intuitive overarching structure to our software designs. We reflect on using frameworks that seek to structure our thinking and therefore our programs, and should allow us to focus on subsequent details inside a proven structure.

Architecture

We then step up to software architecture - dealing with landscapes of interconnected components. We discuss designing these landscapes, replacing specific parts when needed, and providing models of their structure, interactions, constraints and evolution to help with decision-making.

We need to understand the nature of the increasing complexity we face in the emerging systems landscapes, and the strengths and challenges of new approaches, to apply them in an informed way.

Our reflections set the scene for the second part of the paper: a discussion on the nature of the complexity of our current generation of software systems, and the challenges we face with trying to predict and control the emergent properties of these systems.

Complex Systems Science to aid Software Design

Given the complex nature of our systems, I suggest using techniques and tools from Complex Systems Science to understand and design software solutions. I also suggest that Introducing this way of thinking both enhances and disrupts traditional software design approaches.

Artificial Intelligence

I end with a view of software design and development as we enter the age of increasingly informed AI-powered aid. I suggest that there are both opportunities and dangers in embracing this new set of tools. I believe we would do well to understand their strengths and weaknesses, and incrementally add them to the lessons already hard-won in our journey.

Experiencias en el diseño de sistemas de software complejos

Resumen

Los sistemas de software son sistemas complejos.

Constan de muchos componentes interconectados que interactúan de muchas maneras para brindar funcionalidad a sus usuarios y, a menudo, presentan un comportamiento inesperado a partir de dichas interacciones. Esto se está haciendo cada vez más evidente en nuestro mundo de software cada vez más conectado.

Su complejidad está poniendo a prueba las formas tradicionales de diseñarlos.

En este artículo, analizo aspectos de esta complejidad, las diversas formas en que la comunidad de software ha intentado superarla y los desafíos que enfrentamos en el panorama emergente del software. Intento brindar al lector una idea de los desafíos esenciales que enfrentamos al diseñar sistemas de software, analizar las formas en que tradicionalmente los hemos abordado y dar una idea de un panorama de software que ya está llevando estos enfoques al límite.

Necesitamos reflexionar sobre los aspectos de la complejidad del software que hemos encontrado y el valor de las lecciones que hemos aprendido en nuestro recorrido hasta ahora.

La primera parte del artículo es una narración de un recorrido por los tipos de complejidad del software que he experimentado, los desafíos que cada uno presentó y las herramientas y técnicas que usamos para tratar de lidiar con ellos.

Abstracción funcional

El viaje comienza encapsulando la complejidad. Analizamos experiencias en la escritura de una biblioteca de funciones matemáticas, ocultando los detalles detrás de las llamadas a funciones.

Modelado de abstracciones

Pasamos a diseñar sistemas que modelen aspectos interesantes de la realidad desordenada. Analizamos experiencias en el diseño e implementación de sistemas que proporcionen modelos geográficos de características de la superficie de la Tierra.

Marcos de trabajo

A continuación, reflexionamos sobre cómo intentar proporcionar una estructura general intuitiva a nuestros diseños de software. Reflexionamos sobre el uso de marcos de trabajo que busquen estructurar nuestro pensamiento y, por lo tanto, nuestros programas, y que nos permitan centrarnos en los detalles posteriores dentro de una estructura probada.

Arquitectura

A continuación, pasamos a la arquitectura del software, que se ocupa de paisajes de componentes interconectados. Analizamos el diseño de estos paisajes, el reemplazo de piezas específicas cuando es necesario y la provisión de modelos de su estructura, interacciones, restricciones y evolución para ayudar en la toma de decisiones.

Necesitamos comprender la naturaleza de la creciente complejidad que enfrentamos en los paisajes de sistemas emergentes, y las fortalezas y desafíos de los nuevos enfoques, para aplicarlos de manera informada.

Nuestras reflexiones preparan el terreno para la segunda parte del artículo: un debate sobre la naturaleza de la complejidad de nuestra generación actual de sistemas de software y los desafíos que enfrentamos al intentar predecir y controlar las propiedades emergentes de estos sistemas.

La ciencia de sistemas complejos como ayuda para el diseño de software

Dada la naturaleza compleja de nuestros sistemas, sugiero utilizar técnicas y herramientas de la ciencia de sistemas complejos para comprender y diseñar soluciones de software. También sugiero que la introducción de esta forma de pensar mejora y al mismo tiempo altera los enfoques tradicionales de diseño de software.

Inteligencia artificial

Termino con una visión del diseño y desarrollo de software a medida que entramos en la era de la ayuda basada en inteligencia artificial cada vez más informada. Sugiero que existen tanto oportunidades como peligros en la adopción de este nuevo conjunto de herramientas. Creo que haríamos bien en comprender sus fortalezas y debilidades, y en ir agregándolas de manera gradual a las lecciones que ya hemos aprendido con mucho esfuerzo en nuestro camino.

复杂软件系统的设计经验

摘要

软件系统是复杂的系统。
它们由许多相互连接的部分组成，以多种方式交互以向用户提供功能，并且经常在这种交互中表现出意想不到的行为。
这在我们日益互联的软件世界中变得越来越明显。

它们的复杂性正在扩展传统的设计方式。
本文中，我将阐述这种复杂性的各个方面、软件社区为试图攻克这一复杂性而采取的各种方式、以及我们在新兴软件领域面临的挑战。我希望让读者深入了解我们在设计软件系统时面临的基本挑战，看看我们传统上处理这些挑战的方式，并短暂体会一个已经将这些方法扩展到极限的软件格局。

我们需要反思我们遇到的软件复杂性的各个方面，以及我们迄今为止在旅程中学到的经验教训的价值。
本文的第一部分讲述了我所经历过的各种软件复杂性、每种复杂性所带来的挑战、以及我们用来尝试处理它的工具和技术。

函数抽象
旅程从概述复杂性开始。我们探讨了编写数学函数库的经验，隐藏函数调用背后的细节。

建模抽象
我们开始设计系统，后者对混乱现实的有趣方面进行建模。
我们讨论了“设计和实施一系列对地球表面特征提供地理模型的系统”方面的经验。

框架
接下来，我们对“尝试为我们的软件设计提供直观的总体结构”一事进行了反思。我们反思了对框架的使用，这些框架试图构建我们的思维，从而构建我们的程序，并让我们能够在经过验证的结构中专注于后续细节。

架构
然后我们进入软件架构，处理互连组件的格局。我们探讨了：设计这些格局、在需要时替换特定部件，并提供其结构模型、交互模型、约束模型和演化模型以帮助决策。

我们需要了解新兴系统领域日益复杂的本质，以及新方法的优势和挑战，以便明智地应用它们。
我们的反思为本文的第二部分奠定了基础：探讨当前一代软件系统的复杂性本质，以及我们在试图预测和控制这些系统的新兴特性时面临的挑战。

复杂系统科学助力软件设计
鉴于我们系统的复杂性，我建议使用复杂系统科学的技术和工具来理解和设计软件解决方案。我还建议，引入这种思维方式既可以增强又可以扰乱传统软件设计方法。

人工智能
随着我们进入人工智能辅助时代，我将软件设计和开发的看法作为本文的结尾。我认为，采用这套新工具既有机遇也有危险。我相信，我们应该了解它们的优势和劣势，并逐步将它们添加到来之不易的经验教训中。

Introduction

My whole career as a software professional has been about battling complexity. Software development is confronted with different kinds of complexity, including in the business domain, software components and their interactions, increasingly complex deployment infrastructure, and consequent project dependencies as we seek to evolve each of these. It seems that in the software business, your primary challenge is making sense of, and managing, complexities in these and between these areas.

I studied Computer Science in the early 80's. I submitted stacks of mainframe punch cards for assignments, programmed using the first Pascal compilers, and marvelled at the first Macintosh, with its amazing user interface, but having to endure its stiffy disk shuffle before they introduced a hard disk.

Since then, I've been around in IT companies and corporate departments for close to 40 years. We developed geographical information systems on early mini-computers, and map and aerial photograph library management systems on early Unix workstations. I loved the power in simplicity of Smalltalk, and survived the convoluted object-oriented frameworks of C++, before some sanity prevailed in early Java. That was a temporary respite - web development broke like a wave over component-based client-server development just as we were getting the hang of it, and the complexity of development has multiplied since then.

Developers nowadays have their work cut out for them, needing to master a wide conglomeration of technologies from no-SQL databases, APIs and query layers, swarms of micro-services, stylesheets, callbacks, and black booklets of web script incantations we collect from different web frameworks and how-to sites.

Designing and developing software has always been a battle with complexity. As Fred Brooks explained [Brooks], you can take some of it away, through higher level abstractions, better programming languages, and software development tools. He calls this accidental complexity - taking away the translation difficulty between the design in your mind and how you express it in code. But there's always that complexity that is essential to the problem at hand - it's in the life expectancy and product pricing calculations that actuaries grapple with in insurance companies, the intricate paths through tax rules that tax experts grapple with in accounting practices, the nuances of causes and symptoms that doctors grapple with in diagnosing diseases, the complex cost and time optimisation calculations in logistics, and the force calculations and trade-offs between strength of materials and air and light that architects grapple with in designing skyscrapers. This is what Fred Brooks calls essential complexity - it is part of the domain, and cannot be abstracted away. When we try to express this in software systems that we provide to our clients, we have to get to grips with that complexity somewhere. It could be in the code, in the details we need to capture even in the most advanced software design environment, in the spreadsheets that illustrate the calculations, or in the process and data analysis diagrams that express the domain requirements.

Some think we can get away from it by buying a software package that handles the complexity, while business-oriented users drag and drop simple components into place. Software package salesmen over the years have peddled their magic black boxes that you put down in the middle of your organization, they make this whooshing sound, and they structure and simplify everything. I've yet to witness that working in practice outside of the carefully curated demos in software fairs.

There's no simplifying away the essential complexity of a domain. But we have learnt to understand it, and structure it, through careers where we've learnt a thousand ways of not succeeding, and changed our ways of thinking and working through the calm unpacking of pioneers who taught structured programming, object orientation, component-based development and the like.

That's been the case from Fortran that gave us expressions that did away with manually moving variables between registers, but we still had to code Fast Fourier Transform formulae correctly. It's been the case in Integrated Development Environments with their help around the complexities of the language and frameworks at our fingertips, but we still had to design the intricacies of the software well. It was the case with Model-Driven Architecture environments that magically generated code from design diagrams, but left us in the dark trying to debug subtle errors.

Even the new possibilities with data in the cloud, while taking away many infrastructure provision and sizing limitations, have given us data lakes which often just move our data quality issues to servers in Ireland.

It is my contention that even the promise in ChatGPT-driven software development follows this pattern. Being able to compose our programs from pieces of code generated for us by learning from what others have done on the whole internet will be hugely beneficial. It will take away some difficulties, but will present us with others. I contend that there will be huge advantages in having access to an extensive library of code which others have used to solve similar problems, but that the difficulties we will experience will still have to do with understanding and designing the essential complexity of our particular problem domain.

Part 1: A Journey

J.R.R. Tolkien's 'The Hobbit' starts off with a strange party of hobbits, dwarves and a wizard setting off from the Shire on a series of adventures. Driven only by tales of old, remembered dimly, and a vaguely exciting mission, they have no idea of the challenges and difficulties that lie ahead.

A young aspiring developer sets off on a series of computer software adventures, driven only by a fascination with the recently discovered possibilities of modelling real world structures and processes in software to solve real-world problems.

How Difficult Can it Be?

Writing computer software is firstly about understanding the problem you're trying to solve.

Conventional software development wisdom will tell you that before you specify the technical details, you need to capture what you understand about what your users want. You need to know what you want to do before you decide how to do it. In contemporary practice, this is often done in a text document, with drawings that illustrate the process to be followed, and unpacking the structure of the information involved.

Let's say the need is for a dentist booking system. The information involved is, conceptually: a practice has a number of dentists, each with a number of slots a day. An appointment can be booked with an available or favoured dentist by a client, with an indication of the dental work required. The process should be as follows: a client either telephones in or visits a receptionist, or logs on to a mobile app or a web site. Once we establish the client's particulars, we show a calendar view of open slots, and they can request one. Of course, dentists may request additional slots for follow-up work. The practice will confirm appointments via email, and remind clients of upcoming appointments. Billing will be done on the basis of appointments booked and materials used during the work done in them.

Writing computer software is then about giving instructions to a machine in a language or languages that allow you to express how you wish to solve a particular problem.

A complete solution consists of a number of related technical aspects. For example, in the domain of website design, you need to specify what the web pages should look like, in a language that specifies web page look and feel (perhaps HTML). You also need to specify the web client behaviour - e.g. what should happen if you press the Submit button (issue a call to a web service to fetch a set of data (using JavaScript), then show it using the look-and-feel language on the page. Of course, then you need to define server behaviour – firstly, you tell the database about the structure of your data in a language that specifies data structures (often SQL: customers have orders for amounts of items), and then you tell the database management software what you want (again in SQL: I'm looking for all of the orders of customer 1234, and their statuses, or here is a new order for customer 1234, for item xyz, for amount abc) and it executes that instruction and returns a result.

This is a somewhat naive linear view of designing a software solution, just to give a flavour. There is of course usually considerably more complexity and nuance in getting to a solution.

There has long been a debate in computer software circles about how we do this - how we should look at software design.

The particularly engineering-oriented among us would say it's just like building something in the physical world - specify exactly what you want, and tell the builders to get on with it.

Others who would say that software development is more exploratory and malleable, say we need to explore our way ahead. Implement a small core, get feedback from the customer, then build on that to grow a solution that you can shape together.

The first approach works well if we know exactly what we want, down to the minute details, and if we can specify all of the complexity we need upfront. This approach is often mandated when there are lives at stake, as for medical devices, or a requirement for mathematically proven precise calculations in time and space, as for real-time aircraft avionics. It is then imperative to work out the critical details up front.

Most often, though, projects do their work in a complex domain where there is a fair degree of initial uncertainty, for example if we are aiming to produce a product with a fair degree of innovation, or where we need to navigate through making many inter-dependent design decisions. It is best then to proceed more like the second approach, building incrementally from a proven core.

Of course, the engineers scoff and tell us that building a commercial aircraft or a skyscraper is way more complex, and those projects work well using engineering standards and processes in a linear fashion, with sign-offs at each stage. It seems some of us are comfortable with meticulously planning everything up front, while others are more comfortable to explore.

Perhaps it depends on context. If you're an engineering advocate, what do you do when you're building a mobile app for your startup, and you just want to release a minimum viable product to enter a rapidly evolving market, and you don't have two years just to perfect the engineering design document?

On the other hand, would you be happy with a couple of guys in a double garage designing your pacemaker software, telling you that they'll iron out any issues as they occur?

The software landscape is large and varied, and consists of many kinds of software. As is the case with different kinds of writing (from social media snippets, to newspaper articles, to legally binding documents), different kinds of software need to adopt a position somewhere along the spectrum from exploring incrementally to upfront planning and formal design.

Let's for now work with what we agree on. Software is made up of many interacting components and these interactions contribute to complexity. As the scale and scope of the software increases, so does the complexity. It is one thing to master the workings of a mobile app for managing a to-do list, and another thing entirely to design the software that controls all of the aircraft in the airspace over continental USA.

That complexity takes different forms. In this first part of the paper, we'll explore some of the types of complexity we find in software, and the approaches we've taken to manage those over the years.

Hiding the details of algorithms

$$\hat{f}(\xi) = \int_{-\infty}^{\infty} f(x)\, e^{-2\pi i x \xi}\, dx$$

Domain

The detailed implementation behind a fundamental operating system level library.

When I started studying Computer Science, I was required to do vacation work, and duly arrived at a parastatal scientific institution doing work in geographical information systems. They had developed their own programming language on one of the then new mini-computers, supported by a mathematical function library.

I was assigned to work on the library, and so became engrossed in the low-level details involved in calculating the outputs of mathematical formulae, whose accuracy and speed was critical for any functionality requiring these calculations.

Complexity, tools and lessons

Examples of the details involved were Fourier approximations of trigonometric functions and using an algorithm to provide a fairly distributed set of random numbers for a pseudo-random number generator.

Both of these involved careful attention to the speed and accuracy of the calculations. In testing floating point storage and calculation precision, I became quite good at spotting accuracy errors in hexadecimal floating point representations!

I will never look at a mathematical function library in quite the same way - behind a simple call to sin(x) is a huge amount of complex mathematics.

Designers of high level languages added two mechanisms to help us abstract away from these complexities. These mechanisms hide the details of calculations, for example the sequence of primitive assembler-level operations, and the movement of intermediate results between registers and memory - accidental complexity which needs to be hidden from us when we want purely to use the logical concept in a calculation.

Firstly, they added function calls (eg func(x, y, z)) - we can call a function, passing it a number of parameters, which would go through its detailed process using those variables, and return a result which we can use in further calculations. Hiding that complexity behind a function call lets us ignore its details, and get on with reasoning about the next level of complexity in the domain, like geometry calculations in a geographical data set.

Secondly, they added expressions (eg sin(x) / 2 * cos(x)) that allow us to express mathematical calculations in a style that is closer to the notation we are familiar with.

This experience taught me three design principles:

1) Hide details away behind concepts that make logical sense.
2) Combine these logical concepts in a model that uses them to describe structure and behaviour at a required level.
3) But, you need to understand the properties of the implementation well, so that you can guarantee, for example, speed and accuracy of calculations.

Complexity in Modelling the Earth's Surface

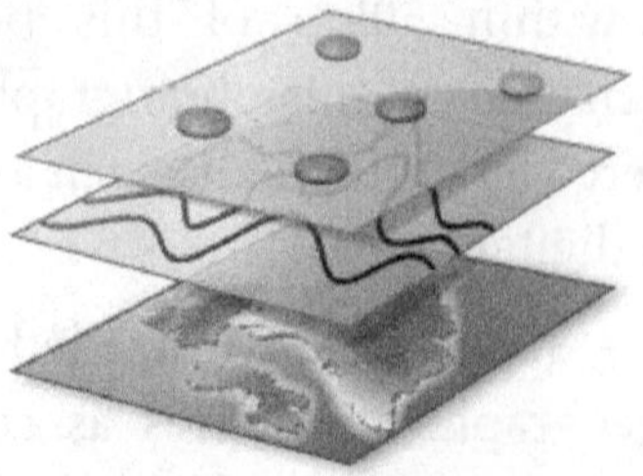

Domain

Air Reconnaissance Intelligence

After my undergraduate degree, I was required to undergo military service, compulsory in South Africa at the time.

I was assigned to an air reconnaissance intelligence unit. There I was part of a team that worked on a library system for maps, photographs and earth observation images.

Complexity, tools and lessons

This was an exercise in modelling the complexity of real world phenomena. Digital and physical media containing different representations of data from observing the earth's surface - from detailed physical photographs at different heights above the earth, to physical topographical maps at different scales and using different projections, to digital satellite images of different formats and taken from different oblique observation angles, to digital geographical maps.

In this library, we had to represent geographical features e.g. buildings, roads, fields and towns in models of the earth's surface. We then had to project those onto flat surfaces, then display them digitally (using specified map symbols), and perform calculations on them. (e.g. how far is it from this point to this one? Or which towns are within 50km of this point? Or which areas of this photograph are also covered by other media such as physical and digital maps?)

To do this, we needed to model geographical features as collections of geo-located mathematical objects (points, line segments and areas) in databases. Then we had to perform spatial operations on these features (e.g. find me all intersections between rivers and roads in this area, or give me a list of the towns I will visit along this road).

We then needed to visualize the features in digital maps. That required querying the appropriate features for the type of map required (for a travel map, one might retrieve the towns and roads, and for a land use map, one might retrieve areas of crops, suburban housing and industrial use). We then rendered them on digital media by mapping them according to defined symbology (make all rivers blue), and at the appropriate scale (at a small scale, towns will be shown as dots; at a larger scale, we'll show all of the streets).

The complexity of Geographical Information Systems is reflected in the complexity of its data structures, the calculations in different projection spaces, and the required speedy and intuitive rendering of geographical features on digital maps or overlays.

If you had shown me Google Maps on a cell phone back then, I would not have believed that was possible on a small hand-held device.

My experience in Geographical Information Systems has given me an appreciation of what it takes to enable direct manipulation of Geographical Information Systems user interfaces (interactive queries, distance calculations, even zooming in and out and seeing a town change from a dot to a network of roads). The complexity and sheer processing power hidden behind user gestures navigating interactive map user interfaces is remarkable, yet so simple that even my mother-in-law can navigate around a map on her cell phone.

In summary, what this experience introduced me to was data modelling - being able to model the real world as data structures containing and referring to other data elements. I had started on a learning curve of representing and reasoning about information in the language of a domain.

Frameworks & Design Notations

Domain

Financial Services

Complexity, tools & lessons

Interacting Objects

At around this time, I moved to software development in Financial Services. With this career change came a learning curve in the world of insurance policies, actuarial calculations, accounting transactions, call centres and claims processes. On the software side, it came with a significant shift in my thinking around software design and implementation.

Around this time too, object orientation started to become popular. The ideas of procedural abstraction were joined with those of data abstraction, allowing software designers and developers to both think of and program systems using objects, which packaged the data structure and procedural behaviour of elements of the domain into one.

While this change applied broadly to any programming (e.g. using Smalltalk or C++), the earliest significant changes occurred in how we designed user interfaces. An Application object was now composed of objects such as Button and Menu (which had several Buttons as children). Objects contained properties such colour and label, and behaviour such as press(). The initial design patterns taught us to inherit from the Button class, and rewrite the press() function to get our particular code called. This was called inheritance - a way to say this object was all of that object over there, except for these specific changes.

That was good for simple cases, but unravelled in more complex cases, so another significant development in programming languages arrived. We started thinking of events and writing event handlers. You could write an object which subscribed to an event to be published by a user interface object – the user interface object would notify your object that an event of interest had occurred, calling a piece of your code e.g. onPressed() for a button pressed event. Your code could then perform any functionality required when that button was pressed.

Development became easier for a little while, as we thought of user interfaces just as a collection of objects notifying our event handlers. Then, complexity struck again, as we were faced by huge collections of objects interacting to do anything from laying out the whole interface to reacting to each other's events (e.g. synchronizing different views - like providing zoom factor buttons which changed the current zoom factor, and also updated the detail level of a map data view).

Diagrams that express design specifications visually

We started doing diagrams of these objects and their interactions, so we could visually understand what we were designing. This was my introduction to modelling software behaviour.

Integrated Development Environments arrived, where we could visually compose and configure user interfaces. These started allowing us to graphically specify the object configuration we wanted, and then generated the code patterns behind to actually do it. Borland's Delphi was a firm favourite in this regard.

Frameworks to structure complex programs

Object-oriented design and development spread everywhere, not only in user interfaces. Frameworks (skeletons of already composed code that allowed us to reuse proven structures and 'flesh out' parts where we wanted specific behaviours) appeared, for more and more parts of applications. They gave us ways to store and retrieve our objects to databases and communication between the client and server parts of our programs. Objects became larger and became components (independently deployable objects which we could use to compose whole programs).

C++ gave us C with objects - we could conceptually take our favourite C code and start structuring it using object oriented principles and mechanisms. Initially, the idea was great - C needed an intuitive object mechanism. Many of us will remember the crippling complexity of the initial frameworks (which required you to know exactly how virtual tables - the mechanism that C++ used to implement multiple inheritance - worked).

To cope with the complexity, framework and Integrated Development Environment providers gave us catalogues of examples that we could use as templates to start our development. 'How to' manuals showed us basic object interaction diagrams to help us understand how the frameworks worked conceptually, but did not cover everything, and didn't show us how to combine things. So we copied the templates, where the framework code had '<fill in your details here>' markers. That was an easy way to start programming using a new framework. But, as one scaled up and changed the scope of the starting example, it was all too easy to get to a place where your code just stopped working. Debugging through the whole code base, you had no idea why an event in one part of the framework ended up in a completely inexplicable part of your code.

The programming abstractions provided by frameworks were great until you needed to know exactly how the details of the framework worked to make use of it.

Visual Modelling

Along with the rising adoption of object-orientation came the increasing need to visualize our software designs, not only to understand graphically what we were designing and how it would work, but also so we could learn from others who had thought more deeply than we had, and had published their work in books about best practice design patterns.

The visual modelling of aspects of software grew to modelling not only the structure but also the behaviour. We hankered after the idea that we could express what we wanted at a conceptual level. State charts allowed us to design behaviour within an object or component, and process flow diagrams allowed us to specify how users should interact with the programs.

The modelling notation wars calmed down after a battle for mindshare, and produced the Unified Modelling Notation (UML) [UML], an all-encompassing standard graphical software modelling notation. UML tools proliferated, and we all had our favourite. To be completely honest, none of us knew or understood the whole of UML, and most of us got by with just the basics - a class diagram or two, and object interaction diagrams to illustrate the flow of data.

Design Patterns

Several authors published catalogues of design patterns - each phrased in the style: 'if you find the following problem to solve in your design, use the following configuration of objects and interactions to solve it'. Many were extremely useful, especially in broader structuring of object oriented programs, and we all walked around with copies of *Design Patterns* (fondly named the Gang of Four book [GoF]), and Martin Fowler's *Analysis Patterns* [Fowler-AnalysisPatterns] and *Patterns of Enterprise Application Integration* [Fowler-PatternsOfEnterpriseApplicationArchitecture] under our arms.

Towards Model-Driven Development

On our more optimistic days, we even began to speak of, and play with, tools that promised Model-Driven Development [OMG-MDA], where we would be able to graphically specify software completely, and the code would be generated in its entirety. We wished for model compilers, which would raise the level of software design to where design patterns would become part of the language, as had been the case for high level language compilers, where structured programming constructs became part of high level languages.

In summary, I think my time as an object oriented designer and developer taught me how to think of any domain I encountered as a collection of objects, interacting to achieve overall behaviour. The major challenge was to make sure that overall behaviour was what you actually wanted. This, if I think back, was the start of my fascination with complex systems - how large numbers of interacting objects could give rise to surprising or unexpected behaviour.

Refurbishing a Software Landscape

Domain

Financial Services

And then I became an architect.

My responsibility increased to a number of software components, each with its own team. I moved up from merely designing one program at a time, to needing to structure whole collections of programs that make up the application portfolio of a business.

While quietly minding my own business learning to develop systems in Borland's Delphi, I found myself a newly minted architect, leading a software landscape reconstruction project in a sister company.

The application portfolio of a financial services company typically consists of a product administration system, surrounded by orbiting systems that interact and correspond with customers, manage the work of the administrators, integrate to payment systems, and produce reports.

The customers wanted more visibility into, and control of, their financial affairs than physical correspondence and overnight batch processes were providing. They were demanding web interfaces and real-time transactions. The existing application portfolio was aging, overnight batch-based, brittle, developed in an ancient technology, and most of the developers had fled.

'Build up a team and fix it' they said. The new CIO and I, holed up in a broom cupboard at our new headquarters, peered out at the world wondering what we had got ourselves into.

But, over the next three or so years, we did that. We built up a team of developers, project managers, business analysts and operational staff. We wrapped the old administration system in a layer of services, developed a new web interface, and put in place workflow, correspondence and document management components.

Complexity, tools and lessons

I learnt how to show our systems as a layered software architecture: here's broadly where we are, here's where we want to go, and here's how to get there.

This application architecture became the blueprint that everyone referred to. Of course, application architectures are pretty conceptual, and mapping that to the detailed business process, integration and infrastructure deployment views was challenging, with many stakeholders wondering how the conceptual view helped them at all except for initial conceptual positioning. All of that is fluff they said - how does it actually work?

And we had to work out the details, painstakingly, and learnt that while you needed to start with a conceptual view to help you decide the overall direction, even the best conceptual models gloss over rather important icebergs in the details that you didn't even know were there, and arrived at inopportune times, forcing you to change course mid-voyage.

I discovered architecture views, first from Krutchten [Krutchten-4+1Views], then Bass, Clements and Kazman [Bass-ArchitectureInPractice], then Rozansky and Woods [Rozansky & Woods]. I learnt to show different views of the system, depending on who was looking and what they were interested in. Different stakeholders wanted to understand different aspects of the system, at different levels of detail, and at different times.

I learnt to define an architecture roadmap that showed what the architecture looked like now, what it would look like in the future, and the steps to take to get there. When you are able to articulate a strategic journey of understandable steps with benefits in each, but still keeping the business running, people will follow you on that path.

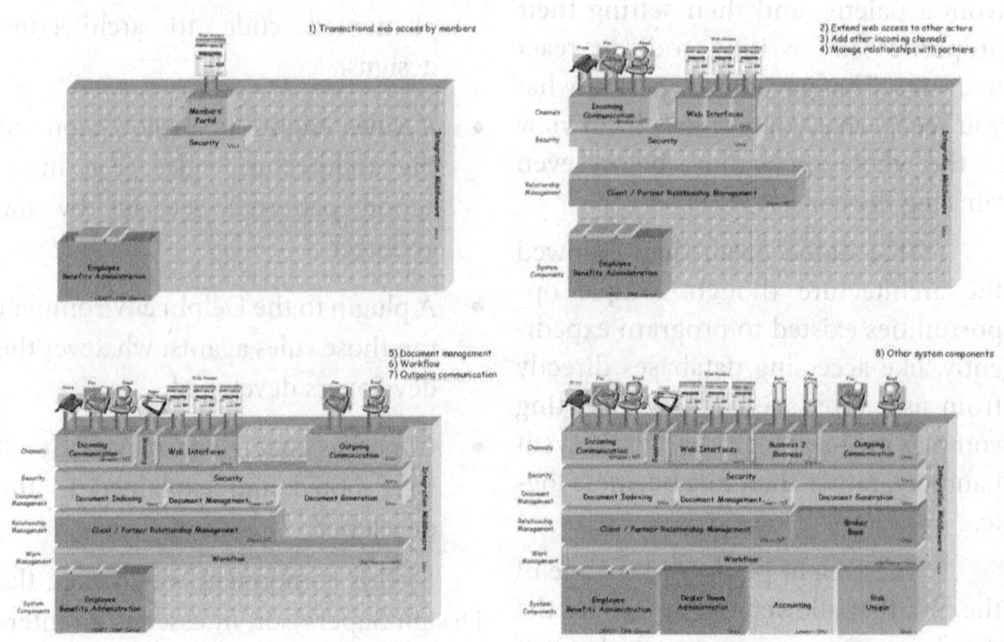

I learnt the value of having over-arching architecture principles, such as a system-wide integration strategy. That allows you to plug components into a landscape that defines component interactions at the level of exposed interfaces, so that you can plug in the next component, knowing where it will go, who will talk to it, and how.

Perhaps the most valuable lesson was the value of architecture itself - in stepping away from the code to a collection of useful models that allow you to abstract away from the detail, you can understand and articulate the overall picture.

A Design Supervisor

Domain

Software Architecture

Complexity, tools and lessons

Learning to do software architecture, I saw first-hand the disparity that exists between what was defined at the architecture level, and what actually exists on the ground. So many levels of interpretation seems to breed significant deviation and local decisions that counteract the interests of the whole.

I've always been interested in tools to aid the software engineering process. Before I moved to the architecture rebuild project, as I mentioned, we started to write systems in Delphi.

Delphi was the pioneer of a new breed of integrated development environments. One designed the user interface canvas by dragging components from a palette, and then setting their properties and writing code to react to events. That gave developers a 'what you see is what you get' graphical view of the whole application, before even running the code.

That didn't mean they followed the architecture though. Ample opportunities existed to program expediently, like accessing databases directly from user interface code, or inserting complex business logic directly in event handlers, rather than in a business logic.

The Delphi platform was one of the first that allowed one to extend the development environment with what they called plugins. Your plugin code could subscribe to and react to events from the development environment itself. So, one could write software that analysed events such as a new component being added to the canvas, a property being set, or event-handling code being written. Your plugin could reflect on what was being designed, and guide those decisions.

An initial set of experiments in that direction grew into a PhD project [Boake-DesignSupervisor] and [Boake-ArchitectureDecisions].

- An architecture meta-model captured software designs, decisions and rationale.
- A model of the design of a software base was built up from intercepting design events such as adding or configuring a component.
- Model analysis was then done to establish correspondence of implemented code to architecture designs.
- A rules engine in Prolog captured the architecture rules (e.g. interaction patterns) set out by the architect.
- A plugin to the Delphi environment ran those rules against whatever the developers developed.
- Concerns (eg pattern violations) were noted and explained to the developer.

This component was named the Design Supervisor, in essence an interactive architectural equivalent to the lint-style code analysis tools of the C and C++ world.

The architecture pattern meta-model ideas in the rules engine had some of their roots in early UML meta-models, and the design reflection rules had their roots in the early model-driven architecture work in the OMG.

From this grew a fascination with tools and techniques for representing and analysing software designs.

Heart Transplant

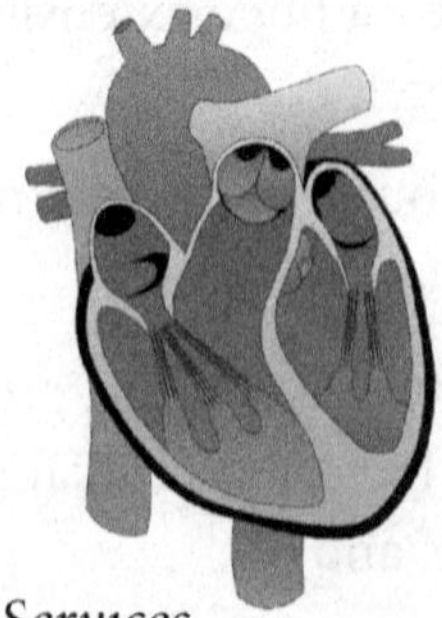

Domain

Financial Services

I moved to a large bank, seeking experience away from insurance. When I arrived there, they said 'You know about insurance, don't you?' and placed me as a solution architect in the insurance division.

Complexity, tools and lessons

One of the most challenging architecture assignments was to design and oversee the replacement of a legacy administration system in the middle of a landscape consisting of a multitude of satellite systems.

This is equivalent to a heart transplant operation. To do this, you have the business in intensive care, keeping it alive while you take out a vital system, replace it with another, and reconnect all of the necessary pipes and veins.

The planning of such an operation requires:

1) *Data storage and flow analysis*: A careful analysis of the landscape, including what data the target system stores, and then following and documenting detailed data flows both up and downstream of the target system.
2) *System requirements and replacement choice*: One must then match the requirements of the business both met and not met by the existing system, with the characteristics of several candidate replacement systems. This involves getting beneath the usual marketing promises to the hard questions: 'How does it actually work?' and 'What does it do well, and what does it do badly?'). In effect, these are architecture reviews, as described by the SEI [Kazman-ATAM]. One of the most important things to insist on is not to change too much: first replace the existing system with equivalent functionality, then phase in enhancements afterwards.
3) *Data migration*: Then, one must plan and execute a data migration - data from the source system, in its data schema, and bearing all of the warts and omissions of an aging incumbent system, must be transformed to the equivalent target data schema, and it must be carefully verified that policyholders end up in a comparable state on the target system.
4) Once chosen and all of the corporate procurement processes have completed, the project commences.

This is essence a five-way conversation between the core product development team, the product implementation team, the internal IT team, the internal business team, and those auditing the process.

Much of the complexity in this effort is in ensuring the communication is smooth between these parties. The overarching business change communication must be informative and timely, the demands of the corporate IT (e.g. deployment patterns and governance processes) must be communicated clearly to the product implementation team, and the on-site team must be in constant touch with the product developers back at the factory. The auditors must be involved right from the decision in the beginning to the testing at the end - signing off a system replacement is essential to national insurance licensing authorities.

Despite several rocky periods, we did in fact replace the system. In hindsight, we made several mistakes, easy to make but with significant consequences.

1) Our communication among the parties was guarded and superficial, and fraught with friction from different mandates and interests (financial, delivery timescale, and architectural).

2) Perhaps the most significant oversight was a lack of essential functionality in the chosen system - they said it was there, but it wasn't – they needed to develop it. We made a couple of errors of assumption, without testing them. As a result, we ended up having to implement an additional system to make up for that lack - a huge extension in time and budget.

I learnt, through many late nights and grey hairs that

1) architecture decisions, grounded in verified facts, are critical and costly if wrong, and

2) an architectural understanding is central to all of the necessary communication, and the architect needs to be a clear and simple communicator, far more than merely a technical problem solver.

Mapping the Territory

Domain

Managing a Complex Application Landscape in A Bank

Complexity, tools and lessons

After a few years of designing different solutions in the bank's insurance landscape, I was made the Chief Architect, responsible for the application landscape.

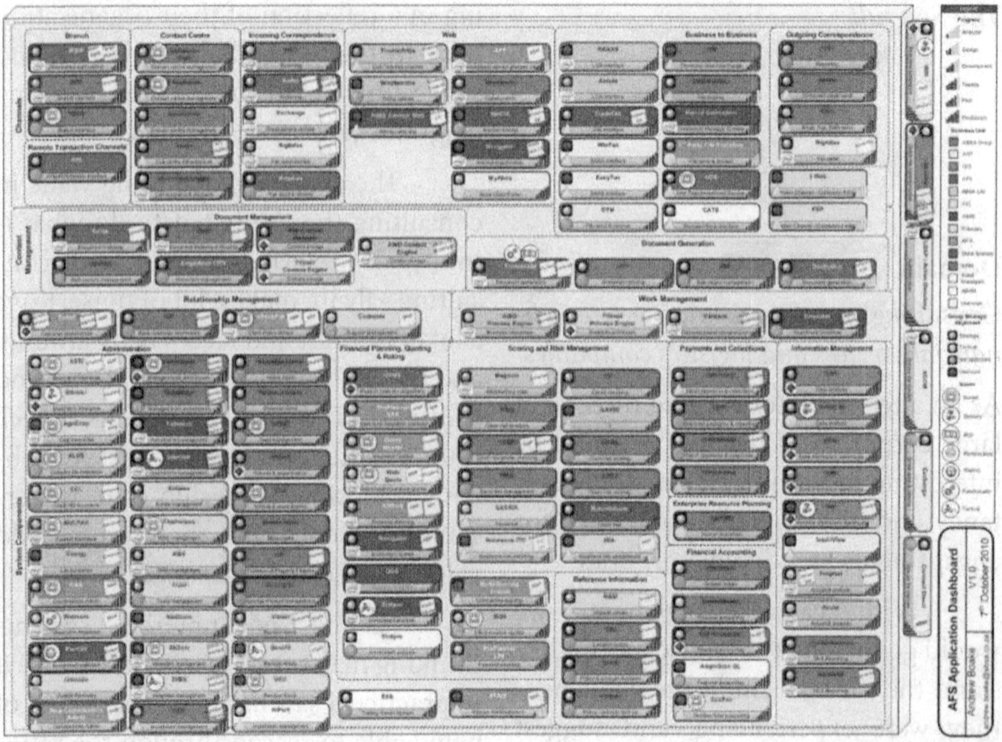

The first and best decision was to choose a stakeholder and really add value to them. I made it my mission to provide the CIO with an up-to-date A3 map of the application landscape. That map showed every system, who was responsible, the current operational state, and its strategic direction. It also showed every project and where it was impacting the landscape. He carried that map into every meeting, insisting that the participants point out where their proposal would add to or make changes to the landscape, or where a project was in getting to where he wanted the landscape to be.

Managing changes to that landscape by many projects, including both internal development teams and vendors was a full-time job. I learnt that capturing an accurate view of a large application portfolio, including ownership, operational status, technical and business health, and intended strategic direction is painstaking and that trust in the model is critical. I also learnt that it takes hard work uncovering the underlying details to maintain a useful accurate model of a complex system.

Accuracy of that landscape was of utmost importance - I became an investigative librarian, tracking and documenting changes religiously. The best sources of that information were both formal and informal - the weekly architecture governance forum, where new projects were required to present their solutions, and of course frequent visits to the smokers' area where the reality behind projects is discussed.

The Seagull

Domain

Consulting on software architecture to financial services and logistics companies.

As an alternative to working directly at large corporates, I decided it would be interesting to work for a small consultancy, and from there be contracted for engagements at different corporates.

With each engagement, we would go in, map the landscape, understand the causes behind the challenges they were experiencing, and suggest opportunities to improve things.

Complexity, tools and lessons

I was amazed to discover the same kinds of challenges in each organization we visited - the names of those involved would change, and the degree and priority of the challenges would be slightly different.

When you've worked through the systems challenges in different organizations, you begin to see patterns, and build up your own list of approaches that work, and those that don't, seeing as you've already lived through those experiences.

It was intellectually challenging work to spot the problem patterns and to match potential solution archetypes, understanding the essence through the specific details. It was a very interesting experience to bring that understanding in a reflection of their organization back to them, highlighting issues, and suggesting architecture roadmaps using diagrams that spoke to them.

The challenge of adding value in consulting though is not to do what is informally referred to as seagull consulting - fly in, make a lot of noise, leave a lot of feathers and faeces lying around, and fly off, leaving everyone dazed and confused. The best consultants, I feel, immerse themselves in the messy problems, working alongside and understanding deeply. Only then can you add value as a trusted advisor.

Having encountered systems thinking in theory, I learnt how to use it in practice. I saw firsthand the power of being able to reason through the rationale of why a system consisting of people, processes and software components was exhibiting undesirable behaviour. More often than not there were good people just stuck in a system that wasn't working as a whole.

The skill is to model the system, understand how it works, and identify the appropriate remedy (which may well be a new software system, or may just be using the existing components in a better way).

You also need to analyse the proposed system to determine impacts of change. You don't want to get even more undesirable outcomes!

Then, one has to convince and help the participants to modify their behaviour to get different outcomes. This was new and ground-breaking: Systems Thinking is of course the subject of many a business school course, but I'm not aware of any that covers this way of thinking when dealing with software architecture.

Commonwealth Diplomacy

Domain

Central Legislation Compliance Services for a Large Financial Services Group

One of the consulting engagements involved designing and implementing a system (of people, processes and software components) to ensure compliance in a large financial services organization, with many business units, to anti money-laundering legislation.

We had to gather significant business events, from all business units involved, that indicated money laundering risk (like onboarding a new client, accepting a payment, moving money between accounts, or making a payment). We then had to quantify the risk, and take mediating actions (like gathering additional information and documents from those involved, or reporting the risk to the regulator).

Complexity, tools and lessons

The technical complexity of this system was inherent in that it used a new architecture pattern (*event-based architecture*) to integrate to the business units' line of business systems to source the relevant business events, and then *complex event processing* (running rules against the gathered events) that would determine their risk and the mitigating actions.

An example might be: if someone is on, or is related to someone on, an international sanctions list, their risk profile increases significantly, possibly to the extent that we should not do business with them. Another example might be if someone deposits a large amount of cash into his investment account, then moves it to an offshore account before allowing it to gather any interest, that might constitute a suspicious set of transactions that should be checked.

The business units involved had very different business models, processes and data. Each had its own terminology, and kinds of transactions. Examples were investment product providers, life insurers, providers of credit loans, and business units managing armies of financial advisors to investment and insurance clients. Each would be subject to the legislation in different ways, being party to different aspects of risk - onboarding possibly risky clients, or performing transactions with various degrees of vulnerability to money laundering.

This meant that the business complexity was in understanding the intent of the legislation, and mapping that to the different business units' processes, software systems and their data, so that you could ask them to provide specific information at the right time in their process, and not allow the transaction to proceed until they got the go-ahead.

The first level of software complexity was to provide a general enough systems integration interface to cater for all of the different businesses' data and events.

The second level of software complexity was to provide a central store of all that information so that it could be processed. There they needed a powerful enough rules engine to express the nuances of money laundering risk determination and mitigation rules. It also needed to be flexible, because the legislation typically changed every 6 months, and a legislation change should preferably just require a configuration change in the rules or the required information.

The third level of software complexity was to integrate back into the business processes with requirements to gather more information or documents, or to perform regular follow-up checks on the client over the next few years.

And the fourth and most challenging level of software complexity was data quality. The line of business systems provided data with different accuracy and currency, and often different data for the same client. The system had to decide which information was more trusted, to build up a 'golden record' of trusted information for each client, to be used in further processing.

Centrally coordinated legislation compliance is a challenging exercise. To convince a whole financial services group of architectural decisions such as an integration approach must be similar to trying to lobby for a new law to go through the US senate! Communication and negotiation skills are the deciding factor of success or failure. You have to simplify a complex architecture to its essence so that decision-makers can easily buy in to a vision, and then you need to be able to flesh it out to the levels of detail required for experts from many different domains to be confident in the aspects that interest them (security, performance, privacy legislation compliance, ...). In a baptism of fire I learnt the true complexity involved in providing architecture views for a myriad of different stakeholders!

Riding the Tsunami

Domain

A Financial Services Startup

The one thing I hadn't done in my career was to work at a startup. When the opportunity arose, I jumped at the chance.

An investment platform (a business that matches people and their financial needs to investment products, and manages all of the transactions between them) had just released their minimum viable product into the market, with a few available products and very few clients. They were looking to scale.

I joined their architecture team, who were looking at bolstering the technical platform's support for many more clients, and many more products. They also wanted to be able to support different distribution channels integrating to the platform via an API layer, and then eventually provide the platform as a service to different providers, branded differently, and with their data absolutely segregated.

Complexity, tools and lessons

My favourite video clip from many years ago showed three guys sitting around a desk with a personal computer screen, in a typical double garage. The screen showed the management view of a web site, with a dashboard showing 'Number of users: 0'. They sat glumly, obviously having just gone live with their site, and no one was visiting.

Just then, the dashboard ticked over, and went to 1, then 2, then 5 users. Celebrations broke out as the numbers started to climb - the company was off the ground!

Zooming through the celebrations, the camera picks up the face of one of them, who keeps looking at the count of users increasing, and then at the little server under the desk. He begins to look very worried.

Scaling

Scaling up a system involves improving a number of aspects, loosely termed non-functional requirements (NFRs).

Functional requirements of a system specify what the system must do, and non-functional requirements how well it must do it. For example, *performance* specifies how fast it must be, like how quickly it comes back to the user with the results of a query, or if it can do the batch fee run over all accounts in a certain time window. *Availability* requires stability under all sorts of conditions, e.g. if a server or network fails, or a piece of software crashes - the system must be able to recover and continue operating. *Security* requires that only verified users may see certain data, or access certain functionality.

Scaling requires that all of the functionality is still available, still subject to security vetting, and with acceptable performance, when you increase the scale of use, e.g. scaling the number of users, number of accounts, or number of transactions.

These non-functional requirements are most often stated in business terms - this business process should take no longer than this time. Then, one has to design the technology layers - at the application level, the data structures, the data flow between application components, the calculations performed, so that they follow scalable patterns. At the infrastructure level, you need to measure and optimise processor capacity, memory capacity, disk storage capacity, network bandwidth, and put high availability and load balancing mechanisms in place where needed.

When all of these detailed technical pieces interact, the result is acceptable end to end performance, or a system that is resilient against certain kinds of failure, or a system that can deal with the required number of simultaneous logons, or that is secure from certain kinds of attacks. In a manner of speaking, system quality attributes emerge from the complex behaviour at the details, and when measured, must meet the stated overall requirements.

To be able to scale in this way, one has to understand the architecture of the system, down to the details. One then needs to specify quite exactly what is to be measured, and where, and what would be acceptable measurements. Then, one needs to instrument the system - in modern systems, that means instrumenting different technology layers - web protocols, integration protocols, network throughout and latency, processor activity, disk activity. Those measurements are sent to a data store, then aggregated and visualized. The challenge is to design your instrumentation so that that aggregation yields measures that make business sense.

If (when) you find issues, you then need to pinpoint where the issues occur, and work on fixing those i.e. finding and improving specific performance bottlenecks, or fixing a specific security vulnerability, or preventing a specific vulnerability to failure, down to the detail.

It helps if you've documented design decision rationale (*I'm putting two load-balanced servers here to achieve the following web refresh performance)*. This will guide you to seeing which aspects have not been addressed, or places where two decisions are perhaps counteracting one another (*I've put in this sophisticated data encryption,* or *This call goes through 5 levels of API.* Understanding this can explain why your performance is suffering). Otherwise, you need to look for patterns with a seasoned eye for spotting causes of issues.

Once you've fixed the details, you measure again, and observe the overall effect once again.

In this process, we have learnt to annotate and analyse our architecture to be able to more easily manage this process:

- We annotated the business processes with non-functional requirements.
- We annotated the infrastructure landscape with corresponding design decisions.
- We also annotated the infrastructure landscape with measurements.
- And we annotated the business processes with aggregated measurements to be able to compare those with the stated requirements.

Refactoring

Releasing a minimal viable product most often means taking certain shortcuts to meet aggressive market targets. But, scaling and expanding initial requirements means the need to revisit what is called technical debt - pieces of the system that, like a line of credit, can get you somewhere in the short term, but you then need to pay it back.

Our investment platform started with a single web site for a particular type of investor. Hastened delivery timescales led to putting business logic, e.g. validating investment combinations and limits, into the web code, to ensure legal investment transactions before the expensive submission via the administration system API.

Other distribution platforms (mobile, other platforms calling our API) were standing in the queue to access our platform functionality. Our existing design meant that the other channels would not have access to the transaction checks in the web site - they would either need to duplicate those in the different channels, or, a far better design idea, we needed to move it to a common validation layer just under a comprehensive API to be consumed by all channels.

This kind of refactoring of course diverts resources from new functionality (which is often what prospective customers are clamouring for), and often pits the sales and marketing team against the internal architecture team. 'Our competitors will get ahead of us' fights for funds against 'Our system will be badly designed which will hurt us in the long run'. It takes wise company management to be able to balance these demands for resource and attention.

In working at a startup, I learnt that an architect needs to be very aware of business priorities, especially for funding. One needs to be acutely aware of the value which is most valuable to them in the current context. A business desperate for scaling use of their platform will obviously like to first gain the new business, so that it can pay for system upgrades. The other side of the coin, where it is imperative to upgrade the system to handle new business, will need to be substantiated very clearly.

This is typical of a startup - I would give anything to have been a fly on the wall when the Facebook architects said they needed to replace the entire data storage mechanism when the number of users went above several million, while the quest for critical mass of users said they should be investing in other features that attracted users rather than working on the system's innards.

And so we come to now. We've looked at different real world examples of system complexity, and how we've approached that in the past. It seems though, in this world of connectedness, of a web of financial systems, a web of cloud infrastructure, a web of software as a service offerings, our old thinking has become a little frayed. How do we deal with this very real interconnected complex system, adding new parts without breaking the existing, using the existing parts in new and innovative ways?

In the next part of the paper, I take a step into this world.

Part 2 – The Challenge

In The Hobbit, Bilbo Baggins comes face to face with the dragon Smaug, lying sleeping as he guards his treasure. Smaug opens one eye, and begins asking the in-

truder questions. The questions reveal a whole lot more about Bilbo than he is willing to admit.

Having seen many different forms of software complexity and ways of approaching it thus far, perhaps it is time to reflect on the challenges of today's software, as we are confronted by crippling complexity on one hand, and promising ways of thinking and tools on the other.

We will in particular first look at software systems through the lens of complex systems science.

Then, we will consider what the world-changing force of AI brings to us in our quest for effective software design and development.

Back of the Tapestry

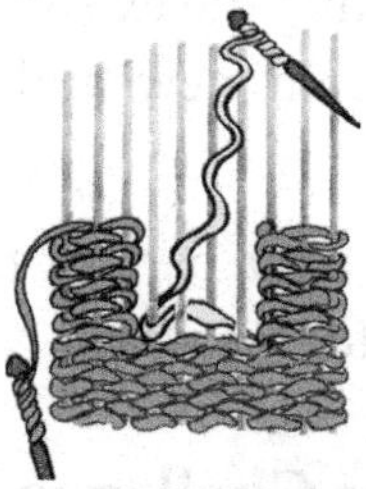

Crippling Complexity behind the Scenes

The mystery and beauty of a giant tapestry, with intricate threads of different colours weaving a beautiful scene, is somewhat disappointingly tarnished when you turn it over. That scene is not beautiful, somewhat chaotic, with threads overlapping, jagging across to contribute elsewhere, and ending suddenly and visibly. The emerging picture of the front is seen to be made up of seemingly chaotic details behind, the exposed workings not easily reconciled with the intent of the front.

Complex Systems

Some systems in the world (like ecosystems, or economies, or brains) consist of many interacting components, whose local interactions give rise to system-wide behaviour that is very difficult to understand, to predict or to control overall, even when we understand the individual interactions. These are called complex systems.

They are different from simple systems (like a ball bouncing according to Newtonian physics, or a balloon filled with gas, obeying the laws of pressure and temperature), or merely complicated systems which we can break down into their parts and easily understand the whole. The complex behaviour of these systems arises from the local interactions of their components, and it is not obvious how the individual interactions (someone buying something) contributes to emergent behaviour (a worldwide recession). The study of these systems is called Complex Systems Science.

Unexpected Consequences

A tale is told in the days of British rule of India, of a certain area which had its medical establishments stretched by villagers suffering from cobra bites. The governor of that area decided something needed to be done, and put a bounty out on cobras. Bring us a dead cobra and we'll pay you. For a while, the cobra population declined, and fewer villagers were bitten.

But, the governor noticed that the amount paid out for dead cobras was steadily increasing. Investigating, he found that the villages had started breeding cobras for supplementary income! Angry, he stopped all bounty payments. The villages let out all of their captive cobras, which then proceeded to bite many more villagers, and the medical establishments were stretched far more than before.

A field studying such complex systems is Systems Thinking. That field gives us tools to model the structure and interactions of large complex systems, then match that to known system archetypes. The field also gives you tools to simulate and visualize this behaviour.

Systems Thinking describes system behaviour using patterns. The one described above is predictably called *unexpected consequences*, and is well known in systems where an unexpected feedback loop is discovered to be working behind the scenes.

Software landscapes in large corporates are a rich ground for examples of this. We have all witnessed a software system put in to encourage a desired behaviour, but what emerges is just the opposite.

Tragedy of the Commons

Another tale is told of a village with a beautiful green in the middle of all of the houses. People let their cattle graze there - it was provided for all to use. But greed reared its ugly head. You see, as a villager you benefited from a free resource, and you could sell your cow at a higher profit, not having had the expense of feeding it. So you soon bring two cows, then three, to graze. Soon everyone has too many cows grazing while not tending to the green. Its grass has no time to recover, and it becomes a dust bowl. Nobody can graze there anymore.

This is a pattern, or archetype, called the *Tragedy of the Commons*. This happens whenever individual gain happens at the expense of the common good. Examples abound in ecology: polluted water supplies and over-fishing our oceans come to mind.

I have seen this pattern so many times with centralized IT services. Individual business units use (and abuse) the central IT resource, without replenishing it (hiring new people is put on hold to cut costs, and there is no time for training, or even leave). The people feel exploited and burnt out, and leave in their droves. Soon the business units consider the central IT to be useless and hire their own teams at far higher cost to the company.

Systems thinking is a powerful way to understand complex behaviour. It is being increasingly adopted as a way to think about complex problems in many fields, such as business and environmental sustainability.

Software architecture has not typically adopted this way of thinking. It is my contention that it should. Architecture design decisions are often about trade-offs and trying to encourage certain emergent system properties, such as increased security, or better overall performance, availability or scalability. These properties affect one another in feedback loops, which can be analysed in this way.

Complex Software Systems

We are increasingly being called on to design, implement and operate complex software systems. I use the word *complexity* in the very strictly defined sense of many interacting parts, which exhibit often unexpected behaviour that emerges from their interactions. The challenge in dealing with creating, adding to and modifying these complex software systems is: how do we understand such systems, and when we design new parts, or replace parts, how do we know that we're following the right path, or that we aren't introducing undesired behaviour?

We are surrounded by an increasingly complex set of technology components, which interact in ecosystems. Technology is complex. It has many domains and stakeholders. It has many components interacting to achieve its goals. And the emergence of unexpected outcomes is frequent.

An example is the mobile app landscape, contributed to by a huge diverse army of app developers. How do we ensure each is a good citizen of the landscape, and that they work well together on your phone? Apple runs a tight ship in its IOS app community, trying to control quality and standards in that way, Android less so. Which is the better approach? For innovation? For consistent user experience?

We have spent some time in Part 1 unpacking the sources of complexity I have personally experienced in software systems design. To summarize, I would suggest that there are a number of contributing factors.

- *Many Components and Interactions*

  The number of moving parts, number of dependencies, and the heterogeneity of the components and their interactions increases the difficulty of understanding such systems exponentially.

  To understand a complex system, it's not just about taking the system apart, and understanding the pieces. That doesn't really tell you about the system as a whole. In most systems, it is the dynamic behaviour, the interactions between the pieces in the structure that are the key.

- *Scale*

  As the scale of a system increases, the number of participating components increases, and the volume of stored and communicated information in interactions increases. This provides so much more opportunity for unintended consequences.

- *Trade-offs*

  System design decisions do not often have clear-cut winners and losers. There are mostly pros and cons for all alternatives, and one needs to be able to articulate these, and make informed choices based on these.

- *Uncertainty*

  A popular definition of an architectural decision is one that has system-wide impacts and is not easily changed. Added to that, software architects are often faced with such decisions early in a project, when there are many unknowns in the supporting information and implications of decisions.

- *Agility*

  Being able to change your mind, to evolve design direction, is a much sought-after property of modern systems development. Our business users often do not have a crystal clear understanding of what they want, and modern software development methods prefer to cooperatively and incrementally grow the system from a small proven core, giving all involved opportunities to provide feedback and influence the desired direction.

  While this certainly encourages innovation and evolution of the system, the difficulty lies in providing the technology platform that allows such evolution. Here I include understanding the domain well from a significant architectural requirements point of view, having a comprehensive suite of tests to give you confidence that changes did not break anything, and rapid redefinition of the deployment environment as required (i.e. flexible cloud infrastructure).

- *Urgency*

  When we are tasked to design and develop software, it is more often than not due yesterday. The identified market window is closing, competitors are looming, funding is limited and has strings attached. In that atmosphere, there is significant urgency attached to estimation of required resources, and architects need to make their upfront decisions at speed, often before they are fully informed and ready.

- *Return on Investment*

  There is more often than not a debate around tactical vs strategic investment. Why don't we just get something to work so we can show return on investment sooner - we'll fix it later. Unfortunately, later there is always something more important, also paramount to return on investment.

The Internet

Given these attributes, it is informative to consider the design of the Internet.

While the Internet exhibits most of these characteristics, it is designed simply (a very simple set of protocols is at the heart of all internet components), it is scalable (incredibly so - it has grown from a single defence network, then an inter-university network, to global high volume communication), it is malleable (we now use the internet for so much more than when it was originally designed), and it is robust (it survives local outages every day, and even survived the unprecedented outages of 911 and peaks of use in Covid).

Perhaps the secret lies in the simple and robust protocols that very clearly define interaction contracts, beyond which you can innovate to your heart's desire?

Corporate IT

Consider in counterpoint, typical corporate IT.

Most corporate IT landscapes I know consist primarily of impossible to renew legacy and packaged software that has been shoe-horned and customized, with layers of temporary fixes, and are held together by point to point integration, with implicit dependencies that make the whole system brittle and resistant to change.

Does it have to be this way?

With their inherent heterogeneous complexity, how can we design corporate architectures better?

Does the example of the internet suggest that corporate architects need to find simple design rules that lead to desired system qualities? How do we find these?

Some Models are Useful

Architecture Models can aid us in our Understanding and Design of Systems

Modelling Software Architecture

All models are wrong

George Box, a British mathematician, famously said: "All models are wrong, but some are useful".

In our context, I take this to mean that all models are an abstraction of reality, leaving out some details and emphasising others. I think this is an insightful statement on the usefulness of developing a model of some complex part of the real world, and then using it to reason through aspects of how it works, or how it could be made to work.

It also lets us understand that there is no one model for all purposes - different models are for different purposes. You will need to carefully select which to use depending on that purpose.

The vanishing art of modelling software designs

I think it is also a fair statement to consider when we look at the state of software design modelling employed in practice.

It is my experience that modelling software systems is decreasing, and is not seen as valuable.

After the hype of model-driven architecture and parallel UML and code views in some IDEs, the world went on to modern web development, with its layers of diverse technologies, and agile development, with its emphasis on the value of working software - and people model very informally these days. In fact, most agile practitioners I know say that models belong on whiteboards to illustrate designs, and are then erased. They do not have lasting value – the only true reflection of value is working code.

In my experience with many IT projects in corporate financial services organizations, we are seeing less and less modelling being used to help with capturing and reasoning through complex system designs.

In a quick poll of a software architecture class, with the students all being experienced programmers, I was met with a stunned 'why would we need to do that?' when I asked them how and what they model during software development.

That has made me think long and hard: What has made people lose faith in models? Could it be the emphasis of agile methods on the code? Could it be that our current models are not rich enough - only the code captures both the structure and behaviour of the system unambiguously, and allows it to be run to see it work? Could it be the fact that most people do their design documentation reluctantly after the coding, rather than using it for thinking, visualization and refinement during the process?

I find this sad, because I have found such value in models of the architecture of systems - they have allowed me to express what's in my head in an unclear form, to clean it up as I visualize different aspects and scenarios, and thereby to develop my thinking, and allow me to express that more clearly to others.

Modelling Architectures

What do we require to model architectures effectively? Here is a list of the aspects and mechanisms that I consider important:

- Being able to represent models of the different enterprise architecture layers and the inter-relationships between them.
- Being able to visualize spatially and using simple intuitive notation to represent all of the important elements of such models.
- Being able to query architecture models, to obtain views of the architecture from the viewpoints of important stakeholders.
- Abstraction - being able to model at different levels of detail (conceptually, logically and physically), and relate and navigate between them.
- System qualities - being able to represent important aspects of system qualities such as security, performance and availability.

A Modelling Notation

ArchiMate is one of a number of architecture modelling notations. It was born in the research departments of Dutch universities, and then refined in the fire of Dutch corporates (Royal Dutch Shell and Phillips among them). It has been formalized and refined further, and adopted as a standard by the Object Management Group [ArchiMate-OMG].

ArchiMate is a useful middle ground notation to express important aspects of modelling software systems. It balances the power and flexibility of models that require configuration of powerful meta-models and the complexity of trying to combine a number of diverse specialized detailed models.

I have used ArchiMate as a notation to show different aspects of business systems. ArchiMate is a powerful common vocabulary and way of thinking of and visualizing relationships between components in the different architectures in an enterprise (eg business, application, data and infrastructure architecture), and between these different architectures (eg application components being used by business processes, application components being deployed on an infrastructure landscape). ArchiMate also shows the rationale behind architecture decisions, and work breakdown required to implement them.

It is by far the most useful notation for software architecture that I have found. It is also proving a valuable tool to use as a base to add aspects such as the Systems Thinking we discussed earlier.

Analysing and visualizing software architectures

Model-Driven Design

In our experience, we have found the usual drawings in presentation packages, or even in advanced drawing tools, to be of limited use. They are still just drawings, and do not easily afford reuse, programmatic navigation or reasoning.

We currently design software solutions using a combination of text and diagrams. These are typically at varying levels of detail and are materially inconsistent. We have to re-draw these and re-write the underlying rationale every time we implement a change.

We are moving from designing software systems using drawings, to using design models. We are moving our way of doing architecture towards model-driven design - we are busy implementing a different approach that employs visualizable analysable reusable design models.

These models may be visualized to show important views, to allow us to make design decisions. These models may also be analysed to check our designs, and to derive further important aspects to inform our decisions. These models may be stored, retrieved and queried for re-use. We also keep track of changes over time.

In a nutshell, the principles behind our approach can be articulated as:

- We are moving from designing software systems using drawings, to using models of systems.
- These models may be visualized to show important views, to allow us to make design decisions.
- These models may be analysed to check our designs, and to derive further important aspects to inform our decisions.
- These models may be stored, retrieved and queried for re-use.
- These models are versioned, to allow us to keep track of changes over time.

Network Graphs

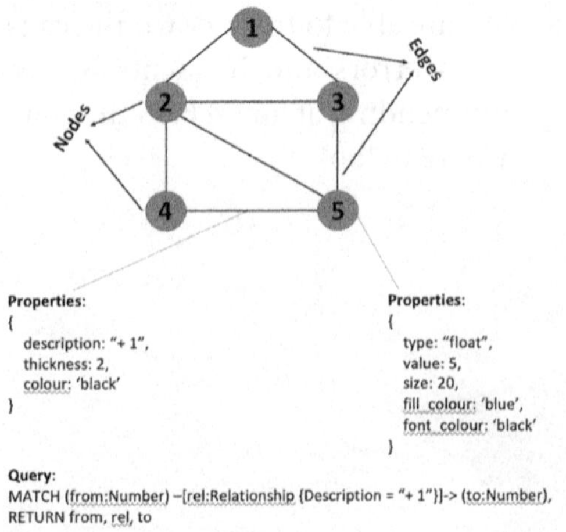

We have found that the best way to model software-related system architectures is to use network graphs. Duncan Watts' book *Six Degrees – The Science of a Connected Age* gives a very good introduction to viewing systems as networks, and the power of understanding that gives you [Watts].

Network graphs more easily depict and allow analysis of relationships and emergent properties than tabular or relational models. Network graphs can be used to depict the important components of an architecture, their relationships and their interactions. Network graphs can also depict the relationships between elements of different architectures.

There are several really excellent suites of tools, pioneered by the data science community, that allow us to input, visualize and analyse network graphs.

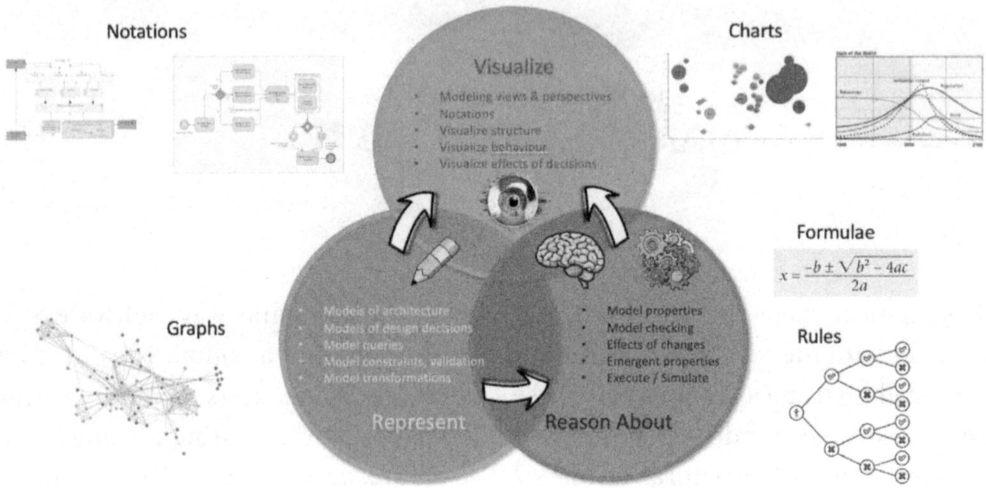

We believe architecture modelling using network graphs gives us powerful tools to take on software complexity.

In order to have a handle on complexity, we need to be able to model the components of an architecture and the links between them, visualize these models, do analysis on them, run simulations using them, and again visualize what we've found.

We have done quite a bit of work in representing, analysing and visualizing architectures.

- We visualize our landscapes.
- We visualize impacts of changes (e.g. major component changes).

- We document reference architectures and recommended design patterns.
- We are able to visualize risks and understand required mitigations (e.g. information security, performance, reliability concerns).
- We are able to track down the causes of errors and incidents by recommending at an architecture level where to look.

Inter-related Architecture Graphs

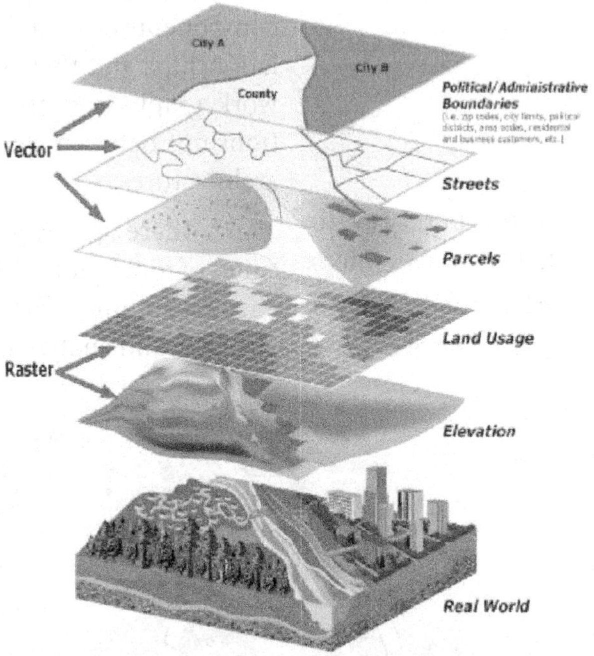

Geographical maps try to depict and make sense of the reality on the ground by modelling using a set of layers. These are geo-located models that address focussed aspects (eg natural features / boundaries / land use). They all refer to, and describe aspects of, the same complex reality.

In the same way, software systems are part of a complex reality containing business users, communicating pieces of software and supporting infrastructure, and we need different, but related, models of that reality to make and understand the implications of system design decisions.

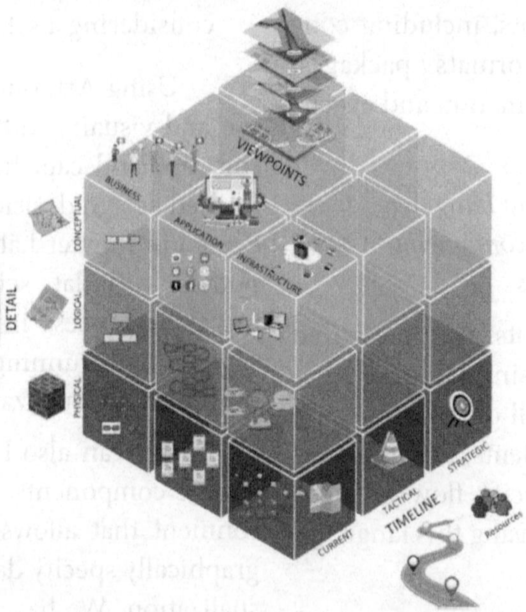

We consider enterprise architecture to be a collection of interrelated graphs, as depicted in the cube above.

The enterprise architecture landscape can be visualized in three dimensions:

- Graphs that capture aspects of different domains - business, application, data, infrastructure.
- Graphs of different levels of detail (abstraction) - conceptual, logical, and physical.
- Graphs at different periods in time - the current state, the target state, and a roadmap of changes that will get you from one to the other.

We need to query the graph models to extract or highlight aspects of interest.

We need to visualize the different graph models, using symbols and visualization techniques to depict aspects of interest.

Analysing Software Architecture Graphs

We can analyse architectures using graph operations and visualization.

We are busy developing Art (which stands for *Architecture Rationale Tool*), an environment for exploring aspects of a software architecture design based on architecture graphs.

Art is a library of Python software, divided into a number of layers:

- *Graph functionality*

  Everything in Art is based on modelling software architectures as network graphs. These graphs use NetworkX, a popular data science community graph library for structuring, manipulating and querying network graphs.

- *Graph Components*

  Art has a layer of graph-manipulating components, which we can compose into graph processing solutions. There are a number of graph components, including connectors to other formats / packages, analysis, transformation and execution of graphs.

- *A Domain-Specific Language for representing and configuring Graph Component Flows*

  These components are configured and composed using a domain-specific language. All of the properties of these components, and the connectors that specify flow between them are set up using this language.

- *Interfaces*

  Art then has a layer of interfaces through which you can visualize and manipulate graphs. Currently, we have integrated with Jupyter Labs and Knime. Dash applications are being worked on. We are also considering a set of REST APIs.

Using Art, one can model, analyse and visualize different aspects of a software landscape in order to make informed design decisions. Art can be executed in Jupyter Lab (an environment popular with data scientists documenting their process in markdown interspersed with running python code, for example for visualizations).

Art can also be used as a set of Knime components. Knime is an environment that allows data scientists to graphically specify data analysis and visualization. We have implemented Art as a Knime node, which allows us to integrate Art to all of Knime's functionality. This allows us to obtain graph data from, and send graph data to Knime data sources, and to use Art analysis and visualization in our Knime workflows.

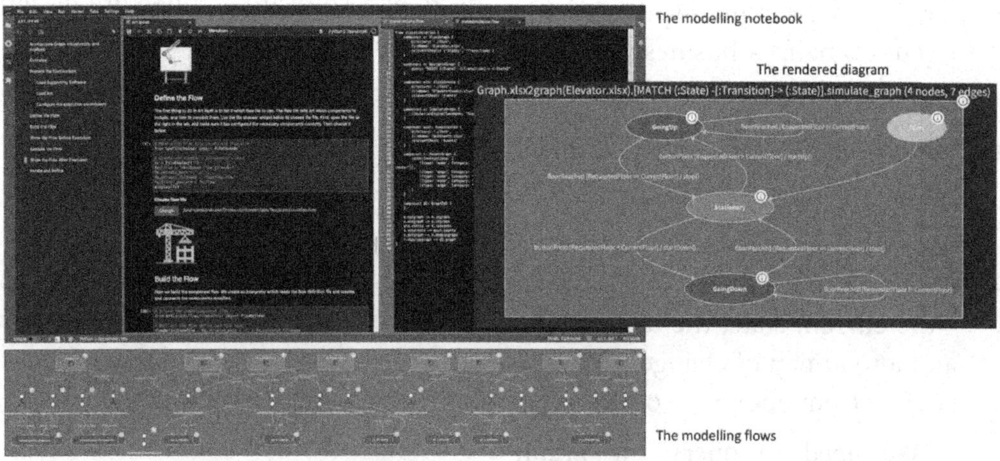

Art can analyse and visualize different aspects around software design. Many of these aspects can be understood and visualized as a particular kind of graph. As an example, here we are visualizing a simulation of a state machine, helping us to understand a system's dynamic behaviour.

We can run analyses and simulations on architecture graphs:

- Single point of failure (graph path analysis)
- Analysing impacts
    - o Transitive closure
    - o impact of failure
    - o implications of decisions
    - o implications of changes
- Analysing the flow of data
- Analysing for design constraints
    - o Model checking
- Analysing for refactoring
    - o Graph transformations
- Analysing for emergent properties

  We are refining the platform to see (represent, visualize, reason about) how design decisions affect emergent system qualities such as performance, reliability, maintainability.
- Simulating to understand and predict behaviour.

We can reason through architecture design rationale

- Choosing between options, e.g. using a radar graph depicting the dimension of choice and the relative option evaluations.
- Systems Thinking reasoning.
- Systems Thinking simulations - running the simulation can yield graphs of variable values over time that show the effects of a certain structure on inter-related properties.

We still have a number of research challenges in this way of modelling architecture.

- We are working on a full ArchiMate-based graph model for all enterprise architecture models and inter-relationships.
- We are working on how to best visualize aspects of architecture, for example auto-layout of graphs and ease of navigation in and between models.
- We have implemented a standard graph query and navigation language (Cypher) - we are still working on how to use Cypher to define the required navigation and transformations of architecture graphs.
- We are working on representing graphs at different levels of abstraction and navigating between them, in a manner similar to navigating into and out of levels of detail in geographical maps.
- We are working on relating Systems Thinking-style architecture decision rationale graphs and the architecture elements they describe.

Complex Systems Science has many aspects beyond analysis and visualization using network graphs, and analysis of rationale using Systems Thinking. A recent course I attended at the New England Complex Systems Institute [necsi.edu] was tremendously informative, and opened a number of further research directions.

For the moment, however, we turn our attention to Artificial Intelligence and its promise.

The Man Behind the Curtain

Dorothy, the Scarecrow, the Tin Man and the Lion return to Oz with the broomstick of the Wicked Witch of the West. They bring it to the Wizard of Oz. He had previously promised that in return for the broomstick, he would grant them a ride home for Dorothy, a brain for the scarecrow, a heart for the Tin Man and courage for the Lion.

But the Wizard tries to stall. He tells them to return the following day.

While they plead with the Wizard not to send them away, Dorothy's dog Toto notices some activity behind a nearby curtain. Toto pulls back the curtain to reveal that the Wizard is not who Dorothy and the others thought he was. "Pay no attention to the man behind the curtain!" the "Wizard" yells in vain. He has been discovered and they see him for who he really is.

The Lure of Intelligent Automated Software Development

We have been, and are, lured by the wizard as he talks to our hopes and fears in software design and development. Take no notice of what's going on behind the scenes, he says. Just adopt this method / this tool and all your wishes will be granted.

I find there are two extremes to dealing with new technologies.

One of them is to jump right in and see. I have a friend, probably the best programmer I know, who has been experimenting with using generative AI in his programming tasks. He showed me a demo a while ago - you're busy with programming something, and you know you need some complicated code here. You have ChatGPT open in the next window, and you just chat to it: "Find me some python code to transform such and such into such and such" - it comes back with a suggestion that it has generated. You look at it and see it's not quite what you were looking for, so you refine the query, it refines its recommended code, and you can copy and paste it. On to the next step...

No more searching through stackoverflow questions and answers. It's actually really quite impressive, and he is sold.

Another approach is to observe and understand what this is all about before being all in. I admit I am in this camp.

The Hype Curve

I've seen so many technologies going through the famous Gartner hype curve - they start by being the next big thing, everyone jumps on the bandwagon, and the hype goes into overdrive.

Then people discover its limitations, and complexities, and the enthusiasm slows and drops off.

Then, with a more informed and careful approach, some people start using it well and refining it, so that a second curve starts and picks up, slower, but more sustained.

I thought that would be the case with the current wave of AI. I'm still waiting for the slow-down.

Generative AI

Generative AI jumped to centre-stage with experiences of intelligent human-like conversations and really informative, insightful answers going viral.

That conversational interface spread to a number of specific applications, like writing aids in word processing applications. Now, we have AI-powered everything from writing reports so much better than you can, to summarizing meetings in real time, to generating really realistic pictures.

The big tech giants all have an AI-powered assistant. Companies are hastily adding AI to their strategies, and salesmen speak in hallowed tones of intelligent functionality in any number of products. Share prices of hardware companies have overheated, because AI needs a bunch of processing power. People urging caution are seen as nay-sayers. The curve is showing little signs of abating.

Let's see if we can make sense of this - perhaps we can take an initial look at what the man is doing behind the curtain.

Put these Things into Piles

There have been two main approaches over the years to get artificial intelligence to understand domains and convert that understanding to recommendations of actions.

The first approach used explicitly defined *rules.* We would consult domain experts, who would reflect on their reasoning when navigating their domain. "When I see pattern X, I know fact Y, and I must act by doing action Z", they would tell us. Often they would cascade the rules: "When I find out that I know fact Y and fact A, I know fact B, and I must act by doing action C". We would express those rules in something like first order predicate logic, and use a tool like Prolog to use them to navigate the facts we know to reach conclusions, to act like an expert in the field.

Expert systems got very good at what they did - they could out-diagnose most doctors, identify complex underwriting risks for insurance companies, and discover deposits of minerals for mining that no one knew about.

They just got very complex as we added to the rules, difficult to test against actual data on the ground, difficult to understand if they got something wrong, and brittle when we wanted to change them.

The second approach was to unleash what came to be called *machine learning* on examples. A neural network (a data structure that mimicked a human brain) would learn patterns by reinforcing weights as it saw more of the same pattern. It could then be shown an example of the pattern, it would compare it to its internal weights, and say 'Ah, that's one of these.'

In the rules approach, an expert would tell you: a chair consists of a back, legs, and a seat. A leg is a straight vertical piece, a seat is a square horizontal piece, ...

In the machine learning approach, the computer would be shown example after example of chairs, and reinforce the patterns that it saw, until it learnt to recognise a chair, without being explicitly told what the parts were.

To try to understand these approaches, let's consider our knowledge to be concepts in a knowledge space, with relationships between them - a knowledge 'graph'. In the rules approach, we express those concepts and the relationships between them explicitly, and codify them in a knowledge base. In the machine learning approach, we let the computer cluster the examples it has seen into *its* concept space, without us explicitly naming them. It annotates the relationships it found with probability weights, which it reinforces or diminishes as it learns.

Machine learning has also taken off, especially in the big data space, where there is just too much data for us to analyse manually, and the relationships too complex to understand, so we have started to rely on machine learning to identify patterns we have missed, or even haven't realised yet.

There are significant challenges when we don't know what the machine has learnt and we treat it like a black box. They can have learnt wrongly, or at least not wisely.

An actual example was a machine learning algorithm that was developed to vet CVs for senior management positions. It learnt what was being sought from examples of successful hires in the past, and then was unleashed to wade through piles of candidates, to select the most promising ones. The problem was, it saw that the most important characteristics of a senior manager was being old, white and male, seeing as all the examples it saw were just that. So it went with the inherent biases of the past, and recommended accordingly going forward.

Machine learning systems were also battling then to learn more conceptual patterns. Working to overcome the weaknesses in that approach, it was found that if you put several of these machine learning components in a pipeline, each one getting its inputs from the previous one's outputs, you could achieve what was called 'deep learning', a far more powerful approach. So, you could for example compose a really effective computer vision system by having one component that did the primitive shape detection in images, then subsequent ones that sorted those shapes into concepts.

Concept Spaces, Patterns and Conversations

Large Language Models (part of a field called Generative AI) are an extension of the machine learning approach. [Adams].

They also consist mainly of deep learning layers of machine learning models. These layers may deal with recognising syntax, then phrases, then semantics, then even sentiment.

They start with being trained:

- Training data is prepared carefully, syndicating from different sources for purpose, cleaning it to ensure quality, tokenising it (i.e. converting it into partially processed pieces), and organising it.
- The models learn from that data, organising it into sequences, and frequencies.
- As more data is processed, the weights are adjusted, so that outliers and errors are 'averaged' so that the model reflects most likely cases.

The Language Model is then ready to converse with you:

- As you type, it parses your sentences (called prompts) to understand them. Natural language understanding from text is a problem that has been worked on for years in the AI community - they are using quite a proven set of approaches and technologies for this task, including idiom, nuance and sentiment.
- The Language Model feeds that understanding into its model, looking for matches in its learnings, using the probability weights to find the most likely answer. It keeps both the prompts and the query results as context for the current conversation.
- It renders the query results into natural language. Again, natural language generation is a mature set of technologies, including style and idiom, put to good use in this application.
- What results is a conversation between you and the Language Model - it understands your questions and the context it has built up in the conversation so far, gets pertinent facts from you, and answers you, casually in conversation.

The amazing thing is the quality of that conversation - most who have conversed with a Language Model have a nagging feeling of speaking to a real intelligence.

One concerning thing is sometimes it fabricates things. Not on purpose - there is no 'intent' here. The algorithms have just been found to 'hallucinate' under certain circumstances. To test this, ask ChatGPT about yourself - it sometimes tells you things that are so obviously wrong. Much work is being done, including selecting training data in a far more controlled way, to prevent this problem.

Another problem being worked on is that of focus or attention. Sometimes the context of a conversation, and the use of a word in that context, is subtle and needs to be inferred from that context. Much work is being done on doing this better.

Perhaps at this point, it is pertinent to summarize what we're dealing with here.

- There is no magic, or sentience in Language Models.
- They have pretty slick ways of ingesting large quantities of text to learn from.

- They are mathematically clustering the concepts they find into concept space by seeing how often this concept is used with this other one, and therefore how likely it is to be related.
- They also are pretty good at understanding natural language questions you pose.
- When you ask about something, they are just going to that part of concept space and retrieving the most probable match to what you're asking.
- Then of course, they then use some pretty slick ways of talking to you about what they've found.

Coding from Everywhere

Generative AI has had pretty impressive results in text-based applications, starting with the written word, but now extending into other areas.

It was realised pretty soon that code was just another set of text, and could be analysed for patterns just like the written word. If generative AI could analyse enough code, it would work out the nuances and could then write code itself, pretty well.

Watching my friend's coding conversations with ChatGPT, I see that a coding expert can work with the model as assistant, generating pieces of code from what it has seen as the most likely way of solving the given problem. But I think it's important that the expert carefully inspects the returned code with an experienced eye, looking out for potential problems with logic, or perhaps performance, security or reliability issues.

Do we think that a swamped beginner programmer could be given a leg-up by such a coding assistant? Perhaps, but I would be very concerned of the danger of cobbling together precarious solutions from unscrutinized pieces. A few companies I know have taken the step of mandating no generative AI-sourced solutions allowed in production code.

Designing from Everywhere?

It won't be long though, and the initial work is already being seen, where software designs could be treated in the same way.

If you think about it, designs are just sentences in a graphical language, which can also be analysed, understood, and pieces recommended. Architecture design is just a language, so LLMs could be quite suited to be trained on a selection of software architecture designs, and extract commonality, to help people design software better.

So, soon, AI-powered design recommendations could very likely make their appearance in your favourite design tool.

I recently started looking at Google AppSheets, a low code / no code application development environment, intended to provide reasonably competent business users with a drag and drop application composition ability to put together solutions that use the rest of Google's component stable (Email, Docs, Sheets, Workflow, Search, Maps), all hosted on Google's cloud.

I became really interested when, beyond the usual and expected drag and drop composition from a component palette, I found Google AppSheets AI, an AI-powered application design assistant.

You start a conversation, and it chats to you as an analyst would - extracting your requirements. What kinds of information are you working with, and what kind of user navigation would you expect?

It then generates a suggested app design by composing existing patterns that meet those requirements. That gives you a head-start: an app that does basically what you want, complete with screens, data model, data store and retrieve, and integration to other Google technologies. You can get to that very quickly to test the concepts and then you can polish and refine that as you wish.

I had the weird feeling as I experienced that way of very quickly putting together a meeting app, with reminders over email, maps of where the meetings were, related docs, and consequent action items, that the world of business analysis and the speed of putting together normal business applications was about to be radically changed.

I wondered that evening what value we normal corporate software development lifecycle beings actually bring, given that kind of tool. Is the meeting and document-heavy way of developing what are honestly not rocket science applications, finally under threat, as it should be?

And so it seems we are on the brink of a wave of intelligent software design tools.

But, there are challenges too.

What's really required for LLMs to analyse software designs?

People model very informally these days. Most architecture is just drawings, with no consistent notation used, and no clear rationale given for design decisions.

So, even if we feed LLMs with all the architecture designs out there, how will they learn the architecture intent?

I think there are a number of things we will have to overcome to be able to deal with architecture designs using LLMs. As it stands, it is not clear how to train LLMs so that they can have informed design conversations with us.

- *Documented designs*

  We're going to have to get to better documented designs, so that LLMs can learn from them.

- *Accurate designs*

  Most software design is a conceptual approximation of what was originally aspired to.

  We will probably need software archaeology (reverse engineering designs from patterns used in the source code) to uncover actual designs, in addition to what we hoped to be implemented.

- *Reasoned designs*

  We need to document design intent and choice rationale so that we can understand the reasons for designs.

- *A language of design prompts*

  We need to be able to ask the right design questions of design models - prompts which may require considerable insight into design intent and patterns.

  eg "How do I make sure this design has the required performance characteristics?" is a very difficult question to ask a design consulting LLM at this stage.

The Echo Chamber

The dangers of not thinking clearly are much greater now than ever before. It's not that there's something new in our way of thinking - it's that credulous and confused thinking can be much more lethal in ways it was never before. (Carl Sagan)

Finally, a comment on the dangers of being in an echo chamber - where we are surrounded by a great volume of voices shouting, and echoing one another. It's very difficult to think clearly in that noise.

But let's make an attempt to do that here.

When we're talking about AI, it is far broader than just machine learning models. The field encompasses other disciplines, which are experiencing their own successes and challenges. Let's learn from those.

Self-driving cars

The other really impressive AI-driven technology is self-driving cars. It is also very ambitious - automating our road use. It has had a more measured take-up though, and is grappling with, and having some success in, some very difficult problems.

A car equipped with sensors captures information, including images, of its environment. It processes those to match features like the sides of roads and the middle line. It updates its view of the world around in real-time. Then, it drives in that world, following directions to get to destinations, while avoiding obstacles.

The self-driving car journey has been a bit less of a meteoric rise - initially these cars managed to drive in very controlled environments, only in consistent lighting, and safe from anything untoward happening.

But they progressed in increments in dealing with a complex physical world, and amazingly, they are now pretty safe, reliable, if a bit slow given that they are inherently not as aggressive as we are in taking gaps.

There are risks - there have been some fatalities.

And there are nay-sayers and detractors. In an amusing twist, people like to 'cone' Google's cars (they place a traffic cone on the bonnet) - that apparently makes the car panic and shut down because it can't handle an obstacle that keeps following it around.

Parts of the technology are making their way into ordinary cars. My run of the mill SUV observes the road ahead and warns us of road hazards and unexpected lane changes. It also dims the brights at night when it sees another car approaching.

You don't have to deploy the

whole package at once - parts of the technology are very useful on their own.

Limitations

Language Models have limitations. It seems though that we are not very clear on exactly what those are, and how we should avoid using them beyond certain boundaries.

I recently read that a professor of Philosophy at a London University enrolled ChatGPT into his first year Philosophy class. It really battled with the fundamental concepts, compared to the other human students grappling with the notoriously subtle nuances of Philosophy, and came bottom of the class in the final evaluation. Perhaps some subjects are more challenging than others, and don't need to be targeted now.

Language models are very good at giving answers based on analysis of existing language artefacts. It is also unclear whether they are at all capable of novel or creative thought.

Perhaps this gives us a clue of whether they will be able in the near future to give good design advice?

Personification

We should be very careful of personifying them, as if we are talking to an intelligent being, reasoning in the same way as us.

In summary, I would hope that we would treat them less like the wizard of Oz, the all-knowing dispenser of knowledge, and we would open the curtain, understand what they do, how they do it, and use them well, where they are useful.

And that might mean we start by using parts of their technology right now - they have definitely pioneered an exciting way of communicating with computers conversationally - imagine where that on its own would be revolutionary.

Conclusion

So, if I met you in a lift and had five floors to tell you what this paper is about, I would say I've learnt some stuff by doing, which is how it should be.

I can and will try to list these here, as take-aways. But there's a real danger that they might sound true enough, but trite. You might say – "That's all been said before, but the real world doesn't work like that." And you might say "I'm smarter than that - I've never found complexity I couldn't handle". Perhaps you are, and you can handle the dependencies of 400 applications on each other, at the level of file interchange formats and API signatures. But I'm not. I also don't handle all of the dimensions we need to think in and talk around in large meetings (business, software, technology, infrastructure), at the detail that each stakeholder needs – those conversations easily overwhelm and degenerate. I've needed to find ways of handling this complexity. So I thought I'd share, but with some context from experience, not just building up from textbook models that fit nicely on a page.

Back to the lift conversation. What would I want you to take away from this? Here are a few summarizing thoughts:

- Encapsulation (hiding the details) is great, but you need to know the properties of the internals well - e.g. in the example of a mathematical library, accuracy and speed of calculations.
- A good data model can help you understand what the domain is about; a good data model abstracts away from the noise. In the example of geographical data, a useful map concentrates on specific features of interest, and simplifies them to a specific scale.
- All models are wrong because they are deliberately deficient in some detail. But they can be useful if they abstract away the noise and show you something useful. For that, you need to really understand who wants to see what, at what level of detail.
- Models hide more complexity than you think. There is always more detail in the coastline (a reference to the famous philosophical question: 'How long is a coastline?', to which the answer is 'it depends on the size of your ruler'. There are always more detailed bays and pebbles at a finer scale than your measurement.)
- The map is not the territory – it is both wise and humble to sense-check against others' maps, and measure in reality. Sometimes we think the model in our head is the only true reflection. Remember - we are also looking at things from one particular viewpoint, and with a particular maturity of understanding.
- Models are excellent for allowing you to manifest accurately on paper what's in your head, so you can look at it, reflect on it, and refine it. Shared models are however elusive. Too many times I've proudly presented a detailed diagram that I've worked on for months, and which I know contains so many pearls of hard-won wisdom, only to be met with frowns and questions of confusion, and hours of starting from scratch and having to debate all of the reasoning again and again. You've got to take them with you on the journey, get them to contribute so you can learn too. If you can then get to a shared model, you have a shared language that facilitates high bandwidth conversations.
- Complexity is exponential - it escalates suddenly. How many of us have thought 'how hard can it be?', only to be shown how apparent simplicity is actually naively hiding all sorts of complexities, especially when you add in interactions with the context, and the next level of detail on how it actually works.
- There is naive simplicity at the beginning, moving through increasing complexity, until you get to informed simplicity, born out of understanding the underlying complexity. You can tell where you are in that journey by seeing whether you're managing to simplify, or discovering more and more complexity.

- Generalization is hard, especially simple powerful generalization. Start with simple specifics first, then find appropriate generalizations, where they are actually helpful. It is a real art though - one only has to reflect on coding frameworks we've used to see how one can be beautiful, apt and simple, and another seems contorted and complex.
- Abstraction is hard and fraught with inaccuracy. It is hard because by definition, it involves leaving out unimportant details. Before you know the details (in the uncertainty in the beginning of a project), you have a naïve view of what is required, and therefore you can't judge what's really important or not. After the details have been worked out, it is still hard because often your conceptual model doesn't reflect a correct abstraction of the current details, and you need to change it. But we never do, so the conceptual views often remain naïve and out of touch.
- Patterns are like hammers. When you have one, and you like it, everything looks like a nail. It seems that our thinking easily gets into a rut, finds previous wheel tracks and it's difficult to get out of those. How do we approach design problems with a beginner's mind?
- There are never simple causes and effects - there are always feedback loops. If you think there is a clear cause and a simple fix, you're probably missing some hidden feedback that will cause unexpected consequences down the line.
- There is never one clear direction for a design decision - there are always trade-offs, consequences both bad and good of a design decision. If you decide one way, perhaps security will be improved, but usability will suffer.
- Trade-offs pit one person's needs against another's. Trade-offs mean conflict - people don't like to be traded off. In the example above, the security guy will be happy because the security risks are diminished, but the user experience guy may be fuming because of the extra security screens users will have to go through. Being the arbiter of trade-offs means you have to be good at conflict resolution.
- Decisions based on trade-offs will need to be re-evaluated if and when circumstances change. That's the real challenge behind the agile value of being open to change. We should be open to our architecture customers learning and changing their minds, but we need to know clearly what the knock-on effects will be. That means the most valuable thing you can do as an architect is articulate the design reasoning clearly, so that you (or your successor) won't have unexpected consequences by changing something with important dependencies.
- We need to improve the state of the art of our architecture tools. They are too shallow to allow us to capture design rationale and reason

through its consequences clearly. I believe there is a huge opportunity to substantially improve software architecture practice by introducing better thinking, supported by better tools.

Bilbo returns to Elrond and then goes on to his house, which is being sold at auction, because he is presumed dead.

The story ends with Bilbo settled once again in his hobbit-hole, more comfortable than ever before and yet thinking back on his great adventure.

In this final chapter, Bilbo reflects on the adventurous year he has spent in the company of the dwarves. Although he is returning home, Gandalf tells him what Bilbo himself knows, that he is not the hobbit he once was. It is somewhat symbolic of his new self that his house and furnishings are being sold; there has been a sort of death to the old Bilbo Baggins.

We are told that from this time onward, Bilbo is thought to be unusual, even a bit odd; that he likes to write poetry and visit elves. You understand, then, that his adventures have indeed changed him in some permanent ways.

(Cliff Notes on The Hobbit)

References

[Adams] AI Foundations of Large Language Models, Adams J., Green Mountain Computing, 2024.

[Albin] The Art of Software Architecture - Design Methods and Techniques, Albin S., Wiley Publishing, 2003.

[Alexander-Notes] Notes on the Synthesis of Form, Alexander C., Harvard University Press, 1964.

[Alexander-PatternLanguage] A Pattern Language, Alexander C., Oxford University Press, 1977.

[Alexander-Timeless] The Timeless Way of Building, Alexander C., Oxford University Press, 1979.

[ArchiMate-OMG] Archimate 3.0 Specification, The Open Group, https://pubs.opengroup.org/architecture/archimate30-doc/, accessed August 2024

[Bass-ArchitectureInPractice] Software Architecture in Practice, 4th Edition, Bass L., Clements P. & Kazman R., Addison Wesley, 2021.

[Boake-ArchitectureDecisions] Improving Architectural Design Decisions, Boake

A., Festschrift: dedicated to Derrick Kourie, South African Computer Journal 2008, Issue 41, Dec 2008

[Boake-DesignSupervisor] A Knowledge-based Software Design Supervisor, Boake A., PhD Thesis, University of Pretoria, 1999.

[Boake-FrameworkCompexity] Complexity in Object Oriented Frameworks, Boake A., 1998.

[Boehme] Balancing Agility and Discipline - A Guide for the Perplexed, Boehme B. & Turner R., Addison Wesley, 2003.

[Booch] Object-Oriented Design with Applications, Booch G., Maksimchuk R., Engel M., Young B. Conallen J & Houston K., Addison Wesley, 2007.

[Brooks] The Mythical Man-Month, Ch 16: No Silver Bullet- Essence and Accident in Software Engineering, Brooks F., Addison-Wesley, 1995.

[Clements-DocumentingArchitectures] Documenting Software Architectures - Views and Beyond, Clements P., Bachmann F., Bass L., Garlan D., Ivers J., Little R., Merson P., Nord R. & Stafford J., Addison Wesley, 2010.

[Fowler-AnalysisPatterns] Analysis Patterns - Reusable Object Models, Fowler M., Addison Wesley, 1997.

[Fowler-PatternsOfEnterpriseApplicationArchitecture] Patterns of Enterprise Application Architecture, Fowler M., Addison Wesley, 2002.

[GoF] Design Patterns: Elements of Reusable Object-Oriented Software, Gamma E., Helm R., Johnson R. & Vllisides J., Addison Wesley, 1995.

[Kazman-ATAM] The Architecture Trade-off Analysis Method, Kazman R., Klein M., Barbacci M. & Longstaff T., 4th International Conference on Engineering of Complex Computer Systems (ICECCS '98), August 1998.

[Krutchten-4+1Views] The 4+1 View Model of Architecture, Krutchten P., November 1995, IEEE Software 12(6).

[Lankhorst-Anatomy] The Anatomy of the ArchiMate Language, Lankhorst M. et al, International Journal of Information System Modeling and Design 1(1)

[Lankhorst-AtWork] Enterprise Architecture at Work: Modelling, Communication and Analysis, Lankhorst M. et al, Springer, 2012

[OMG-MDA] Model-Driven Architecture, Object Management Group, https://www.omg.org/mda/, accessed August 2024.

[Rozansky & Woods] Software Systems Architecture - Working with Stakeholders Using Viewpoints and Perspectives, Rozansky N. & Woods E., Addison Wesley, 2005.

[Rumbaugh] Object-Oriented Modelling and Design, Rumbaugh J., Blaha M., Premerlani W., Eddy F. & Lorensen W., Prentice-Hall, 1991.

[UML] The Unified Modelling Language Reference Manual, Rumbaugh J., Jacobson I. & Booch G., 2nd Edition, Addison Wesley, 2005

[Watts] Six Degrees - The Science of a Connected Age, Watts D., Norton, 2003.

The Transformative Effects of AI on International Economics

Rafael Andersson Lipcsey
hunrafael@gmail.com

1. Introduction

It is clear that artificial intelligence (AI) is a transformative force of a magnitude that will greatly affect the lives of humans in the decades to come. While media attention around the topic has truly ramped up only since Open AI's public release of ChatGPT in 2022, AI technologies are already widely employed within healthcare, retail, banking, manufacture and several other sectors. Having established the importance of AI in the years up ahead raises essential follow-up questions in most fields of research, including economics, to which this paper belongs. What exactly is coming, and what does it imply for the world's economies and the field of economic theory? Is AI a force of infinite wealth to be welcomed, or is it just hype, to be treated with caution? This literature review formulates two research questions:

Firstly, it asks, what does the path towards transformative AI look like, and what is the timeframe within which we can expect to see such effects take place? Secondly, it inquires, how much wealth can AI create, and how will that wealth be shared?

Throughout the review, a specific focus will be dedicated to international trade for two reasons. It has been identified that the sectors most impacted by AI are also the most tradeable sectors. At the same time, research on AI's impacts through international value chains, and attempts at integrating AI into international trade theory is rather limited. As such, an international trade lens was deemed valuable.

Los efectos transformadores de la IA en la economía internacional

Introducción

Está claro que la inteligencia artificial (IA) es una fuerza transformadora de una magnitud que afectará en gran medida la vida de los seres humanos en las próximas décadas. Si bien la atención de los medios en torno al tema realmente ha aumentado solo desde el lanzamiento público de ChatGPT por parte de Open AI en 2022, las tecnologías de IA ya se emplean ampliamente en la atención médica, el comercio minorista, la banca, la fabricación y varios otros sectores. Una vez establecida la importancia de la IA en los próximos años, surgen preguntas de seguimiento esenciales en la mayoría de los campos de investigación, incluida la economía,

doi: 10.18278/jpcs.9.1.6

a la que pertenece este artículo. ¿Qué es exactamente lo que viene y qué implica para las economías del mundo y el campo de la teoría económica? ¿Es la IA una fuerza de riqueza infinita que debe ser bienvenida, o es solo una exageración que debe tratarse con cautela? Esta revisión de la literatura formula dos preguntas de investigación:

En primer lugar, se plantea la cuestión de cómo es el camino hacia una IA transformadora y en qué plazo podemos esperar que se produzcan esos efectos. En segundo lugar, se plantea la cuestión de cuánta riqueza puede crear la IA y cómo se repartirá esa riqueza.

A lo largo de la revisión, se dedicará un enfoque específico al comercio internacional por dos razones. Se ha identificado que los sectores más afectados por la IA son también los sectores más comercializables. Al mismo tiempo, la investigación sobre los impactos de la IA a través de las cadenas de valor internacionales y los intentos de integrar la IA en la teoría del comercio internacional son bastante limitados. Por lo tanto, se consideró valioso un enfoque del comercio internacional.

人工智能对国际经济的变革性影响

导论

人工智能(AI)显然是一种巨大的变革力量，将在未来几十年极大地影响人类的生活。尽管自2022年OpenAI公开发布ChatGPT以来，媒体对这一话题的关注才真正升温，但AI技术已广泛应用于医疗保健、零售、银行、制造业和其他几个行业。确定了AI在未来几年的重要性后，引出了在大多数研究领域（包括本文所属的经济学）中的重要后续问题。究竟会发生什么，这对世界经济和经济理论领域意味着什么？AI是一种值得欢迎的无限财富力量，还是只是炒作，需要谨慎对待？本篇文献综述提出了两个研究问题：

第一，通往变革性AI的道路是什么样的，我们能预期在什么时间范围内看到这种影响发生？第二，AI能创造多少财富，这些财富将如何被分享？

整个综述过程将特别关注国际贸易，原因有二。研究发现，受AI影响最大的行业也是最能进行贸易的行业。同时，鲜有研究聚焦于AI通过国际价值链产生的影响，以及将AI融入国际贸易理论的尝试。因此，国际贸易视角被认为是有价值的。

2. How does the path towards transformative AI look and what is the timeframe within which we expect such changes to take place?

2.1 What is transformative AI?

Before embarking on the path towards transformative AI, a precise understanding of its definition is required. “Transformative AI”, has been described in several ways, such as “*...potential future AI that precipitates a transition comparable to (or more significant than) the agricultural* *or industrial revolution*" (Karnofsky, 2016), or "*...advanced AI that could lead to radical changes in welfare, wealth or power*" (Dafoe, 2018).

The most comprehensive review of what transformative AI actually entails, however, can be found in Gruetzemacher and Whittlestone (2022), who break down its definition into three levels of impact: narrowly transformative AI, transformative AI, and radically transformative AI. For the purpose of this study, their definition of transformative AI, namely "*Any AI technology or application with potential to lead to practically irreversible change that is broad enough to impact most important aspects of life and society.*", which, according to the authors may be indicated by "*...a pervasive increase in economic productivity*" (Gruetzemacher & Whittlestone, 2022), is chosen.

2.2 Integrating AI impacts into economic theory

Another necessary step in answering the questions above is briefly examining attempts at integrating AI impacts into economic theory in general, and trade theory in specific. A function popularly used in literature is the Cobb Douglas production function, which describes output as a function of labour and capital. Building on these theoretical fundamentals, Allan Dafoe (2018) created an AI production function, where AI development is deduced as a function of data, talent, compute, time, investment and other indicators such as prior progress and achievements. The use of a modified Cobb Douglas function of that nature however is questioned by some, due to its limits in accounting for shared dependencies and interactions between the various factors of production, or in this case, AI development. Langenkamp (2022) suggests the use of Wardley Maps instead which are built around a three-step process of describing the case, defining technological capabilities and finally ordering capabilities on a map. Perhaps the most ambitious attempt to date however comes from Trammell and Korinek (2023), who focus on three types of transformative AI impacts in economics, namely output growth, wage growth and on the labour share, aiming to bridge the gap between shorter-term economic theory and more longtermist thinking using a variety of theoretical scenarios.

As for attempts at integrating AI impact into international trade theory, literature is still very limited. The only paper identified in this review is by Hazari et al. (2022) who use a Jones and Manuelli production function to introduce effects of automation and AI into an international trade framework. Both Trammell and Korinek (2023), as well as Hazari et al. (2022)'s work will be covered in more detail at a later stage in this review.

2.3 Supply chain and sectoral perspectives from international trade

When trying to predict the path of transformative impacts of AI on international trade, a supply chain/sectoral perspective is worth discussing. A twofold, yet intertwined dilemma is presented: Firstly, what are the sectors which produce things that can be used as inputs to an AI-based transformation? Secondly, which sectors are most likely to be enhanced by AI technology first, or, put differently, in which sectors are AI innovations the most common? It is clear for example, that the manufacturing sector will be heavily affected, as it uses for instance sensors, IoT devices, advanced analytics and, now also AI, to function in the most efficient way possible (Manyika et al., 2017; Stackpole, 2020). At the same time, many of the outputs of the manufacturing sector, such as sensors and chips are being increasingly used to aid the ever-increasing hunger of AI for data and computation.

Process industries like agriculture, chemicals, metals and mining too, have a lot to benefit from AI technologies, such as AI-powered demand sensing (Ferencz et al., 2022). These sectors don't necessarily produce direct inputs into AI, but their output moves through value chains to the manufacturing sectors, which then in turn supply AI with inputs. An enhancement of efficiency can also be seen in service supply chains, where AI offers personalized recommendations, customer support and other innovations (Ferencz et al., 2022).

A further important perspective concerns the observation that AI innovations are highest for sectors which are also the most tradable, hence the most deeply integrated into global value chains. As found by Ferencz et al. (2022), sectors with the highest foreign value added in final demand, a measure for global value chain integration, also have the highest patents, trademarks and publications share in AI innovations.

What can be concluded from the above? Firstly, we can expect AI impact to happen both through forward and backward linkages in global value chains. Furthermore, we have some idea of the sectors that will be impacted and will impact the AI transformation the most. We also know that AI and international trade are heavily interlinked, as the most tradeable sectors are the ones most impacted by AI. One key question however remains: How quickly can we expect the transformative impacts of AI to appear?

2.4 Turning to past disruptions

If we attempt to take a global value chain perspective in tackling the above question, using similar datasets from the OECD which Ferencz et al. (2022) used for tradability, we don't get very far. Databases such as the ICIO (Inter-Country Input Output Tables), and the Leontief input-output methodologies behind it can show the ultimate effects of shocks to the global economy (and individual countries and sectors) however they do not provide any time perspective of when these are expected to happen.

One option is to turn to past technological disruptions and assume that AI impacts will look somewhat similar. Mateos-Garcia (2020) theorizes that AI impacts will take longer to materialize than newspaper headlines make us believe. Jobs will not disappear completely, but will rather change and evolve over time, similarly to the evolution of the internet. He argues that prediction machines like AI do not only increase the amount of decisions to be made based on AI recommendations, but also the number of decisions which need to be made in order to integrate AI into our economies and societies in a safe and regulated manner. More about the decision-making bottleneck will be discussed below, however the comparison of the AI revolution to the impacts of the internet should be nuanced. On August 6, 1991 the World Wide Web as we know it became commercially available to consumers (Bryant, 2011), and it reached a hundred million users in a little over 8 years, or about 100 months later, on November 12, 1999 (The New York Times, 1999). Meanwhile, Bing AI, powered by Open AI's ChatGPT engine reached 100 million users in about a month (Mashable, 2023). While the above is undeniably not a completely fair comparison, it may give us an indication regarding the sheer magnitude of the rate of AI adoption.

2.5 Feedback loops

Another way to attempt to quantify the leap towards transformative AI is by investigating feedback loops. One such loop is linked to the automation of computer production. If AI could theoretically replace all the labour needed in the production of computers, it could technically produce itself, which would fuel a loop leading potentially to exponential growth in adoption. This review did not find any research exploring such a scenario with a time frame included. According to a study by McKinsey Global Institute, half of today's work activities could be automated by 2055 (Manyika et al., 2017). In addition, it is predicted that physical activities, such as those found in manufacturing have the highest (81 percent) automation potential. Krishanswamy meanwhile explores the possibility of fully automating semiconductor assembly and testing. He concludes that full (level 5) automation is no longer an unreachable myth but provides no timeline for when this could be achieved. A last perspective stemming from the field of molecular biology comes from Kriegman et al (2021), who managed to create an AI designed, self-replicating and configurable organism called a xenobot, which marks one of the very first steps towards a future where self-replication of organisms is no longer just a concept of science fiction.

Feedback loops however need not to be limited to manufacturing but can also be knowledge based. Davidson (2021) explores how AI could affect growth over the long term. He introduces an additional feedback loop apart from the well-known *more ideas → more people → more ideas*, which has traditionally driven economic growth. The new loop, *more ideas → more AI systems → more ideas* could potentially lead to exponential growth, and thus significant impacts of AI on the world. Davidson (2021) assigns a higher than 30% probability that human-level AI has been developed in time for economic growth to reach 30 percent by the year of 2100. Furthermore, he theorizes that over a third of that growth would happen due to the birth of human-level AI.

2.6 Bottlenecks

A further approach that can be taken is to consider possible bottlenecks for rapid AI adoption. These, along with an evaluation of their solvability can provide us with valuable information regarding the feasibility of transformative AI within the next decades.

Bottlenecks can be broadly classified into four categories: supply chain, regulatory, technological, and knowledge based. To keep up with exponential economic growth, inputs to production such as raw materials (Davidson, 2021), will need to be extracted, as well as intermediate products, such as chips and semiconductors will need to be produced, at a rate that can keep up. In addition, logistics lines and power grids will also need to be scaled up to a very significant extent. Next, as covered earlier, the number of decisions on how to safely integrate AI into our economies and societies will vastly increase (Mateos-Garcia, 2019). This also relates to Davidson (2021)'s argument regarding the possibility that humanity will simply decide to harness the potential of AI in a sustainable and more controlled way, even if it was possible to choose exponential growth. Furthermore, technical and technological limits, such as a roof to the type and percentage of tasks automatable by AI, or the requirement of technologies for upscaling that we do not yet possess could slow down progress (Davidson, 2021). Finally, perhaps too few new innovations will be made and too slowly, and perhaps we will lack the resources to upskill and reskill people at a rate fast enough to keep up. All of the above could prove to be detrimental for fast paced, AI supported growth, however at the same time, many could be alleviated by AI technologies themselves.

2.7 AI problems require AI solutions?

When it comes to specific benefits of AI for economies, the literature is fairly vast, and some of the improvements discussed could alleviate, or completely eliminate bottlenecks discussed above. For instance, AI helps the development of more proactive and efficient global supply chains through its predictive capabilities (Jayathilaka, 2022; Achar, 2019; Ferencz et al, 2022), which may alleviate supply chain and logistical bottlenecks. AI is also used for boosting the efficiency of compliance software, streamlines contract creation (through simplifying legal language) (Jayathilaka, 2022; Jones, 2023), and bolsters trade negotiations (through advanced translation) (Achar), all of which could reduce regulatory and decision burdens. Furthermore, technological capabilities already are, and will be further improved using AI technology, such as significant advances in computing power and decreasing costs (Anderson & Rainie, 2018). Finally, AI is to an increasing degree used for education management and delivery. AI technologies can both be employed to reduce regulatory and administrative burden on educators, freeing up precious time for teaching, as well as enhance students' learning through adaptive learning techniques (Miao et al., 2021).

3. How much wealth can transformative AI create and how will that wealth be shared?

Based on the first part of this review, it is clear that while faced with large uncertainty, and several bottlenecks, AI has the potential to strongly boost the efficiency of global value and production chains and bring about strong economic growth. Is it possible however to predict how much wealth transformative AI can create and how that wealth will be shared?

3.1 Scenarios of growth

Predicting how much growth a technology in its beginning stages can bring to the world economy is exceedingly difficult, hence we must rely on scenario building and assumptions. Furthermore, outcomes vary widely depending on the type of model used. Both Davidson (2021) and Trammell and Korinek (2023) employ various models in their analyses, such as complete or partial substitution of AI into a production function, inclusion of AI into task-based functions, as well as standard and exogenous growth models. While a variety of scenarios are used, broadly speaking we can discern between three main ones: standard growth, explosive growth and stagnation. Standard growth is exponential, as has been over the last 150 years, meanwhile explosive growth can be much higher than that. Combined with historical evidence concerning the increasing pace of growth, and the above detailed idea-based feedback loops leads Davidson (2021) to assign a 10 percent probability to explosive growth occurring by 2100. Trammell and Korinek (2023) conclude that AI aided explosive, even super-exponential growth is possible for a certain time, until production reaches limiting factors such as energy production or land usage. Still, Trammell and Trammell and Korinek (2023) note that as of now, we can't put a timeframe to transformative impacts from AI, if these even were to take place.

Apart from standard and explosive growth scenarios, both Davidson (2021) and Trammell and Korinek (2023) consider possibilities of stagnation, and they also introduce an interesting and relevant gap between futurist research and economic theory, noting the absence of considerations regarding existential risks of AI. This omission, they argue, is not due to lack of interest, but rather the inherent challenges in incorporating such risks into growth models. More broadly, they theorize that the key here is the degree to which AI will replace human labour. As long as human labour will remain a bottleneck for AI growth, and AI self-replication feedback loops won't take place, humans will maintain control over AI, and not vice versa. Early attempts at bridging this gap have been made by Acemoglu and Lensman (2023), as well as Jones (2024). The former seek to predict optimal adoption rates of AI technologies by considering costs firms would incur in reverting back to non-AI technologies in the event of an AI catastrophe, while Jones (2024) employs welfare functions to trade off growth and existential risk. Future research in this field stands to benefit from more concrete forecasts of the costs incurred from various types of

AI disasters, for which, methodologies like inoperability analysis, originally developed for natural disasters (Haimes & Jiang, 2001; Santos & Jaimes, 2004) may prove useful.

A somewhat more concrete attempt at predictions of growth comes in the form of a 2018 discussion paper by Bughin et al. from McKinsey Global Institute. By 2030, the value-added gains boost stemming from AI is predicted to be 26 percent, with externalities and transition costs bringing the net impact to 16 percent. An important point brought forward in the paper is the magnifying power of competitive pressure on AI adoption. By 2030, competitive pressure is expected to boost AI adoption by 13 percentage points, from 25 to 48 percent (Bughin et al., 2018). Goldman Sachs Research, meanwhile, takes a more conservative stance, forecasting a cumulative boost to GDP of 7 percent in the period 2023-2033 (Goldman Sachs, 2023).

3.2 Scenarios of growth: Lessons from the history of general-purpose technologies

Predictions of significant short-term accelerations in productivity and growth may be somewhat nuanced by insights from studies on productivity gains from previous general-purpose technologies (GPTs). GPTs can be described as technologies that spread to all sectors of an economy, improve over time, and completely transform the ways in which we invent and produce (Bresnahan et. al, 1995). Examples include steam power, electricity and computers, which despite wide adoption did not yield significant productivity benefits, at least not in the short to medium term. Questions have been raised about whether this perplexing phenomenon, coined the Solow Paradox (Solow, 1987), might also apply to transformative AI (Brynjolfsson et. al, 2017; Ding & Dafoe, 2023). It is plausible that, akin to previous GPTs, the productivity benefits of AI will manifest only after a significant time lag, due to more time needed for its wide diffusion, and the development and implementation of complementary innovations like cloud infrastructure and service-based business models.

3.3 Trade frictions: lessons from the present and past

Many of the benefits that AI brings to global value chains have already been discussed above. Most of the examples brought up all have one common theme: reduction of trade frictions. Thus, taking a trade frictions perspective in attempting to answer how much wealth transformative AI can bring to the world economy is worthwhile.

In looking at the scene of online trade, some conclusions can be drawn. For example, it has been found that trade frictions caused by physical geographic distance when it comes to trade in goods are lower for online trade than for offline trade, with distance coefficients nearly halved (for the EU) of -0.747 for online, and -1.294 for offline trade (Gomez-Herrera et al, 2014). A study on a Norwegian dataset meanwhile found that a high degree of internet availability could actually lead to a slight increase in elasticity of trade when it comes to distance, and thus make trade even more sensitive to distance than it was before (Akerman et al., 2018). It seems, given the above, that even when it comes to more historic technological advances such as the adoption of internet, consensus is lacking on whether, and if so, how much such technologies have reduced trade frictions. Much of this can most likely be attributed to the sheer magnitude and diversity of the online trading space, and the lack of datasets that might be used to tackle this problem.

That being said, even for AI, specific use cases can provide proof of concept for its potential in reducing trade frictions, specifically when it comes to AI language translation models. Brynjolfsson et al. (2018) found that the introduction of improved machine translation systems could increase international trade on eBay by 10.9 percent, a clear testament for the usefulness of AI in this specific case. While research in this field is still in its infancy, it can be expected that an increasing number of studies relating to specific cases will be published in the years to come. Provision of a macro perspective will however surely prove to be a difficult challenge.

3.4 Sectoral divide

When trying to answer the question of how AI induced wealth will be shared, it is a good exercise to take a sectoral perspective first. It is clear, as one might also have read in one of numerous media articles, that some sectors will benefit more from AI innovations than others. The list of sectors is long, and predictions varied, however a few clear winners, such as manufacturing, education, healthcare, agriculture, computer manufacturing and transport seem to emerge (Forbes, 2022; Miao et al., 2021; Ferencz et al, 2022). Based on earlier findings in this review, it can also be hypothesized that sectors in which AI innovations are the highest are also sectors where AI innovation is needed the most, and these are consequently also the most tradeable sectors.

Focus is therefore once again directed towards global value chains, and the role of international trade in progressing, or hindering AI induced growth. That being said, while hypothesizing about which sectors will be the most affected provides some value, this review is not aware of any papers that aim to quantify differences of magnitude in economic impact between sectors. In Bughin et al. (2018), the macroeconomic impact of AI is predicted to be 2.3 times the magnitude for telecom and high-tech sectors than healthcare, which is a substantial difference. It is also noted in the paper, that more firm- and sector-level data is needed for a more comprehensive analysis of sectoral impacts.

3.5 Country divide: Lessons of history

Another dimension to consider is the country divide, more specifically the gap between developed and developing countries. Will AI induced growth close the gap or widen it further? Again, lessons of history should be examined, with internet access an obvious choice for a proxy. Again, literature seems to be scarce. According to a 2022 review by the World Bank, some studies have found that internet enabled technologies, such as mobile money in Kenya have managed to increase incomes and reduce poverty. Furthermore, five studies seem to support the theory that internet infrastructure has increased incomes and consumption in Africa. At the same time, it was also found that subsidizing internet access to individuals already possessing a phone contract, but who did not use roaming data, had limited effects on well-being (Hjort & Sacchetto, 2022). It is concluded that while research is scarce, effects seem to be promising.

3.6 Country divide: General predictions

Perhaps the most prominent perspective in research relating to sharing of AI induced wealth is that of a country divide, between developed and developing countries. Some findings are favourable towards developing countries. For instance, it is speculated that an AI aided shift towards more skill intensive industries could be utilized by developing countries to transform the structure of their own economies and can penetrate sectors that were not previously available to them, because their resources had been tied up (Kouka & Magallanes, 2022). It is also theorized that developing countries, which are more integrated into global value chains than developed ones (both backward and forward linkages of non-OECD countries are stronger than OECD economies'), will benefit greatly from reductions in international trade frictions (for instance through AI powered translation). In addition, reduced compliance costs and an overall decreased regulatory burden brought forward by AI technology can increase accessibility of trade financing (Jayathilaka, 2022), which in combination with reduced trade barriers could disproportionately benefit especially the least developed countries.

That being said, an overwhelming share of the research in the field points towards a bleak future for developing countries, if we follow the trajectory currently lined out. A common theme that can be identified is control over technology. Those who control the production (for example chip production), and those who control the development of AI technologies, and technologies adjacent to AI, will be the big winners of the next few decades. Firstly, as AI is introduced into economies and societies, those in control of the technology will have a very high economic and political bargaining power against those who don't (Brynjolfsson et al, 2019; Kouka & Magallanes, 2022).

Risks of onshoring also await developing countries. As AI enabled automation of production reduces the need for cheap labour, multinationals could choose to bring production closer to home, which can lead to further decrease on growth potential and comparative advantage for countries which depend highly on foreign direct investment (FDI) (Artuc et al, 2023; Spence, 2022). As a result, large labour market adjustments would be needed, at a pace that many countries may not be able to keep up with. Further disparities may be created in developing countries through the widening gap between more advanced, internationally active firms that account for a large portion of exports and small informal firms that account for a large share of low skilled and manual employment (Artuc et al, 2023). Furthermore, as access to up to date, advanced databases becomes essential for competitiveness, SMEs, especially in less advanced economies, will suffer (Jayathilaka, 2022). Finally, obstacles of international law also prove to be detrimental. Tariff rates are the highest in developing countries, many of which do not participate in the WTO Information Technology Agreement. This in itself will act as a barrier for adoption of AI technologies via trade, as well as for the development of in-house AI technologies. Bughin et al. (2018) come to similar conclusions, where net GDP impact of AI adoption hovers around 20 percent for advanced economies, but doesn't even reach 10, for the least advanced economies by the year 2030.

3.7 Country divide: International trade theory perspective

A final perspective on wealth sharing can be examined through the only known attempt at integrating AI impacts into international trade theory. Hazari et al. (2022) find that AI could reverse trade patterns and lead to factor intensity reversals, resulting in the creation of a Leontief paradox (Hazari et. al, 2022). This finding resonates with the conclusions in Kiyota and Kurokawa (2021), who conclude that factor reversals already exist, based on an analysis of Japanese prefectural data. A factor intensity reversal essentially entails a scenario where the relative abundance of specific factors shifts in a direction opposite to a country's competitive advantage (Hillman, A.L. and Hirsch, 1979). A historical example of this is the decline in manufacturing in developed countries alongside its rise in developing countries, leading to a relative abundance of labour in developing countries, thus giving them a comparative advantage in manufacturing.

A Leontief paradox occurs when a country with a higher capital per worker ratio has a lower capital per labour ratio in exports rather than imports. In other words, if a country is labour abundant, it would have capital intensive exports and imports of labour-intensive goods. The exact implications of a scenario where developing countries experience factor intensity reversals are hard to predict. However, generally speaking, a factor reversal for developing countries would imply a shift away from their competitive advantage, namely exports of labour-intensive goods, and also be in line with predictions of increased onshoring by developed countries, putting developing countries under high pressure to adapt in a short amount of time.

4. Discussion and Summary

Perhaps the most overarching conclusion that can be drawn from this review is the need for more research. When it comes to integration of AI into economic theory, we are very much at the beginning stages, and that applies to international trade especially. As for impacts of AI, specific use cases have been discussed in detail, however overarching perspectives weighing benefits against costs and timeframes have been provided to a much lesser extent, rather unsurprisingly so.

Still, some conclusions can be drawn, which are presented below. The path towards transformative AI looks complex, as expected. It seems that certain sectors will both be impacted and drive AI innovation to a larger extent than others, such as manufacturing and high technology. It is also clear that most of these sectors are highly tradeable, which implies the importance of international trade in driving AI innovation forward. Past disruptions such as the introduction of the internet point towards a more gradual adoption of AI, and thus more gradually appearing impacts. Yet, some examples, such as the adoption rate of Bing AI could imply that something entirely different is about to unfold. If certain feedback loops become reality, such as the self-replication of machines, or AI based rapid knowledge enhancement, a scenario of rapid integration of AI into our economies and societies could occur, where human level AI has been developed, and economic growth could reach 30 percent by the year 2100 (Davidson, 2021). Several supply chain, regulatory, technological, and knowledge-based bottlenecks stand in the way however, some of which could be solved or alleviated by AI technology itself, and some which can't.

Predicting how much wealth AI can create is difficult, too. We may employ various growth scenarios, starting from the current norm of exponential growth to explosive growth, or even stagnation. Some predict explosive growth to take place by 2100 with a 10 percent probability (Davidson, 2021), while others simulate a global value-added boost of 26 percent by 2030 (Bughin et al., 2018). Growth predictions in the short-to-medium term are further complicated by historical observations of similarly transformative technologies failing to produce promised productivity benefits, and the lack of research considering catastrophic AI impacts as a limiting factor.

Taking an international trade perspective, AI technologies show potential in reducing trade frictions, which could in turn reduce supply chain bottlenecks in the way of explosive growth. Still, more overarching studies are needed to be able to state this with any confidence.

The division of wealth created by AI can be viewed on for instance a sectoral level, or with a developed versus developing countries perspective (while recognizing that all countries are different and will need to make decisions on how to best parry the AI revolution based on their economies' individual characteristics). It can be speculated that sectors in which AI innovations are the highest, and which contribute the most to AI innovation, will see the most growth, and thus gain an increasingly dominant position in national and international value chains. Interestingly, sectors with the highest level of AI innovation are also most integrated into global value chains, and therefore international trade will most likely become a key battling ground where rapid adoption of AI technologies will be one of the key factors to ensure competitiveness.

Looking at a historical perspective, we see some proof that the introduction of new technologies can create wealth in disadvantaged countries, however more research is needed for conclusive evidence. While AI technologies will surely bring some opportunities to such countries, such as the chance for a shift towards more skill intensive economies, and a reduction in trade frictions, the former may also lead to their doom, if they can't adapt on time. Furthermore, those in control of the knowledge, and manufacturing capabilities linked to AI will gain further bargaining power against those who don't. Lastly, as AI replaces increasing shares of the workforce, offshoring may turn to onshoring, further decreasing the competitive advantage for countries exporting labour intensive goods. It is estimated that the net impact on advanced economies from AI technologies will be up to 4 times larger than for the least advanced economies (Bughin et al., 2018).

Integration of AI impacts into international trade theory is still very limited, however emerging research raises the question: What may happen if the adoption of AI technologies leads to factor intensity reversals? The implications, again, for developing countries could be more negative than positive.

5. Conclusion

What then, can we conclude from the above? We are currently at a point where research in this field remains significantly underdeveloped. In other words, we do not yet fully comprehend the economic implications AI has in store for us. Some studies suggest the potential for explosive growth, which could greatly benefit the development of humanity. However, it is evident that more research, particularly with considerations of AI risk, and costs of AI-induced catastrophes is necessary to add nuance to the overly optimistic projections of current models. Additionally, based on the knowledge we currently possess, it appears that the divide between developed and developing countries will widen as a consequence of AI adoption.

In light of this, it is recommended to apply the precautionary principle and select a measured path of AI adoption. Policymakers should ensure that introduction of AI technologies into economies and societies happen in a controlled manner. Emphasis must be placed on AI safety and the numerous unknowns in this domain. Simultaneously, policy frameworks must be established to better equip developing countries for the transformative effects of AI. This can be achieved by ensuring their access to AI technologies, easing trade barriers for ICT goods, and preparing economic safety nets to mitigate labour market impacts. Rather than fully replacing labour, our focus should be on augmenting it with AI, thereby ensuring that the bargaining power of workers in less advantaged countries is preserved.

References

Acemoglu, D. and Lensman, T., 2023. Regulating transformative technologies (No. w31461). *National Bureau of Economic Research.*

Achar, S., 2019. Early consequences regarding the impact of artificial intelligence on international trade. *American Journal of Trade and Policy*, 6(3), pp.119-126.

Akerman, A., Leuven, E. and Mogstad, M., 2022. Information frictions, internet, and the relationship between distance and trade. *American Economic Journal: Applied Economics, 14*(1), pp.133-163.

Anderson, J. and Rainie, L., 2018. 3. Improvements ahead: how humans and ai might evolve together in the next decade. *Pew Research Center: Internet, Science & Tech.*

Artuc, E., Bastos, P., Copestake, A. and Rijkers, B., 2022. Robots and trade: implications for developing countries. In *Robots and AI* (pp. 232-274). Routledge.

Bresnahan, Timothy F., and M. Trajtenberg. 1995. General Purpose Technologies 'Engines of Growth'?. *Journal of Econometrics* 65 (1): 83–108

Bryant, M., 2011. "20 years ago today, the World Wide Web opened to the public," *The Next Web*, 6 August.

Brynjolfsson, E., Rock, D. and Syverson, C., 2017. Artificial Intelligence and the Modern Productivity Paradox: A Clash of Expectations and Statistics. *National Bureau of Economic Research*, pp.23–57.

Brynjolfsson, E., Hui, X. and Liu, M., 2019. Does machine translation affect international trade? evidence from a large digital platform. *Management Science*, *65*(12), pp.5449-5460.

Bughin, J., Seong, J., Manyika, J., Chui, M. and Joshi, R., 2018. Notes from the AI frontier: Modeling the impact of AI on the world economy. *McKinsey Global Institute, 4.*

Dafoe, A., 2018. AI governance: a research agenda. *Governance of AI Program, Future of Humanity Institute, University of Oxford: Oxford, UK, 1442*, p.1443.

Ding, J. and Dafoe, A., 2023. Engines of power: Electricity, AI, and general-purpose, military transformations. *European Journal of International Security*, 8(3), pp.377-394.

Davidson, T., 2021. Could advanced AI drive explosive economic growth. *Open Philanthropy.*

Ferencz, J., González, J.L. and García, I.O., 2022. Artificial Intelligence and International Trade: Some Preliminary Implications. *OECD publishing.*

Forbes, 2022. Council Post: 16 Industries and Functions That Will Benefit From AI In 2022 and Beyond. *Forbes Magazine.* Available at: https://www.forbes.com/sites/forbestechcouncil/2022/01/13/16-industries-and-functions-that-will-benefit-from-ai-in-2022-and-beyond/?sh=38076131477d.

Goldman Sachs, 2023. Generative AI Could Raise Global GDP by 7%. *Goldman Sachs.* Available at: www.goldmansachs.com/intelligence/pages/generative-ai-could-raise-global-gdp-by-7-percent.html.

Gomez-Herrera, E., Martens, B. and Turlea, G., 2014. The Drivers and Impediments for Cross-Border E-Commerce in the EU. *Information Economics and Policy, 28,* pp.83-96.

Gruetzemacher, R. and Whittlestone, J., 2022. The Transformative Potential of Artificial Intelligence. *Futures, 135,* p.102884.

Haimes, Y.Y. and Jiang, P., 2001. Leontief-Based Model of Risk in Complex Interconnected Infrastructures. *Journal of Infrastructure Systems,* 7(1), pp.1-12.

Hazari, B., Lai, J.T. and Mohan, V., 2022. A Note on the Implications of Automation and Artificial Intelligence for International Trade. *Arthaniti: Journal of Economic Theory and Practice,* p.09767479221129186.

Hillman, A.L. and Hirsch, S., 1979. Factor Intensity Reversals: Conceptual Experiments with Traded Goods Aggregates. *Weltwirtschaftliches Archiv, 115*(2), pp.272-283.

Hjort, J. and Sacchetto, C., 2022. Can Internet Access Lead to Improved Economic Outcomes?, *World Bank Blogs.* Available at: https://blogs.worldbank.org/digital-development/can-internet-access-lead-improved-economic-outcomes.

Jayathilaka, U.R., 2022. The Role of Artificial Intelligence In Accelerating International Trade: Evidence From Panel Data Analysis. *Reviews of Contemporary Business Analytics, 5*(1), pp.1-15.

Jones, C.I., 2024. The AI Dilemma: Growth Versus Existential Risk. *National Bureau of Economic Research.*

Jones, E., 2023. Digital Disruption: Artificial Intelligence and International Trade Policy. *Oxford Review of Economic Policy, 39*(1), pp.70-84.

Kiyota, K. and Kurokawa, Y., 2022. Factor Intensity Reversals Redux: Feenstra is Right!. *Review of International Economics, 30*(4), pp.885-914.

Kouka, M. and Magallanes, M.C., 2022. Technological Trivergence and International Trade: A Literature Review. *Harvard University.*

Kriegman, S., Blackiston, D., Levin, M. and Bongard, J., 2021. Kinematic Self-Replication in Reconfigurable Organisms. *Proceedings of the National Academy of Sciences, 118*(49), p.e2112672118

Karnofsky, H., 2016. Some Background on our Views Regarding Advanced Artificial Intelligence. Blog. Available at: https://www.openphilanthropy.org/blog/some-background-our-views-regarding-advanced-artificial-intelligence.

Krishnaswamy, S. (no date) Challenges and Strategies to Achieve Full Automation in Semiconductor Assembly and Test, *SEMI.* Available at: https://semi.org/en/about/AMAT.

Langenkamp, M. and Yue, D.N., 2022, July. How Open Source Machine Learning Software Shapes AI. In *Proceedings of the 2022 AAAI/ACM Conference on AI, Ethics, and Society* (pp. 385-395).

Manyika, J., Chui, M., Miremadi, M., Bughin, J., George, K., Willmott, P. and Dewhurst, M., 2017. A future that works: AI, automation, employment, and productivity. *McKinsey Global Institute Research, Tech. Rep, 60*, pp.1-135.

Mateos-Garcia, J., 2021. The Economics of Artificial Intelligence today. *The Gradient.* Available at: https://thegradient.pub/the-economics-of-ai-today/

Mauran, C., 2023. Bing, yes that Bing, now has 100 million daily users. *Mashable*, 9 March. Available at: https://mashable.com/article/microsoft-bing-100-million-daily-users-ai-chatbot.

Miao, F., Holmes, W., Huang, R. and Zhang, H., 2021. AI and Education: A guidance for Policymakers. *UNESCO Publishing.*

Santos, J. R., & Haimes, Y. Y., 200). Modeling the Demand Reduction Input-Output (I-O) Inoperability Due to Terrorism of Interconnected Infrastructures. *Risk Analysis: An International Journal*, 24(6), 1437-1451. DOI: 10.1111/j.0272-4332.2004.00540.x

Spence, M., 2022. Automation, Augmentation, Value Creation & the Distribution of Income & Wealth. *Daedalus, 151*(2), pp.244-255.

Solow, R.M., 1987. We'd Better Watch Out. *New York Times Book Review*, July 12:36.

Stackpole, B., 2020. 5 Supply Chain Technologies that Deliver Competitive Advantage, *MIT Sloan*. Available at: https://mitsloan.mit.edu/ideas-made-to-matter/5-supply-chain-technologies-deliver-competitive-advantage.

The New York Times, 1999. Internet Users Now Exceed 100 Million. *The New York Times*, 12 November, 1999.

Trammell, P. and Korinek, A., 2023. Economic Growth under Transformative AI: A Guide to the Vast Range of Possibilities for Output Growth, Wages, and the Labor Share. *Global Priorities Institute*.

Developing Interest in Complex Systems: It's Where the Wicked Problems Live

Tim Craske

Systems Thinking Consultant, Geoscientist and Ore Discoverer

timcraske50@gmail.com

You may be curious as to how and why people get interested in Systems Thinking and its use in understanding the world in which we live. Working with Complex Systems thinking involves a holistic understanding of the interconnections within systems, the ability to analyse their dynamics, and a willingness to embrace uncertainty to tackle wicked problems and foster innovation.

But I am already diving too deep. My own interest in holistic thinking started over 30 years ago when I became a project generation geologist for Western Mining Corporation in Australia. By the 1980's, for a project to be accepted into the exploration portfolio, it had to be supported by a holistic integration of likely geological processes with empirical observations and regional data.

As with successful study of other complex systems, this holistic modelling process involved an interdisciplinary approach, drawing on the skills and wisdom of geophysicists, geochemists and other specialists. This collaborative process required trust, candour and support between peers and management, augmented by mentoring from internal experts.

This approach pushed targeting beyond the simple cookie cutter approach of looking directly for features seen in other deposits, towards an out-of-the-box perspective of what could be and most importantly where it could be. That said, it was still considered fundamental to start with building a list and mental model of mappable features at each type deposit. Both large and small deposits were studied in an attempt to determine what features, geometries could be used to differentiate between targets that could be giants from those that might be small or low grade and not be economically mineable.

Western Mining's exploration division had a very strong culture that made you feel like family. This encouraged people to take risks and try different approaches. We always tested a range of targets before leaving a project. Management understood it takes several years in a region to begin to get to grips with the limits and opportunities. Often where you end up is some distance from where you start as you learn from your failures. Key here is to fail fast and learn quickly. You learn nothing by being timid. Fortune favours the brave.

After I left Western Mining in 2001, I worked for a number of junior

doi: 10.18278/jpcs.9.1.1

companies during the industry downturn before the China led super-cycle took off, and continued even through the Global Financial Crisis. In 2011 I read an interesting, perhaps seminal article in Economic Geology Newsletter by a former peer and technical manager, Dr Jon Hronsky. Jon's article described how orogenic gold hydrothermal deposit systems could be the result of self-organised complex system (SOCS), whereby the fluid self-organises to overcome a local barrier or trap, resulting in a cascade of energy and fluid release that would result in deposition of metals.

I was fascinated by the new terminology, and the possibility that mineral systems could have goals, overcome barriers to fluid movement to reach the goal of deposition, all the while shedding energy and increasing entropy but locally concentrating metals. This set me on a journey from about 2015 to try and understand mineral systems better. Strangely enough through this journey I now understand that Hronsky's model is limited, likely flawed, and better models exist to explain ore geosystem phenomena.

In 2015, I organised the first workshop retreat to address learning more about systems thinking and applications in exploration geoscience. Whilst trying to go from zero to hero in one weekend, we did have a lot of fun. One of the participants, Deborah Lord, connected the group to an environmental systems scientist at CSIRO named Ashley Sparrow. We followed up with a Saturday at University of Western Australia to listen to Ashley and think about applications in geoscience. I did not know then what I learned at NECSI course this February, 2024, that is the Law of Universality. This systems "law" is what makes all knowledge useful.

What is the Law of Universality?

The Law of Universality is at the core of understanding complex systems that are all around us. Put simply the law says that it is possible to understand a variety of patterns and behaviours in different systems as they often share the same underlying concepts. This is where Ashley's contribution to our story fits in.

At the core of Universality is scale. As we move up scales in complex systems, we start to see the important simple rules that give rise to the diverse patterns. That is to say there are only a few properties that are important at a larger scale perspective, that you can never map all the details and you don't need to.

Further, it also means that gathering diverse groups of people together who have knowledge gained in different disciplines, life experiences or cultures is probably the best way to make progress in understanding systems, how patterns form, and what are the key leverage points for change or impact.

So, we can take ideas from other disciplines to understand the patterns in, say geology and mineralising systems.

This should be considered a key breakthrough in progressing the understanding of complex geosystems. It means we can look at a science like astronomy that has been around for several thousand years and apply some of the principal rules to solving the problems in geology, a science that is only 200 years old. It also means that the progress that was made in social, biological, financial and ecological science over the last 50 years should be able to be applied to understanding the behaviour and patterns in geosystems and mineralising geosystems. Knowing anything suddenly becomes useful!

As "discovery scientists" who study complex mineralising systems, we need to work out the things that truly matter, what is important and what is not, and study and treat these important things carefully. As a blog commentator reminded me, Steve Jobs once said, "Innovation distinguishes between a leader and a follower." Applying principles from various disciplines to understand complex systems truly embodies this spirit of innovation. I now believe that this approach to bridging gaps across different fields will lead to more discoveries.

Complex Systems thinking encourages a focus on emergent phenomena

Complex Systems thinking encourages a focus on emergent phenomena – patterns and behaviours that arise from interactions among system components. By understanding the underlying mechanisms driving emergence, we can identify opportunities for innovation.

This involves fostering conditions (organisational culture) that promotes serendipity, diversity, and experimentation within the system. There is an ongoing exploration of how to innovate in systems, i.e. acknowledging that the linear way of innovating does not work in complex situations and for transforming systems. A systemic approach to thinking invites the innovation community to apply for funding aimed at establishing ecosystems or platforms dedicated to challenge-based, adaptive innovation. Systemic innovation should be adaptive, and the most adaptive way to organise innovation processes is in an innovation ecosystem. Such a system can embrace all the actors needed for handling the complexity (industry, research institutions, public agencies, civil society, and media, among others). This brings me to my next growth stage, when I became a member of Systems Innovation, and worked through their excellent online courses and eBooks (https://www.systemsinnovation.network/about).

Ecosystems like SI can inspire portfolios of interventions and activities, bringing together all actors and stakeholders that are needed for change, spanning from industry, research institutions to public sector, government and communities. If rigged for the long-term, as they can orchestrate collaboration across sectors, and collaborations that must continue even after a project ends.

The long-term perspective of an ecosystem, and the actors within it are both beneficiaries when it comes to scaling new innovations.

However, as this work involves paradigm shifts for others to engage and change thinking the final driver of acceptance and change will be deeply human and social in its nature. Change affects people, and paradigm shifts affect things such as they never go back to how they were. In Geoscience the greatest paradigm shift in my lifetime was the advent of Plate Tectonics Theory which arguably has changed all geologist world views of how the Earth works.

Whatever the new idea, difficulties usually come from scaling up from pilot projects, like the first stock and flow mineralising systems map for Hercynian Tin deposits. People are resistant to change and new perspectives. This is often due to the absence of essential actors within their environments to incentivise and lead change. The key is to grow a well-integrated ecosystem, where relevant stakeholders can be engaged as needed, and the composition of stakeholders can evolve in tandem with the concepts progress. This is where the idea for "Thinkercafe" came from, to corral some of the best thinkers in Australia to build, review and model the new way. I am grateful to all those who have participated in this initiative and journey.

So where to next? We need to follow The Five Answers

So where to next? This is where we need to go as an industry. We need to follow The Five Answers.

Unearthing Riches: The Five Answers for Mineral Discovery (from my LinkedIn Blog, March 2024) and https://www.thinker.events/blog/tim-craske-the-5-answers-for-discovery/

Mineral discovery intertwines science, exploration, and economics. It's a pursuit that has shaped civilizations, driven technological advancements, and fuelled economic growth through history. But what are the keys to uncovering resources beneath the Earth's surface? The answers lie in a comprehensive framework encompassing cultural values, paradigm shifts, systems thinking, access to ground, and access to financial resources.

1. Culture: The culture of your organisation, or if you are a solopreneur, the culture gained through a career of different roles with a spread of employers, has more influence on your chance of discovery than any other factor including geological understanding. It speaks to supporting risk taking, persistence, curiosity and collaboration. This is a greater factor than good geology skills. Culture can inhibit or accelerate new prescience leading to paradigm shifts.

2. Paradigm Shift: Successful mineral discovery often hinges on a paradigm shift – a departure from conventional wisdom or outdated geological models or a new search space. Embracing innovative technologies and unconventional theories, can revolutionise the way we perceive and explore regions or identify new greenfield search spaces. A willingness to challenge existing paradigms opens doors to new frontiers of discovery.

3. Systems Thinking: Mineral exploration is inherently complex, requiring a holistic understanding of geological, environmental, and socio-economic systems ("value chains"). Systems thinking enables geologists to map the interconnectedness of various factors influencing mineral deposit location, scale and grade. By adopting a systemic approach we can identify patterns, anticipate challenges, predict the size of a deposit from only one or two drill holes and identify locations of missing ore nodes in a network of hydrothermal deposits, thereby optimising project progression through the portfolio pipeline.

4. Access to Ground: Securing access to prospective land is fundamental to exploration success. Whether through land acquisition, partnerships, or government permits, gaining permission to explore and extract minerals is a critical prerequisite. Collaborating with landowners, regulatory authorities, and local stakeholders facilitates responsible exploration practices and high ESG ratings, while maximising the potential for discovery. Working on second grade ground because you cannot deal with stakeholders controlling your primary targets means that you will be much less successful in the short and likely the long term. However, building relationships with landholders and first nation traditional owners can be facilitated by working in a district and building trust over time to gain access to your primary targets.

5. Access to Money: Mineral exploration demands substantial financial investment, from initial prospecting activities to drilling and feasibility studies. Access to capital is essential for funding exploration campaigns, acquiring equipment, and sustaining operations in remote and challenging environments. Private investors, government grants, and venture capital play pivotal roles in financing mineral exploration ventures, ensuring the resources needed to pursue discovery opportunities. You need to build bridges to all these sources of funds. Without consistent funding projects slow, stagnate and investors lose faith and patience.

The Five Answers is a complex system-based model providing a comprehensive roadmap for navigating the complexities of exploration to discover valuable mineral resources, underscoring the enduring significance of mineral exploration in shaping our world. From a complex systems perspective, thinking in the resources sectors needs to match the complexity of the challenges ahead. In the clean energy transition, we all must address complex challenges and the exploration and the extraction industries will need to play their part in mitigating climate change as well as providing the materials for the clean energy transition. The Resources Sector has to deal with complexity, and the exploration arm of the sector needs to be the leaders in this area. In essence, explorers cannot afford to operate without a systems-thinking mindset.

Related Titles from Westphalia Press

The Limits of Moderation: Jimmy Carter and the Ironies of American Liberalism
by Leo P. Ribuffo

The Limits of Moderation: Jimmy Carter and the Ironies of American Liberalism is not a finished product. Yet, this book is a close and careful history of a short yet transformative period in American political history, when big changes were afoot. and continue to shape our world.

Bunker Diplomacy: An Arab-American in the U.S. Foreign Service
by Nabeel Khoury

After twenty-five years in the Foreign Service, Dr. Nabeel A. Khoury retired from the U.S. Department of State in 2013 with the rank of Minister Counselor. In his last overseas posting, Khoury served as deputy chief of mission at the U.S. embassy in Yemen (2004-2007).

Energy Law and Policy in a Climate-Constrained World
by Victor Byers Flatt, Alfonso López de la Osa Escribano, Aubin Nzaou-Kongo

This book presents reflections on concepts, foreign policy, regional and international cooperation, and the specific role the state is to play when it comes to such thing as energy law and policy.

The Zelensky Method
by Grant Farred

Locating Russian's war within a global context, The Zelensky Method is unsparing in its critique of those nations, who have refused to condemn Russia's invasion and are doing everything they can to prevent economic sanctions from being imposed on the Kremlin.

The Lord of the Desert: A Study of the Papers of the British Officer John B. Glubb in Jordan and Iraq
by Dr. Sa'ad Abudayeh

John Bajot Glubb, a British engineer officer, was sent to Iraq in 1920 to resolve the problems which erupted after the Iraqi revolt. He remained in the area for ten years, working with the Bedouins. In 1930, he moved to Jordan for twenty-six successful years. He invented what Dr. Abudayeh calls the Diplomacy of Desert.

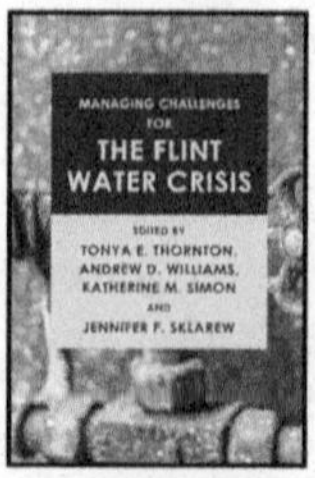

Managing Challenges for the Flint Water Crisis
Edited by Toyna E. Thornton, Andrew D. Williams, Katherine M. Simon, Jennifer F. Sklarew

This edited volume examines several public management and intergovernmental failures, with particular attention on social, political, and financial impacts. Understanding disaster meaning, even causality, is essential to the problem-solving process.

Resistance: Reflections on Survival, Hope and Love
Poetry by William Morris, Photography by Jackie Malden

Resistance is a book of poems with photographs or a book of photographs with poems depending on your perspective. The book is comprised of three sections titled respectively: On Survival, On Hope, and On Love.

Abortion and Informed Common Sense
by Max J. Skidmore

The controversy over a woman's "right to choose," as opposed to the numerous "rights" that abortion opponents decide should be assumed to exist for "unborn children," has always struck me as incomplete. Two missing elements of the argument seems obvious, yet they remain almost completely overlooked.

Geopolitics of Outer Space: Global Security and Development
by Ilayda Aydin

A desire for increased security and rapid development is driving nation-states to engage in an intensifying competition for the unique assets of space. This book analyses the Chinese-American space discourse from the lenses of international relations theory, history and political psychology to explore these questions.

The Athenian Year Primer: Attic Time-Reckoning and the Julian Calendar
by Christopher Planeaux

The ability to translate ancient Athenian calendar references into precise Julian-Gregorian dates will not only assist Ancient Historians and Classicists to date numerous historical events with much greater accuracy but also aid epigraphists in the restorations of numerous Attic inscriptions.

The Politics of Fiscal Responsibility: A Comparative Perspective
by Tonya E. Thornton and F. Stevens Redburn

Fiscal policy challenges following the Great Recession forced members of the Organisation for Economic Co-operation and Development (OECD) to implement a set of economic policies to manage public debt.

China & Europe: The Turning Point
by David Baverez

In creating five fictitious conversations between Xi Jinping and five European experts, David Baverez, who lives and works in Hong Kong, offers up a totally new vision of the relationship between China and Europe.

Issues in Maritime Cyber Security
Edited by Dr. Joe DiRenzo III, Dr. Nicole K. Drumhiller, and Dr. Fred S. Roberts

The complexity of making MTS safe from cyber attack is daunting and the need for all stakeholders in both government (at all levels) and private industry to be involved in cyber security is more significant than ever as the use of the MTS continues to grow.

Freemasonry, Heir to the Enlightenment
by Cécile Révauger

Modern Freemasonry may have mythical roots in Solomon's time but is really the heir to the Enlightenment. Ever since the early eighteenth century freemasons have endeavored to convey the values of the Enlightenment in the cultural, political and religious fields, in Europe, the American colonies and the emerging United States.

Made in the USA
Monee, IL
08 November 2026

67383824R00103